KB054193

직독직해로 읽는

# 어린왕자

The Little Prince

직독직해로 읽는

# 어린왕자

## The Little Prince

개정판 5쇄 발행　2023년 9월 10일
초판 1쇄 발행　　2010년 7월 10일

| | | | |
|---|---|---|---|
| **원작** | 생텍쥐페리 | | |
| **역주** | 더 콜링(김정희, 박윤수, 김해은) | | |
| **디자인** | IndigoBlue | | |
| **일러스트** | 수봉이 | | |
| **발행인** | 조경아 | | |
| **발행처** | 랭귀지북스 | | |
| **주소** | 서울시 마포구 포은로2나길 31 벨라비스타 208호 | | |
| **전화** | 02.406.0047 | **팩스** | 02.406.0042 |
| **이메일** | languagebooks@hanmail.net | | |
| **MP3 다운로드** | blog.naver.com/languagebook | | |
| **등록번호** | 101-90-85278 | **등록일자** | 2008년 7월 10일 |
| **ISBN** | 979-11-5635-039-2 (13740) | | |
| **가격** | 12,000원 | | |

ⓒ LanguageBooks 2010

직독직해로 읽는

# 어린왕자

## The Little Prince

생텍쥐페리 원작
더 콜링 역주

**Language Books**

# 머리말

"어렸을 때 누구나 갖고 있던 세계명작 한 질,
그리고 TV에서 하던 세계명작 만화에 대한 추억이 있습니다."

"친숙한 이야기를 영어 원문으로 읽어 봐야겠다고 마음 먹고 샀던 원서들은
이제 애물단지가 되어 버렸습니다."

"재미있는 세계명작 하나 읽어 보려고 따져 보는 어려운 영문법,
모르는 단어 찾느라 이리저리 뒤져 봐야 하는 사전,
몇 장 넘겨 보기도 전에 지칩니다."


영어 독해력을 기르려면 술술 읽어가며 내용을 파악하는 것이
중요합니다. 현재 수능 시험에도 대세인 '직독직해' 스타일을 접목시
킨 〈직독직해로 읽는 세계명작 시리즈〉는 세계명작을 영어 원작으
로 쉽게 읽어갈 수 있도록 안내해 드릴 것입니다.

직독직해 스타일로 읽다 보면, 영문법을 들먹이며 따질 필요가
없으니 쉽고, 끊어 읽다 보니 독해 속도도 빨라집니다. 이 습관이 들
여지면 어떤 글을 만나도 두렵지 않을 것입니다.

명작의 재미를 즐기며 영어 독해력을 키우는 두 마리의 토끼
를 잡으세요!

〈직독직해로 읽는 세계명작 시리즈〉 기획 단계부터 함께해 준 윤수와 해은, 좋은 디자인으로 예쁜 책이 될 수 있도록 마음 써 주시는 디자인 DX, 이 책이 출판될 수 있도록 늘 든든하게 지원해 주시는 랭귀지북스에 감사의 마음을 전합니다.

마지막으로 내 삶의 주관자 되시는 하나님께 영광을 올려 드립니다.

더 콜링 김정희

# 목차

CONTENTS

Once / when I was six years old / I saw a magnificent picture
예전에  내가 여섯 살 때  나는 멋진 그림을 보았다

/ in a book, / called True Stories from Nature, / about the
책에서,  〈자연의 실화〉라고 불리는  원시림에 관한.

primeval forest. It was a picture / of a boa constrictor / in the
그것은 그림이었다  보아뱀의

act of swallowing an animal. / Here is a copy of the drawing.
한 마리의 동물을 삼키고 있는.  여기에 그 그림의 복사본이 있다.

In the book / it said: / "Boa constrictors swallow / their prey
책에는  쓰여 있었다:  "보아뱀들은 삼킨다  먹이를 통째로,

whole, / without chewing it. After that / they are not able to
그것을 씹지도 않고.  그 후에  그것들은 움직일 수 없다,

move, / and they sleep / through the six months / that they
그리고 잠을 잔다  6개월 동안

need for digestion."
소화하기 위해 필요한."

I pondered deeply, then, / over the adventures of the jungle.
그리고 나서, 나는 깊이 생각했다,  정글 모험에 대해.

And / after some work / with a colored pencil / I succeeded
그리고  몇 편의 작품 후에  색연필로 그린  나는 성공했다

/ in making my first drawing. My Drawing Number One. It
나의 첫 작품을 만드는 데.  나의 작품 1호.

looked like this:
그것은 이렇게 보였다:

---

magnificent 장대한, 멋진 | primeval forest 원시림 | boa constrictor 보아뱀, 왕뱀 | swallow (꿀꺽) 삼키다
| prey 먹이, 사냥감 | chew 씹다 | digestion 소화 | ponder 곰곰이 생각하다 | adventure 모험 |

I showed my masterpiece / to the grown-ups, / and asked them
나는 나의 걸작을 보여 줬다        어른들에게.                    그리고 그들에게 물어봤다

/ whether the drawing frightened them.
그림이 그들을 놀라게 했는지.

But they answered: / "Frighten? / Why should any one be
그러나 그들은 대답했다:        "놀랐냐고?        왜 놀라야만 하는 거지

frightened / by a hat?"
        모자 때문에?

My drawing was not / a picture of a hat. / It was / a picture of a
내 작품은 아니었다        모자에 관한 그림이.        그것은 ~였다

boa constrictor / digesting an elephant. But / since / the grown-
보아뱀의 그림        코끼리를 소화시키고 있는.        그러나    ~때문에

ups were not able to understand it, I made another drawing: I
어른들은 그것을 이해하지 못하기,        나는 다른 작품을 만들었다:

drew / the inside of the boa constrictor, / so that / the grown-
나는 그렸다  보아뱀의 안쪽을,                ~하기 위해서

ups could see it clearly. They always need to have / things
어른들이 그것을 분명히 볼 수 있도록.    어른들은 항상 필요로 한다            설명된 것을.

explained. / My Drawing Number Two / looked like this:
        나의 작품 2호는                이렇게 보였다:

Key Expression

● 감각동사 look
Look은 '~처럼 보이다'라는 뜻을 가진 감각동사입니다.
ex) It looked like this. 그것은 이것처럼 보였다.

감각동사는 2형식 동사로 뒤에 '형용사' 혹은 'like +명사'를 동반해요. look과 같
은 감각동사에는 seem, sound, feel, taste 등이 있어요.
ex) It looks good.
   It looks like a good book.

masterpiece 걸작, 명작 | grown-up 성인, 어른 | frighten 두려워하게 하다 |

The grown-ups' response, / this time, / was to advise me /
어른들의 반응은, 이번에는, 내게 충고했다

to lay aside my drawings of boa constrictors, / whether from
보아뱀 그림을 집어 치우라고, 안쪽이든 바깥쪽이든,

the inside or the outside, / and devote myself instead / to
그리고 그 대신에 몰두하라고

geography, / history, / arithmetic / and grammar. That is
지리, 역사, 산수 그리고 문법에. 이것이 ~한 이유이다,

why, / at the age of six, / I gave up / what might have been a
6살 때, 내가 포기했던 멋진 직업이 될 수도 있었던 것을

magnificent career / as a painter. I had been disheartened / by
화가로서. 나는 낙담했다

the failure of my Drawing Number One / and my Drawing
작품 1호의 실패로 인해 그리고 작품 2호의,

Number Two. Grown-ups never understand / anything by
어른들은 결코 이해하지 못한다 그들 스스로는 아무것도,

themselves, / and / it is tiresome / for children / to be always
그리고 그것은 성가시다 아이들이 항상 그리고 영원히

and forever / explaining things to them.
어른들에게 설명해야 하는 것은.

So then / I chose another profession, / and learned to pilot
그래서 그 후에 나는 다른 직업을 선택했다. 그래서 비행기 조종을 배웠다.

airplanes. I have flown a little / over all parts of the world; / and
나는 날아왔다 전 세계를: 그리고

/ it is true that / geography has been very useful / to me. At a
그것은 사실이다 지리학이 매우 유용했다는 것은 나에게. 첫 눈에

glance / I can distinguish / China from Arizona. If one gets lost
나는 구별할 수 있었다 중국과 아리조나를. 누군가 길을 잃으면

/ in the night, / such knowledge is valuable.
밤에, 그런 지식이 유용하다.

response 응답, 반응 | lay aside 집어치우다, 버리다 | devote oneself to ~에 몰두하다 | geography 지리학
| arithmetic 산수, 계산 | dishearten 낙심하게 하다 | tiresome 성가신, 지치는 | profession 직업 | pilot
조종하다, 조종사 | at a glance 첫눈에 | distinguish 구별하다 | valuable 가치가 있는, 귀중한

12    The Little Prince

**In the course of this life / I have had a great many** encounters
이런 삶을 보내면서                              나는 수많은 만남을 가졌다

**/ with a great many people / who have** been concerned with
수많은 사람들과                    ~과 관련된

**/ matters of** consequence. **I have lived a great deal / among**
중요한 일.                    나는 오랫동안 살아왔다

**grown-ups. I have seen them** intimately, **/ close at hand. And /**
어른들 사이에서.    나는 그들을 면밀하게 관찰했다.    가까이에서.    그리고

**that hasn't much** improved **/ my opinion of them.**
그 경험은 그다지 개선시키지 못했다    그들에 대한 내 의견을.

**Whenever I met one of them / who seemed to me at all** clear-
나는 사람을 만날 때마다                    판단력이 있어 보이는.

sighted, **/ I tried the experiment / of showing him my Drawing**
나는 실험을 시도했다                    그에게 내 작품 1호를 보여 주는,

**Number One, / which I have always kept. I would try to find**
내가 언제나 간직하고 있는.            나는 알고자 했다,

**out, / so, / if this was a person / of true understanding. But, /**
그래서.    이 사람이 ~한 사람인지 아닌지를    진정으로 이해하는.    그러나,

**whoever it was, / he, or she, / would always say:**
누구든지.          그, 혹은 그녀는,    언제나 말했다:

**"That is a hat."**
"이것은 모자네."라고

Key Expression

● 접속사 whether / if

Whether은 '~인지 아닌지'라는 뜻의 접속사에요. Whether은 if와 바꿔 쓸 수 있으며 의미를 확실히 하기 위해 문장 맨 끝에 or not을 붙이기도 해요.

ex) I showed my masterpiece to the grown-ups, / and asked them / whether the drawing frightened them.
나는 내 작품을 어른들에게 보여 주고, 그 그림이 그들을 놀라게 했는지 물었다.
I would try to find out / if this person was a person of true understanding.
나는 이 사람이 진정으로 이해하는 사람인지를 알고자 했다.

encounter 만남, 접촉 | be concern with ~와 관계가 있다 | consequence 중요함, 결과 | intimately
면밀하게 | improve 개선되다 | clear-sighted 명석한, 판단력이 있는

Then / I would never talk / to that person / about boa constrictors,
그러면     나는 말하지 않았다          그 사람에게는          보아뱀에 대해,

/ or primeval forests, / or stars. I would bring myself down / to
원시림에 대해,                혹은 별에 대해.  나는 내 자신을 낮췄다

his level. I would talk to him / about bridge, / and golf, / and
그의 수준으로.  나는 얘기했다          다리에 대해,        골프에 대해,

politics, / and neckties. And / the grown-up would be greatly
정치에 대해,      그리고 넥타이에 대해.  그러면  어른들은 매우 기뻐했다

pleased / to have met / such a sensible man.
만나게 되었다면서      합리적인 사람과.

## ♛ 2 ♛

So I lived my life alone, / without anyone / that I could really
그래서 나는 홀로 살아왔다.          아무도 없는 채로      진정으로 이야기를 나눌 수 있는,

talk to, / until I had an accident / with my plane / in the Desert
사고가 나기 전까지          내 비행기가          사하라 사막에서,

of Sahara, / six years ago. Something was broken / in my engine.
6년 전에.          무엇인가 고장이 났다          내 비행기 엔진에.

And as I had with me / neither a mechanic / nor any passengers,
그리고 내게 없었기 때문에          비행기 정비사도          어떤 승객도,

I set myself to attempt / the difficult repairs / all alone. It was
나는 시도하려고 준비하고 있었다      이 모든 어려운 수리를          혼자 감당해 내려고.

a question of life or death / for me: I had scarcely / enough
이것은 생사의 문제였다          내게는: 나는 겨우 가지고 있었다      마실 만큼의 물을

drinking water / to last a week.
일주일 지속할 수 있는.

sensible 합리적인 | mechanic 기계공, 정비사 | passenger 승객 | attempt ~을 시도하다, 꾀하다 | repair
수리, 수선 question of life or death 생사의 문제 | scarcely 간신히, 겨우 |

**The first night, / then, / I went to sleep / on the sand, / a**
첫 날 밤,　　　　　　　그때,　　　나는 잠이 들었다　　　모래 위에서,

**thousand miles / from any human habitation. I was more**
1,000마일 정도 떨어진　　사람이 사는 곳으로부터.　　　　　나는 더욱 격리되어 있었다

**isolated / than a shipwrecked sailor / on a raft in the middle of**
　　　　　　난파선 선원보다　　　　　　바다 한가운데 있는 구명보트 위의.

**the ocean. Thus you can imagine / my amazement, / at sunrise,**
그러니 상상할 수 있을 것이다　　내가 경악했음을,　　　새벽녘에,

**/ when I was awakened / by an odd little voice. It said: /**
　내가 깨었을 때　　　　작고 신기한 목소리에 의해.　　그것은 말했다:

**"If you please / ——draw me a sheep!"**
"괜찮다면　　　　— 양 한 마리만 그려 줘!"

**"What!"**
"뭐!"

**"Draw me a sheep!"**
"양 한 마리만 그려 달라고!"

human habitation 사람이 사는 곳 | isolate 분리하다, 격리하다 | shipwrecked sailor 난파선의 선원 | raft
뗏목, 구명보트 | amazement 경악 | odd 이상한

I jumped to my feet, / completely thunderstruck. I blinked / my
나는 벌떡 일어났다.　　　　　너무 깜짝 놀라서.　　　　　　　나는 깜박거렸다

eyes hard. I looked carefully / all around me. And I saw / a most
눈을 심하게.　　나는 조심스럽게 쳐다보았다　　　내 주변을.　　　그리고 나는 보았다

extraordinary small person, / who stood there / examining me
아주 특이하게 작은 사람을,　　　　　　거기에 서서　　　　　나를 관찰하고 있는

/ with great seriousness. Here / you may see / the best portrait
아주 진지하게.　　　　　　여기　　당신이 보게 될 것이다　최고의 초상화를,

that, / later, / I was able to make of him. But my drawing is /
　　　나중에,　내가 그를 그릴 수 있었던.　　　　그러나 나의 그림은

certainly very much less charming / than its model.
훨씬 못하다　　　　　　　　　　　실물에 비해.

That, however, / is not my fault. The grownups discouraged me
그러나,　　　　　이것은 나의 잘못이 아니다.　어른들이 좌절시켰다

/ in my painter's career / when I was six years old, / and I never
화가로서의 나의 꿈을　　　　　내가 6살 때,

learned to draw anything, / except boas from the outside and
그리고 나는 그리는 것을 배워 본 적이 없었다.　보아뱀 바깥쪽과 안쪽 외에는.

boas from the inside.

Key Expression 🔑

**⊷ be able to ~ 할 수 있다**
be able to는 가능을 나타내는 말로, can과 같이 쓰입니다.

ex) Here / you may see / the best portrait that, later, / I was able to / make of
him.
여기 / 당신은 볼 것이다 / 최고의 초상화를 / 내가 가장 잘 그릴 수 있었던.
When at last I was able to speak, / I said to him.
마침내 가까스로 말을 할 수 있게 되었을 때, 그에게 말했다.

thunderstruck 깜짝 놀란 | blink (눈을) 깜박거리다 | extraordinary 보통이 아닌, 이상한 | seriousness
진지함, 중대함 | portrait 흡사한 물건, 초상화 | discourage 방해하다, ~하지 못하게 하다

Now I stared / at this sudden apparition / with my eyes fairly
이제 나는 유심히 봤다    이런 뜻밖의 출현을                눈이 머리 밖으로 튀어나갈 듯이

starting out of my head / in astonishment. Remember, / I had
깜짝 놀라서.                기억하라,        나는 불시

crashed / in the desert / a thousand miles from any inhabited
착 했었다    사막에서    사람이 사는 지역으로부터 1,000마일이나 떨어진 곳에 있는.

region. And yet / my little man seemed / neither to be straying
그런데        이 꼬마 친구는 ~해 보였다        길을 잃고 불안해하지도 않고

uncertainly / among the sands, / nor to be fainting from
모래 속에서,            피로로 기절할 것 같지도 않았고

fatigue / or hunger or thirst or fear. Nothing about him gave
혹은 배고픔이나 목마름, 공포로.        그에 관한 어떤 것도 ~을 주지 않았다

/ any suggestion of a child lost / in the middle of the desert, /
길 잃은 아이라는 흔적을            사막 한복판에서.

a thousand miles from any human habitation. When at last I
사람이 사는 곳으로부터 1,000마일이나 떨어진.            마침내 말을 할 수 있게 되었

was able to speak, / I said to him: /
을 때,            그에게 말했다:

"But —— what are you doing here?"
"그런데    — 너는 여기에서 무엇을 하고 있니?"

And in answer / he repeated, / very slowly, / as if he were
그러자 대답으로        그는 반복했다.        매우 천천히.        마치 이야기 하는 것처럼

speaking of / a matter of great consequence: /
대단히 중요한 일을:

"If you please / ——draw me a sheep…"
"가능하다면        — 양 한 마리만 그려 줘…"

When a mystery is too overpowering, / one dare not disobey.
미스테리가 너무 대단할 때.            사람은 감히 따르지 않을 수 없다.

Absurd as it might seem to me, / a thousand miles from any
어처구니 없어 보일 수도 있었지만,            사람 사는 곳으로부터 1,000마일이나 떨어져서

human habitation / and in danger of death, / I took out of my
생명에 위협 속에서,            나는 주머니에서 꺼냈다

---

stare ~을 유심히 쳐다보다 | apparition 유령, 허깨비 | in astonishment 깜짝 놀라서 | crash (비행기) 불시착 |
inhabited ~에 살다, 서식하다 | region 지역 | straying 길을 잃다, 헤매다 | fainting 졸도하는 | fatigue 피로,
피곤 | at last 마침내 | overpowering 저항할 수 없는 | dare 감히 ~하다 | disobey ~에 따르지 않다

pocket / a sheet of paper and my fountain-pen. But then / I
종이와 만년필을.                                              그러나 그때

remembered / how my studies had been concentrated / on
나는 기억했다        내가 어떻게 공부에 집중하게 됐었는지를

geography, history, arithmetic and grammar, / and I told the
지리학,  역사,  산수 그리고 문법에 대한,                    그래서 나는 그 꼬마 친구에

little chap / (a little crossly, too) / that I did not know / how to
게 말했다      (약간 심술궂게)                나는 알지 못한다고      어떻게 그리는지.

draw. He answered me: /
        그가 대답했다:

"That doesn't matter. / Draw me a sheep…"
"괜찮아.                        양 한 마리만 그려 줘…"

But I had never drawn a sheep. So I drew for him / one of the
그러나 나는 양을 그려 본 적이 없었다    .    그래서 나는 그를 위해 그렸다

two pictures / I had drawn so often. It was that / of the boa
두 가지 중에 한 개를    내가 종종 그려왔던.      그것은 그림이었다

constrictor from the outside. And I was astounded / to hear
속이 보이지 않는 보아뱀의.              그리고 나는 깜짝 놀랐다

the little fellow greet it with, /
그 꼬마 친구가 그림에 대해 보인 반응을 듣고,

Key Expression

### 과거완료 had + p.p
과거의 기준시점 이전부터 과거 기준시점까지의 일을 나타낼 때 사용해요.
ex) I had never drawn a sheep. 나는 양을 그려본 적이 결코 없다.

완료, 결과, 경험, 계속을 나타내며, 과거의 어느 시점보다 더 앞서서 일어난 동작
이나 상태를 나타내는 대과거의 용법으로 쓰이기도 해요.
ex) I lost my watch that my father had given me as a birthday present.
나는 시계를 잃어버렸는데, 그 시계는 아버지께서 생일 선물로 주신 것이었다.
→ 시계를 선물로 준 것이 시계를 잃어버린 것보다 먼저 일어난 일이에요!

absurd 불합리한, 어처구니 없는 | fountain-pen 만년필 | chap 녀석, 사나이 | crossly 심술궂게, 토라져서 |
astound 놀라다 | greet ~에 반응을 보이다

"No, no, no! / I do not want an elephant / inside a boa
아니, 아니, 아니!        나는 코끼리를 원하지 않아                보아뱀 속에 있는.

constrictor. A boa constrictor is a very dangerous creature,
보아뱀은 매우 위험한 생명체이고,

/ and an elephant is very cumbersome. Where I live, /
코끼리는 다루기가 너무 힘들어.                    내가 사는 곳에는,

everything is very small.
모든 것이 매우 작거든.

What I need / is a sheep. Draw me a sheep."
내가 필요한 것은        양이야.        양을 그려 줘."

So then / I made a drawing.
그리하여        나는 그림을 그렸다.

He looked at it carefully, / then he said
그가 그것을 조심스럽게 봤다.              그리고 그가 말했다.

"No. This sheep is / already very sickly. Make me another."
"싫어. 이 양은        이미 매우 병이 들었어.        다른 것을 그려 줘."

So I made / another drawing.
그래서 나는 그렸다    다른 그림을.

My friend smiled gently / and indulgently.
그 친구는 부드럽게 웃었다              그리고 봐 주는 듯이.

"You see yourself," / he said, / "that this is not a sheep. This is
"아저씨 자신도 알 거야."      그가 말했다.      "이건 양이 아니라는 걸.              이건 숫양

a ram. It has horns."
이잖아.      이것은 뿔을 가지고 있어."

So then I did my drawing / over once more.
그래서 나는 그림을 그렸다              다시 한 번.

But it was rejected too, / just like the others.
그러나 이것은 또 거절당했다.        다른 것처럼.

"This one is too old. I want a sheep / that will live a long
"이건 너무 늙었어.              나는 양을 원해        오래 함께 살 수 있는."

time."

---

cumbersome 성가신, 부담이 되는 | indulgently 관대하게

By this time / my patience was exhausted, / because I was in
바로 이 때          내 인내심도 바닥이 났다,          왜냐하면 나는 서두르고 있었다

a hurry / to start taking my engine apart. So I tossed off this
비행기 엔진 수리를 시작하려고 .          그래서 나는 이 그림을 쥐 버렸다.

drawing.

And I threw out an explanation / with it.
그리고 나는 설명을 던져 줬다          이것과 함께.

"This is only his box. The sheep you asked for / is inside."
"이것은 양의 상자야.          네가 부탁한 그 양은          이 안에 있어."

I was very surprised / to see a light break / over the face of
나는 매우 놀랐다          밝아지는 것을 보고

my young judge:
그 어린 평론가의 얼굴이:

"That is exactly / the way I wanted it! Do you think that / this
"이게 바로          내가 원했던 방식이야!          아저씨는 생각해

sheep will have to have / a great deal of grass?"
이 양이 먹어야 한다고          많은 양의 풀을?"

"Why?"
"왜?"

"Because / where I live / everything is very small…"
"왜냐하면          내가 사는 곳에는          모든 것이 아주 작거든…"

by this time 이렇게 되자 | patience 인내, 끈기 | exhaust 다 써버리다, 소모하다 | take apart ~을 분해하다 |
toss off 단숨에 해치다 | threw out 넌지시 말하다 | judge 평론가

"There will surely / be enough grass / for him," / I said. "It is a
"그 곳에는 분명히 있을 거야    풀이 충분하게    그를 위한."    내가 말했다.

very small sheep / that I have given you."
"이것은 매우 작은 양이야    내가 네게 준."

He bent his head / over the drawing:
그는 그의 머리를 숙였다    그림 위로:

"Not so small that / ——Look! He has gone to sleep…"
"그렇게 작지는 않은데    — 봐!    양이 잠이 들었어…"

And that is how / I made the acquaintance of the little prince.
그것이 ~한 방식이다    내가 어린왕자와 아는 사이가 된.

<h1>♕ 3 ♕</h1>

It took me a long time / to learn / where he came from. The
오랜 시간이 걸렸다    내가 알게 되는 데에는    그가 어디에서 왔는지.

little prince, / who asked me so many questions, / never seemed
어린왕자는,    내게 수많은 질문을 했지만,    전혀 들리지 않는 것

to hear / the ones I asked him. It was from words / dropped by
같았다    내가 그에게 묻는 질문들은.    바로 말로부터였다

chance that, / little by little / everything was revealed to me.
우연히 흘린,    조금씩    모든 것이 내게 드러난 것은.

The first time / he saw my airplane, for instance / (I shall not
맨 처음    그가 내 비행기를 보았을 때 , 예를 들면    (내 비행기를 그리지는 않겠다;

draw my airplane; / that would be much too complicated for
(내 비행기를 그리지는 않겠다;    그것은 내게 너무 복잡하니까),

me), / he asked me:
그는 내게 물었다:

"What is that object?"
"저 물건은 뭐야?"

"That is not an object. / It flies. / It is an airplane. / It is my
"저건 물건이 아니야. 하늘을 날아. 그건 비행기야. 그건 내 비행기야."

airplane."

And I was proud / to have him learn / that I could fly.
그리고 나는 자랑스러워했다 그에게 알려 줘서 내가 날 수 있다는 것을

He cried out, / then:
그는 소리쳤다, 그러자 :

"What! / You dropped down from the sky?"
"뭐라고! 아저씨는 하늘에서 떨어진 거야?"

"Yes," / I answered, / modestly.
"그래." 나는 대답했다. 겸손하게.

"Oh! That is funny!"
"오! 그거 재미있군!"

And the little prince / broke into a lovely peal of laughter, /
그리고 어린왕자는 사랑스러운 웃음을 터뜨렸다.

which irritated me very much. I like / my misfortunes to be
그러나 그것이 나를 매우 화나게 했다. 나는 원한다 내게 닥친 불행이 받아들여지길

taken / seriously.
진지하게.

Then he added:
그러자 그는 또 말했다.

"So you, too, / come from the sky! Which is your planet?"
"그럼, 당신도, 하늘에서 떨어졌구나! 당신 별은 어느 별이야?"

At that moment / I caught a gleam of light / in the impenetrable
그 순간 나는 한 줄기 힌트를 얻었다 불가사의한 미스테리 속에서

mystery / of his presence; / and I demanded, / abruptly:
그의 출현에 대한; 그리고 나는 물었다, 불쑥:

---

bend (머리를) 숙이다 | acquaintance 익히 앎, 아는 사람 | by chance 우연히 | reveal 드러나다 | for instance
예를 들면 | complicated 복잡한, 성가신 | modestly 조심성 있게 | peal 울림 | irritate 노하게 하다, 자극하다
| misfortune 불운, 불행 | planet 별 | gleam 번쩍임, (생각, 희망 등이) 번뜩이다 | impenetrable 헤아릴 수
없는 | presence 존재 | abruptly 불시에, 갑자기

"Do you come / from another planet?"
"너는 온 거야 　다른 별에서?"

But he did not reply. He tossed his head gently, / without
그러나 그는 대답하지 않았다.　그는 머리를 가볍게 끄덕였다,

taking his eyes / from my plane:
눈을 떼지 않으며　내 비행기로부터:

"It is true / that on that / you can't have come / from very far
"사실　저것을 타고는　올 수 없지　그리 멀리서는…"

away…"

And he sank into a reverie, / which lasted a long time. Then, /
그리고 그는 몽상에 잠겼다,　오랫동안 계속된.　그리고 나서

taking my sheep out of his pocket, / he buried himself / in the
내 양 그림을 주머니에서 꺼내고는　그는 잠겼다

contemplation of his treasure.
그의 보물에 대한 생각으로.

You can imagine / how my curiosity was aroused / by this
상상할 수 있을 것이다　얼마나 내 호기심을 자극했을지

half-confidence / about the "other planets." I made a great
이 확신으로 인해　'다른 별'에 대한.　나는 무척 노력했다,

effort, / therefore, / to find out more / on this subject.
그러므로,　더 많이 알아내려고　이 주제에 대해서.

"My little man, / where do you come from? What is this /
"꼬마야,　넌 어디에서 왔니?　그게 뭐지

'where I live,' / of which you speak? Where do you want to
'내가 살던 곳'이라니,　네가 말한?　어디로 데려가고 싶은 거니

take / your sheep?"
네 양을?"

---

sink into (잠, 망각에) 빠지다 | reverie 환상, 공상 | arouse ~을 자극하다

After a reflective silence / he answered:
잠자코 생각한 후                                           그는 대답했다:

"The thing that is so good / about the box / you have given me
"다행인 점은                                  상자에 대해서          아저씨가 내게 준

/ is that at night / he can use it / as his house."
밤에는                         양이 그걸 사용할 수 있다는 거야  자기 집처럼."

"That is so. / And if you are good / I will give you a string,
"그건 그래.                그리고 네가 착하게 굴면             밧줄도 줄게,

too, / so that you can tie him / during the day, / and a post to
         네가 양을 묶을 수 있도록           낮 동안에,         그리고 묶을 수 있는 말뚝도."

tie him to."

But the little prince / seemed shocked / by this offer:
그러나 어린왕자는                 충격 받은 듯 했다            이 제안에:

"Tie him! / What a queer idea!"
"양을 묶으라니!      정말 이상한 생각이야!"

"But if you don't tie him", I said, / "he will wander off
"그렇지만 양을 묶지 않으면,"        나는 말했다.    "그것이 어딘가로 뛰쳐나가 헤맬 거야,

somewhere, / and get lost."
                그리고 길을 잃을 거야."

reflective 숙고하는, 사려 깊은 | string 끈 | post 말뚝 | queer 이상한, 야릇한 | wander off 벗어나다

**My friend / broke into another peal of laughter:**
내 친구는　　　또 다시 웃음을 터뜨렸다.

**"But / where do you think / he would go?"**
"하지만　어디라고 생각해　　　양이 갈 곳이?"

**"Anywhere. Straight ahead of him."**
"어디든.　　　곧장 앞으로 가겠지."

**Then / the little prince said, / earnestly:**
그러자　어린왕자는 말했다.　　　진심으로:

**"That doesn't matter. Where I live, / everything is so small!"**
"그건 상관없어.　　　내가 사는 곳에는,　모든 것이 정말 작으니까!"

**And, / with a hint of sadness, / he added:**
그리고,　조금 슬픈 모습으로,　　　그는 덧붙였다:

**"Straight ahead of him, / nobody can go very far…"**
"계속 앞으로 가도,　　　아무도 그다지 멀리 못 가…"

Key Expression

**break into a laughter : 웃음을 터뜨리다**
break into은 '~에 침입하다'라는 뜻의 숙어이지만 '갑자기 ~하기 시작하다'
라는 뜻도 있어요.
그 밖에 'break into a run 갑자기 달리기 시작하다', 'break into a
smile 갑자기 미소짓다', 'break into tears 울음을 터뜨리다', 'break
into applause 갑자기 박수치다' 등으로 응용됩니다.

ex) The little prince broke into a lovely peal of laughter.
　　어린왕자는 사랑스러운 웃음을 터뜨렸다

earnestly 진심으로 | hint 미약한 징후, 낌새

## ☆ mini test 1

A. 다음 문장을 해석해 보세요.

(1) It was a picture of a boa constrictor / in the act of swallowing an animal.
→

(2) Whenever I met one of them / who seemed to me at all clearsight, / I tried the experiment of showing him / my Drawing Number One, / which I have always kept.
→

(3) Absurd as it might seem to me, / a thousand miles from any human habitation and in danger of death, / I took out of my pocket / a sheet of paper and my fountain-pen.
→

(4) The thing that is so good about the box / you have given me / is that at night he can use it / as his house.
→

B. 다음 주어진 문장이 되도록 빈칸에 써 넣으세요.

(1) 나는 내 작품을 어른들에게 보여 주고, <u>그 그림이 그들을 놀라게 했는지를</u> 물었다.

I showed my masterpiece to the grown-ups, and asked them

[                    ]

(2) 내게는 <u>정비사도 어떤 승객도 없었기</u> 때문에, 나는 혼자서 어려운 수리를 시도하려고 준비하고 있었다.

As I had with me [                    ], I set myself to attempt the difficult repairs all alone.

(3) 그는 그가 중요한 일을 <u>말하고 있는 것처럼</u> 천천히 반복했다.

He repeated, very slowly, [                    ] of a matter of great consequence.

A. (1) 그것은 한 마리의 동물을 삼키고 있는 보아뱀의 그림이었다. (2) 나는 판단력이 있어 보이는 사람을 만날 때마다, 내가 언제나 간직하고 있는 작품 1호를 보여 주는 실험을 시도했다. (3) 어처구니 없어 보이겠지만, 사람 사는 곳으로부터 1,000마일이나 떨어진 곳에서 생명의 위협을 느낀 채, 나는 주머니에서 종이

(4) 내가 살고 있는 곳에는, 모든 것이 매우 작아.

_____, everything is very small.


**C. 다음 주어진 문구가 알맞은 문장이 되도록 순서를 맞춰 보세요.**

(1) 그게 바로 내가 원하는 방식이야.
(the way / exactly / That is / wanted it / I)


(2) 그가 어디서 왔는지 내가 알아내는 데에는 오랜 시간이 걸렸다.
(a long time / to learn / took / It / he / me / came from / where)


(3) 이 주제에 대해 더 많이 알아내기 위해 많은 노력을 했다.
(to find out / made / I / on / more / a great effort / this subject)


(4) 정말 이상한 생각이야!
(queer / a / idea / What)


**D. 다음 단어에 대한 맞는 설명과 연결해 보세요.**

(1) magnificent ▶        ◀ ① think about something carefully

(2) ponder ▶        ◀ ② see or understand how they are different

(3) isolate ▶        ◀ ③ separated from other people

(4) distinguish ▶        ◀ ④ extremely good or beautiful

I had thus learned / a second fact of great importance: / this
그래서 나는 배우게 되었다    매우 중요한 두 번째 사실을:

was that the planet / the little prince came from / was scarcely
이것이 바로 그 별이다    어린왕자가 온

any larger than a house!
겨우 집 한 채보다 조금 더 큰!

But that / did not really surprise me much. I knew very well
그러나 그것은    그렇게 나를 놀라게 하지는 않았다.    나는 매우 잘 알고 있었다

/ that in addition to the great planets / —— such as the Earth,
큰 행성들 뿐만 아니라    — 지구나,

Jupiter, Mars, Venus / —— to which we have given names, /
목성, 화성, 금성과 같은    — 우리가 이름을 지어주었던,

there are also hundreds of others, / some of which are so small
또한 수백 가지의 다른 것들 것이며,    그 중 어떤 것들은 매우 작고,

/ that one has a hard time seeing them / through the telescope.
어떤 것은 보기가 어렵다는 것을    망원경을 통해서도.

When an astronomer discovers one of these / he does not give
천문학자는 이런 것을 발견하면    이름을 지어 주지 않고,

it a name, but only a number. He might call it, / for example, /
대신 번호만 준다.    그는 이렇게 부를 것이다.    예를 들어,

"Asteroid 325."
"소행성 325라고."

I have serious reason / to believe that / the planet from which
나는 분명한 이유가 있다    믿고 있는    어린왕자가 온 별이

the little prince came / is the asteroid known as B-612.
어린왕자가 온    B-612라고 알려진 소행성이라는 것을.

This asteroid has only once been seen / through the telescope.
이 소행성은 오직 단 한 번 눈에 띈 적이 있다    망원경을 통해.

That was by a Turkish astronomer, / in 1909.
그것은 터키 천문학자에 의해서였다.    1909년에.

Jupiter 목성 | Mars 화성 | Venus 금성 | telescope 망원경 | astronomer 천문학자 | asteroid 소행성
serious reason 분명한 이유 | Turkish 터키의

**On making his** discovery, / **the astronomer had presented**
그의 발견에 대해,      그 천문학자는 발표했었다

**it / to the International** Astronomical **Congress, / in a great**
국제 천문학회에서,      훌륭한 증명과 함께,

demonstration. **But he was in** Turkish costume, / **and so nobody**
그러나 그는 터키 전통의상을 입고 있었고,      그래서 아무도 믿지 않

**would believe / what he said.**
았다      그가 말하는 것을.

**Grown-ups are like that…**
어른들은 그런 식이다…

**Fortunately, however, / for the** reputation **of Asteroid B-612, / a**
그러나, 다행히도,      소행성 B-612에 관한 명성 덕분에,

**Turkish** dictator **made a law / that his subjects, / under pain of**
터키의 한 독재자가 법을 만들었다      그의 신하들은,      위반하면 사형이라는

**death, / should change to European costume. So in 1920 / the**
조건으로,      유럽식 옷으로 바꿔야 한다는.      그리하여 1920년

**astronomer gave his demonstration / all over again, / dressed**
그 천문학자는 증명을 내놓았다      다시 한 번,

**with** impressive **style and** elegance. **And this time / everybody**
인상적이고 멋진 스타일의 옷을 입고.      그리하여 이번에는

**accepted his report.**
모든 사람들이 그의 보고서를 인정했다.

---

---

discovery 발견 | astronomical 천문학의 | demonstration 증명 | Turkish costume 터키의 옷차림 |
reputation 평판, 명성 | dictator 독재자 | impressive 인상적인 | elegance 고상함

If I have told you these details / about the asteroid, / and made
내가 당신에게 자세한 이야기를 했다면                             그 소행성에 관해,

a note of its number for you, / it is on account of the grown-
그리고 소행성의 번호들에 대해 언급했다면,              그것은 어른들 때문이고 그들의 방법이다.

ups and their ways. Grown-ups love figures. When you tell
                              어른들은 숫자를 좋아한다.                          당신이 어른들에게 말하면

them / that you have made a new friend, / they never ask you
          새로운 친구가 생겼다는 것을,                              그들은 절대 어떤 질문도 물어보지

any questions / about essential matters. They never say to
않는다                       중요한 것에 대해서는.                          그들은 절대 묻지 않는다.

you, "What does his voice sound like? What games does he
          "목소리가 무엇을 닮았니?                            무슨 게임을 가장 좋아하니?

love best? Does he collect butterflies?" Instead, they demand:
          나비를 수집하니?" 등의 질문을              대신에, 그들은 묻는다:

/ "How old is he? How many brothers has he? How much does
   "몇 살이니?              형제가 몇 명이니?                          몸무게는 얼마나 되니?

he weigh? How much money does his father make?" Only
          아버지가 돈을 얼마나 버시니?" 등을

from these figures do they think / they have learned anything
오직 저런 숫자로부터 그들은 생각한다                          친구에 대해 알게 되었다고.

about him.


If you were to say to the grown-ups: / "I saw a beautiful house
만약 어른들에게 말한다면:                                        "나는 아름다운 집을 봤어요

/ made of rosy brick, / with geraniums in the windows / and
   붉은 벽돌로 만들어진,              창가에는 제라늄이 있고

doves on the roof," / they would not be able to / get any idea
그리고 지붕에는 비둘기들이 있는," 그들은 할 수 없을 것이다              그 집에 대한 어떤 생각도.

of that house at all. You would have to say to them: "I saw a
                    대신 그들에게 이렇게 말했어야 한다:                "나는 집을 봤어요

house / that cost $2,000." Then they would exclaim: / "Oh,
          $2,000짜리."                          그리하면 그들은 감탄했을 것이다:

what a pretty house that is!"
"오, 정말 예쁜 집이구나!"라고

account 계좌, 장부, 단골, (있었던 일에 대한) 설명 | essential 본질(적인), 중요한 (것) | rosy brick 장미빛 벽돌
geranium 제라늄 | exclaim 소리치다, 외치다

Just so, you might say to them: "The proof that the little
그러므로, 그들에게 말할지도 모른다:           "어린왕자가 존재한다는 증거는

prince existed / is that he was charming, / that he laughed,
                        그가 밝고,                              늘 잘 웃고,

/ and that he was looking for a sheep. If anybody wants a
양을 갖고 싶어 한다는 것이에요.                 만약 누군가 양을 원한다면,

sheep, / that is a proof that he exists." And what good would
            그것이 그가 존재한다는 증거예요."        그러면 무슨 소용이 있을까

it do / to tell them that? They would shrug their shoulders,
그들에게?                              그들은 어깨를 으쓱거릴 것이다,

/ and treat you like a child. But if you said to them: "The
그리고 당신을 어린 아이처럼 취급할 것이다.   그러나 만약 그들에게 말하면:

planet he came from / is Asteroid B-612," then they would be
"어린왕자가 온 별은              소행성 B-612예요,"라고,        그러면 그들은 확신을 가지고,

convinced, / and leave you in peace / from their questions.
            괴롭히지 않을 것이다         질문으로.

They are like that. One must not hold it / against them.
어른들은 그 모양이다.      원망하면 안 된다              어른들에 대해.

Children should always show / great forbearance / toward
어린이들은 항상 보여 줘야 한다            지대한 인내심을

grown-up people.
어른들에게.

exist 존재하다 | shrug (어깨를) 으쓱하다 | convince ~을 확신시키다 | forbearance 인내, 자제

But certainly, / for us who understand life, / figures are a
그러나 분명, 인생을 이해하는 우리에게는, 숫자는 관심없는 문제이다.

matter of indifference. I should have liked to begin this story
나는 이 이야기를 시작했어야 했다

/ in the fashion of the fairy-tales. I should have liked to say:
옛날 이야기 형식으로, 나는 이렇게 말했어야 했다:

"Once upon a time / there was a little prince / who lived on a
"옛날 옛날에 어린왕자가 있었어요 별에 사는

planet / that was scarcely any bigger than himself, / and who
자기 몸집보다 조금 더 큰,

had need of a sheep……"
그리고 양을 필요로 하는……"

To those who understand life, / that would have given / a
인생을 이해하는 사람들에게는, 이 편이 해 주었을 것이다

much greater air of truth / to my story. For I do not want /
훨씬 더 실감나도록 내 이야기에. 왜냐하면 나는 원하지 않는다

anyone to read my book carelessly. I have suffered too much
누군가가 내 책을 가볍게 읽는 것을. 내게는 아주 고통스러운 일이다

grief / in setting down these memories. Six years have already
이런 추억을 꺼내 놓아야 한다는 것은. 6년이라는 시간이 흘렀다

passed / since my friend went away from me, / with his sheep.
내 친구가 내 곁을 떠나가 버린 지도, 그의 양과 함께

If I try to describe him here, / it is to make sure / that I shall
내가 만약 여기에서 그를 설명한다면, 확실히 하기 위해서이다 그를 영원히 잊지 않

not forget him. To forget a friend / is sad. Not everyone has
을 것이라고. 친구를 잊는다는 것은 슬픈 일이다. 모든 사람이 친구를 가지는 것은

had a friend. And if I forget him, / I may become like the
아니다. 그리고 만약 내가 그를 잊는다면, 난 어른이 되어가는 것일지도 모른다

grown-ups / who are no longer interested / in anything but
더 이상 관심이 없는 숫자 외에는 아무것도……

figures……

---

indifference 무관심 | fairy-tale 요정들의 이야기, 동화 | greater ~보다 큰 | grief 슬픔 | anything but ~
외에는 무엇이든

It is for that purpose, / again, / that I have bought a box of
이것은 목적이기도 하다,   다시,   내가 그림물감 한 상자와 연필을 산.

paints and some pencils. It is hard to take up drawing / again
그림을 그린다는 것은 정말 어려운 일이라,

at my age, / when I have never made any pictures / except
내 나이에 다시,   나는 어떠한 그림도 그려 본 적이 없다

those of the boa constrictor from the outside / and the boa
보아뱀의 겉모습 외에는   보아뱀의 뱃속과,

constrictor from the inside, / since I was six. I shall certainly
6살 이후로.   물론 나는 노력할 것이다

try to / make my portraits / as true to life as possible. But I am
초상화를 그리기 위해   가능한 실물에 최대한 가깝도록.   그러나 나는 성

not at all sure of success. One drawing goes along all right, /
공을 자신하지는 못한다.   어떤 그림은 괜찮은데,

and another has no resemblance to its subject. I make some
다른 것은 전혀 닮지 않았다.   나는 잘못 그린 적도 있다,

errors, too, / in the little prince's height: / in one place he is
어린왕자의 키를:   어떤 그림에서는 그의 키가 너무나 컸고,

too tall / and in another too short. And I feel some doubts /
다른 그림에서는 너무 작았다.   그리고 나조차 의심이 든다

about the color of his costume. So I fumble along / as best
그의 옷 색상에 대하여.   그렇게 실수하며 해 왔다   최선을 다해서,

I can, / now good, now bad, / and I hope / generally fair-to-
좋게도, 나쁘게도,   그리고 나는 바란다   대부분 그저 그만하기를.

middling.

take up 계속되다, 다시 시작하다 | go along 잘 돼가다 | resemblance 유사, 닮음 | fumble 실수하다 | fair-to-
middling 그저 그만한(=so-so)

In certain more important details / I shall make mistakes, also.
보다 중요한 부분들에서 모두 잘못 그릴 수도 있다.

But that is something / that will not be my fault. My friend
그러나 그것은 ~것이다 나의 잘못으로 인한 것이 아닌. 나의 친구는

never explained / anything to me. He thought, perhaps, / that I
설명하지 않았다 어떤 것도 내게. 아마도, 그는 생각했겠지,

was like himself. But I, alas, / do not know / how to see sheep
내가 그와 비슷할 거라고. 그러나 난, 안타깝게도, 모른다, 양을 보는 방법을

/ through the walls of boxes. Perhaps / I am a little like the
상자의 벽을 뚫고. 아마도 나는 좀 어른들과 비슷한가 보다.

grown-ups. I have had to grow old.
나도 나이가 들어버렸다.

## 5

As each day passed, / I would learn, / in our talk, / something
날이 갈수록, 나는 알게 되었다, 우리의 대화 속에서 어린왕자의 별에 대한

about the little prince's planet, / his departure from it, / his
것을, 그가 어떻게 떠나 왔는지를, 그의 여행에 관한

journey. The information would come very slowly, / as it might
것을. 정보는 매우 느리게 나오곤 했다, 우연히 나오는 듯이

chance to fall / from his thoughts. In this way, / I heard, / on
그의 생각으로부터. 이런 식으로, 나는 들었다, 3일째

the third day, / about the catastrophe of the baobabs.
되던 날에, 바오밥 나무의 비극에 대해.

alas 아아(슬픔이나 유감을 나타내는 소리) | departure 출발, 벗어남 | chance to 우연히 ~하다 | catastrophe 큰 재해, 대이변 | baobab 바오밥(아프리카 산의 큰 나무) | abruptly 갑자기, 불쑥 | grave 예사롭지 않은, 침통한

This time, / once more, / I had the sheep to thank for it. The
이번에도,　　　또 다시,　　　　어린 양 덕분이었다.

little prince asked me abruptly / —— as if seized by a grave
어린왕자가 불쑥 내게 물었다　　　　　— 예사롭지 않은 의심에 사로잡힌 것처럼 —

doubt —— "It is true, isn't it, / that sheep eat little bushes?"
　　　　"정말이지, 그렇지,　　　　양이 작은 나무를 먹는다는 게?"

"Yes, that is true."
"그럼, 사실이야."

"Ah! I am glad!"
"아!　　다행이야!"

I did not understand / why it was so important / that sheep
나는 이해하지 못했다　　　왜 그렇게 중요한 건지　　　　양이 작은 나무를 먹는다는

should eat little bushes. But the little prince added: / "Then / it
것이.　　　　　　　　　그러나 어린왕자는 다시 물었다,　　　　"그러면

follows that they also eat baobabs?"
양은 바오밥 나무도 먹는 거야?"

I pointed out to the little prince / that baobabs were not little
나는 어린왕자에게 지적했다　　　　바오밥 나무는 작은 덤불이 아니라

bushes, / but, on the contrary, trees as big as castles; / and that
　　　　반대로, 성만큼 큰 나무라고;　　　　그리고 ~하더라

even if / he brought a whole herd of elephants away with him, /
도　　　　코끼리 떼를 데려가도,

the herd would not able to eat up / one single baobab.
코끼리 떼는 먹어 치울 수 없을 거라고　　　한 그루의 바오밥 나무도.

---

Key Expression

**not A but B : A가 아니라 B**

'not~but...'이나 'not only~but also...'과 같이 짝을 이루어 쓰이는 접속사를 상관접속사라고 해요. A와 B에는 같은 형태의 단어나 구, 절이 온다는 점에 주의하세요.
또한 not A but B는 'A가 아니라 B'라는 뜻이므로, 뒤에 오는 B에 인칭 및 수를 일치시켜야합니다.

ex) Baobabs were not little bushes / but trees as big as castles
바오밥나무는 작은 덤불이 아니라 성만큼 큰 나무였다.

---

bush 관목 | contray 반대의 | herd (소, 말 등의) 무리

The idea of the herd of elephants / made the little prince
코끼리 떼라는 발상이                              어린왕자를 웃게 만들었다

laugh.

"We would have to put them / one on top of the other," / he
"코끼리 떼를 놓아야 겠네              한 마리씩 위로 쌓아서"

said.
그는 말했다.

But he made a wise comment: /
하지만 그는 영리한 답변을 했다:

"Before they grow so big, / the baobabs start out by being
"그렇게 크게 자라기 전에는,        바오밥 나무도 작은 것에서 시작하잖아."

little."

"That is strictly correct," / I said. "But why do you want / the
"그건 엄밀하게는 그렇지."            내가 말했다. "그런데 너는 왜 하고 싶은 거야

sheep to eat the little baobabs?"
양한테 작은 바오밥 나무를 먹이는 것을?"

He answered me at once, / "Oh, come, come!" / as if he were
그는 즉시 대답했다.        "오, 이봐요!"              말하고 있다는 듯이

speaking of something / that was self-evident. And I was
                          자명한 사실을.

obliged to make a great mental effort / to solve this problem, /
그리고 나는 많은 정신적 노력을 들여야 했다        이 의문을 해결하기 위해,

without any assistance.
아무 도움도 없이.

Indeed, / as I learned, / there were on the planet / where the
정말로,        내가 배운 대로,        별에는 있었다

little prince lived —— as on all planets —— / good plants and
어린왕자가 살았던      — 모든 행성이 그렇듯 —            좋은 나무와 나쁜 나무가.

bad plants. In consequence, / there were good seeds from
                  결과적으로,            좋은 나무에는 좋은 씨앗이 있고.

---

strictly 엄밀히, 엄격히 | correct 정확한, 옳은 | self-evident 자명한 | be obliged to 어쩔 수 없이 ~하다
mental 마음의, 정신의 | assistance 도움, 원조 | indeed 정말 | consequence 결과

good plants, / and bad seeds from bad plants. But seeds
그리고 나쁜 나무에는 나쁜 씨앗이 있었다.                    그러나 씨앗은

are invisible. They sleep deep / in the heart of the earth's
보이지 않는다.            그것들은 깊이 잠들어 있다        지구의 암흑 깊은 곳에.

darkness, / until someone among them / is seized with the
그것들 중 어느 것인가                  깨어나려는 욕망을 가지기 전까지는.

desire to awaken. Then this little seed / will stretch itself and
그리고 나서 이 작은 씨앗은        기지개를 켜고 시작한다

begin / —— timidly at first —— / to push a charming little sprig
— 처음에는 소심하게 —              매력적인 싹을 틔우기를

/ inoffensively upward / toward the sun. If it is only / a sprout
해가 되지 않게 위쪽으로        태양을 향해서.        만약 그것이 단지

of radish or a sprig of rosebush, / one would let it grow /
무의 싹이나 장미 나무의 싹이라면,            자라도록 둘 것이다

wherever it might wish. But when it is a bad plant, / one must
원하는 장소 어디에서든.        그러나 그것이 나쁜 식물일 때는,        그것을 파괴해야

destroy it / as soon as possible, / the very first instant / that
한다        가능한 한 빨리,              바로 첫 순간에

one recognizes it.
그것을 발견하게 된.

Key Expression

**as if 가정법 : 마치 ~인 것처럼**
as if는 가정법의 특수한 형태로, if절에 항상 과거동사(be동사는 were)가 온
다는 점을 잊지 마세요.

ex) He answered me at once / as if he were speaking of something / that was
self-evident.
그는 자명한 것을 말하고 있는 것처럼 즉시 대답했다.

invisible 보이지 않는 | be seized with ~의 욕망에 사로잡히다 | timidly 소심하게 | sprig 잔가지
inoffensively 해가 되지 않게 | sprout 싹, 눈 | radish 무 | rosebush 장미 나무, 장미 덤불

Now there were some terrible seeds / on the planet / that was
거기에는 나쁜 씨앗들이 약간 있었다　　　　　　　그 별에는

the home of the little prince; / and these were the seeds of
어린왕자의 집이 있는;　　　　　　그리고 이것들은 바오밥 나무의 씨앗이었다.

the baobab. The soil of that planet / was infested with them.
그 별의 토양은　　　　　　바오밥 나무 씨앗들로 가득했다.

A baobab is something / you will never, never be able to get
바오밥 나무는　　　　　결코, 결코 없앨 수 없다

rid of / if you attend to it too late. It spreads over / the entire
　　너무 늦게 알아차리게 되면.　　　　그것은 퍼져버린다　　　별 전체로.

planet. It bores clear through it / with its roots. And if the
그것은 별을 뚫고 들어간다　　　　뿌리로.　　　그래서 별은 너무 작고,

planet is too small, / and the baobabs are too many, / they
　　　　　　바오밥 나무는 너무 많아진다면,

would split it in pieces…
그것들은 별을 산산조각 내 버릴 것이다…

"It is a question of discipline," / the little prince said to me
"이것은 훈련의 문제야."　　　　어린왕자는 내게 말했다

/ later on. "When you've finished your own toilet / in the
　나중에.　　"화장을 끝냈을 때에는　　　　　아침에, ·

morning, / then it is time / to attend to the toilet of your planet,
　　그리고 나면 ~할 시간이야　별의 몸단장을 해야 할.

/ just so, / with the greatest care. You must see to it / that you
마찬가지로, 주의깊게.　　　　　잘 봐야 해

pull up regularly / all the baobabs, at the very first moment /
규칙적으로 뽑아내도록　모든 바오밥 나무를, 아주 초기에,

when they can be distinguished from the rosebushes / which
바오밥 나무는 장미 덤불과 구별할 수 있어

they resemble so closely / in their earliest youth. It is very
서로 매우 닮은　　　　　그것들이 어릴 때는.　　그건 아주 지루한 일이야."

tedious work," / the little prince added, / "but very easy."
　어린왕자는 덧붙였다,　　　　"그러나 매우 쉬워."

infest (해충 따위가) 들끓다 | attend to 정성을 들이다 | bore ~에 구멍을 뚫다, 도려내다 | split 쪼개다 | in pieces 조각을 내어 | discipline 훈련, 규율 | toilet 화장, 몸단장 | regularly 정기적으로, 자주 | distinguish 구별하다 | tedious 지루한, 실증나는

And one day / he said to me: / "You ought to make a beautiful
그리고 어느 날    그는 내게 말했다:    "아저씨는 예쁜 그림을 그려야 해,

drawing, / so that / the children where you live / can see
~할 수 있도록   아저씨가 살고 있는 별의 아이들이    정확하게 볼 수 있도록

exactly / how all this is. That would be very useful to them
이 모든 일이 어떻게 되는지.    그건 매우 유용할 거야

/ if they were to travel some day. Sometimes," / he added, /
언젠가 그 아이들이 여행을 떠나게 된다면.    때로는,"    그는 덧붙였다,

"there is no harm in putting off a piece of work / until another
"미뤄도 해가 없는 일이 있어    다른 날로.

day. But when it is a matter of baobabs, / that always means a
그러나 바오밥 나무의 문제의 경우에는,    언제나 비극을 가져와.

catastrophe. I knew a planet / that was inhabited a lazy man.
나는 어떤 별을 알고 있어    게으름뱅이 한 명이 살고 있는.

He neglected three little bushes…"
그는 바오밥 나무를 세 그루나 내버려 뒀어…"

Key Expression

**so that ~ : ~하기 위해서**
so that이 이끄는 절이 조동사를 동반할 때 '~하기 위하여, ~하도록'이라고 해
석합니다. 여기서 so that은 'in order that'으로 바꿀 수 있어요.

ex) You ought to make a beautiful drawing, so that the children where you live
can see exactly how all this is.
당신은 당신이 살고 있는 별의 아이들이 이 모든 일이 어떻게 되는 건지 정확히
볼 수 있도록 예쁜 그림을 그려야 해.

neglect 소홀히 여기다, 무시하다

So, / as the little prince described it to me, / I have made a
그래서, 어린왕자가 내게 설명해 준 대로, 나는 그 별을 그렸다.

drawing of that planet. I do not much like to / take the tone
나는 그리 좋아하지 않는다 도덕군자의 목소리를 내는 것

of a moralist. But / the danger of the baobabs / is so little
을. 그러나 바오밥 나무의 위험은 거의 알려져 있지 않고,

understood, / and such considerable risks / would be run by
그런 심각한 위험이 사람에게 미칠 것이니까

anyone / who might get lost on an asteroid, / that for once / I
소행성에서 길을 잃은, 이번 한 번

am breaking through my reserve. "Children", / I say plainly,
나는 침묵을 깨려고 한다. "어린이 여러분", 나는 분명히 말한다,

"watch out for the baobabs!"
"바오밥 나무를 조심하세요!"

My friends, / like myself, / have been skirting this danger / for
내 친구들은 나처럼, 이런 위험을 회피해왔다

a long time, / without ever knowing it; / and so it is for them
오랫동안, 알지도 못한 채; 그래서 이것은 그들을 위한 것이다

/ that I have worked so hard / over this drawing. The lesson
내가 열심인 것은 이 그림을 그리는 것에. 내가 전한 교훈은

which I pass on / by this means / is worth all the trouble / it
이런 방법으로 수고할 가치가 있으니까

has cost me.
내게 끼친 만큼.

Perhaps / you will ask me, "Why are there no other drawings /
아마도 여러분은 내게 물을 것이다. "왜 다른 그림은 없어

in this book / as magnificent and impressive / as this drawing
이 책에는 멋지고 인상적인 그림이 이 바오밥 나무만큼?"이라고

of the baobabs?"

moralist 도덕주의자 | reserve 삼감, 제한, 침묵 | plainly 분명히, 솔직하게 | skirt (문제 따위를) 피해가다 | pass
on 전하다 | worh the trouble ~할 가치가 있다

The reply is simple. I have tried. But with the others / I have
대답은 간단하다.                        나는 노력했다.        그러나 다른 작품에서는

not been successful. When I made / the drawing of the baobabs
난 성공적이지 못했다.                  내가 만들었을 때      바오밥 나무 그림을

/ I was carried beyond myself / by the inspiring / force of
  나는 자신을 뛰어넘어 완성했다                    영감의 힘을 받아서

urgent necessity.
절실한 필요성의.

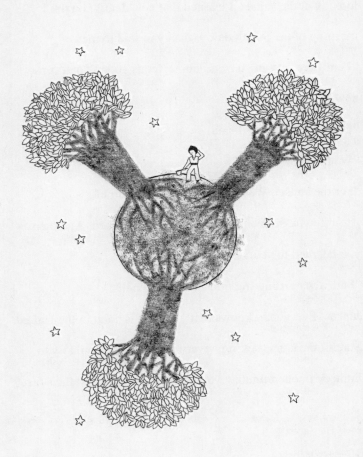

Oh, little prince! / Bit by bit / I came to understand / the
오, 어린왕자야!　　　조금씩　　　나는 알게 되었어

secrets of your sad little life… / For a long time / you had
네 슬픈 인생의 비밀을…　　　　　오랜 시간 동안

found your only entertainment / in the quiet pleasure of
너는 즐거움을 찾았어　　　　　　일몰 보는 것의 기쁨으로부터.

looking at the sunset. I learned that new detail / on the
　　　　　나는 새로운 사실을 알게 되었어

morning of the fourth day, / when you said to me:
4일째 되던 날 아침,　　　　네가 내게 이런 말을 했을 때:

"I am very fond of sunsets. Come, let us go look at a sunset
"나는 일몰이 정말 좋아.　　　　이리 와,　지금 일몰을 보러 가자."

now."

"But we must wait," I said.
"그렇지만 기다려야 해,"　　내가 대답했다.

"Wait? For what?"
"기다려?　무엇을?"

"For the sunset. We must wait / until it is time."
"일몰을.　　　우리는 기다려야 해　　때가 될 때까지 ."

At first / you seemed to be very much surprised. And then /
처음에　너는 매우 놀란 것처럼 보였다.　　　　　그러더니

you laughed to yourself. You said to me:
너는 웃었지.　　　　넌 내게 말했어:

"I am always thinking / that I am at home!"
"나는 아직도 생각하고 있어　　우리집에 있다고!"

Just so. Everybody knows that / when it is noon in the United
그렇다.　모두가 알고 있다　　　　미국이 정오일 때

States / the sun is setting / over France. If you could fly to
　　　해가 진다고　　프랑스 너머로.　　만약 프랑스로 날아갈 수 있다면,

France / in one minute, / you could go straight into the sunset,
　　　1분 안에,　　일몰을 볼 수 있을 것이다.

inspire 고무시키다 | urgent 절박한 | necessity 필요성, 필연성 | bit by bit 점차적으로 | fond (특히 오랫동안)
좋아하는 | twilight 황혼

/ right from noon. Unfortunately, France is too far away / for
바로 정오에.                안타깝게도,              프랑스는 너무도 멀리 있다

that.
그렇게 하기에는

But on your tiny planet, / my little prince, / all you need do is /
그러나 네 작은 별에서는,         어린왕자,          네가 해야 할 것은 오직

to move your chair / a few steps. You can see / the day end and
의자를 움직이기만 하면 돼      몇 발자국만      너는 볼 수 있지      해가 지고 황혼이 물드는

the twilight falling / whenever you like…
것을                 네가 원할 때면 언제나…

"One day," / you said to me, "I saw the sunset forty-four
"언젠가,"        네가 나에게 말했다,      "나는 일몰을 44번이나 보았어!"

times!"

And a little later / you added:
그리고 조금 있다가      덧붙였다:

"You know —— / one loves the sunset, / when one is so sad…"
"있잖아 —           누군가 일몰을 좋아하는 것은,       마음이 울적할 때야…"

"Were you so sad, then?" I asked, / "on the day of the forty-
"넌 슬펐니, 그때?"                   내가 물어봤다,    "그 날 44번의 해넘이를 보았을 때?"

four sunsets?"

But the little prince made no reply.
그러나 어린왕자는 대답하지 않았다.

**be fond of~ : ~을 좋아하다**
be fond of는 '~을 좋아하다'라는 뜻이지만, '~하는 나쁜 버릇이 있다'라는 의
미로도 쓰인답니다. of 뒤에는 명사나 동명사(-ing)가 옵니다.

ex) I am very fond of sunsets. 나는 일몰을 매우 좋아한다.

　I am fond of eating candies. 나는 사탕 먹는 것을 좋아한다. (→ 나쁜 버릇)

# 👑 mini test 2

A. 다음 문장을 해석해 보세요.

(1) This was that the planet the little prince came from was scarcely any larger than a house!
→

(2) I have serious reason to believe that the planet from which the little prince came is the asteroid known as B-612.
→

(3) I did not understand why it was so important that sheep should eat little bushes.
→

(4) The idea of the herd of elephants made the little prince laugh.
→

B. 다음 주어진 문장이 되도록 빈칸에 써 넣으세요.

(1) 천문학자가 이들 중 하나를 발견하여도 <u>그는 그것에게 이름을 지어주지 않고</u>, 오직 숫자만 정해 주었다.

When an astronomer discovers one of these ⬜⬜⬜⬜⬜, but only a number.

(2) 이 천문학자들은 단지 <u>망원경을 통하여</u> 한 번 본 적이 있을 뿐이다.

This asteroid has only been seen ⬜⬜⬜⬜⬜.

(3) <u>조금씩</u>, 나는 네 슬픈 삶의 비밀을 이해할 수 있게 되었다.

⬜⬜⬜⬜⬜, I came to understand the secret of your sad little life.

A. (1) 어린왕자가 온 별은 거의 집 한 채보다 조금 더 크다! (2) 어린왕자가 온 별이 B-612라고 알려진 소행성이라고 믿는 그럴 듯한 이유가 있다. (3) 나는 양이 작은 나무를 먹는다는 것이 왜 그렇게 중요한지 이해하지 못했다. (4) 코끼리 떼라는 발상이 어린왕자를 웃게 만들었다. | B. (1) he does not give it a name

(4) 너는 네가 원할 때면 언제나 해가 지고 황혼이 물드는 것을 볼 수 있다.

You can see the day end and the twilight falling _____ .


C. 다음 주어진 문구가 알맞은 문장이 되도록 순서를 맞춰보세요.

(1) 친구를 잊는다는 것은 슬프다.
   (is / To / forget / sad / a / friend)
   →

(2) 나는 어떻게 박스의 벽을 통하여 양을 보는지 모른다.
   (how to see / through / do not know / I / sheep / the walls of boxes)
   →

(3) 우리는 시간이 될 때까지 기다려야 한다.
   (must / until / time / We / it / wait / is)
   →

(4) 처음에 너는 매우 놀란 것처럼 보였다.
   (very / surprised / you / At first / seemed / to be / much)
   →


D. 의미가 어울리는 것끼리 연결해 보세요.

(1) neglect ▶         ◀ ① the scientific study of the star and planets

(2) astronomy ▶       ◀ ② to fail to give them proper attention

(3) inhabit ▶         ◀ ③ the time when the sun goes down and night begins

(4) sunset ▶          ◀ ④ to live in a particular place

## ♔ 7 ♔

On the fifth day, —— again, as always, / it was thanks to the
5일째 되던 날.　　　— 언제나처럼 다시 한 번,　　　양 덕분이었다 —

sheep —— / the secret of the little prince's life / was revealed to
　　　어린왕자의 삶의 비밀이　　　　　　　　내게 밝혀진 것은.

me. Abruptly, / without anything to lead up to it, / and as if the
불쑥,　　　　밑도 끝도 없이　　　　　　　　비롯된 질문인 것처럼

question had been born / of long and silent meditation / on his
　　　　　　　　　　오랜 침묵의 숙고 끝에　　　　　　그의 문제

problem, / he demanded:
에 대해,　　　그는 물었다:

"A sheep / —— if it eats little bushes, / does it eat flowers, too?"
"양은 말이지　　— 그게 작은 나무를 먹는다면,　　　꽃도 먹는 거야?"

"A sheep," / I answered, / "eats anything / it finds in its reach."
"양은 말이지,"　　나는 대답했다　　"아무거나 먹어　　발견하는 것은.'

"Even flowers / that have thorns?"
"꽃이라도　　　　가시를 가진?"

"Yes, / even flowers that have thorns."
"응,　　가시를 가진 꽃이라도."

"Then the thorns / —— what use are they?"
"그러면 가시는　　　— 무슨 소용이 있어?"

I did not know. / At that moment / I was very busy / trying to
나는 알지 못했다.　　　그 순간　　　　나는 매우 바빴다　　　나사를 풀려고 시

unscrew a bolt / that had got stuck in my engine. I was very
도하느라　　　엔진에 꽉 끼어버린 나사를.　　　나는 매우 걱정됐다.

much worried, / for it was becoming clear to me / that the
　　　왜냐하면 분명해졌기 때문이다

breakdown of my plane / was extremely serious. And I had so
내 비행기의 고장이　　　극도로 심각하다는 것이.　　　그리고 마실 물이 거의

little drinking water left / that I had to fear the worst.
남지 않아서　　　　　　최악의 상황을 걱정해야 했다.

---

thanks to ~의 덕택에, ~의 결과 | abruptly 갑자기, 불쑥 | meditation 명상, 숙고 | thorn 가시 | unscrew ~
의 나사를 빼다 | breakdown 고장 | extremely 극도로

"The thorns / —— what use are they?"
"가시는              — 무엇에 쓰는 거야?"

The little prince never let go of a question, / once he had
어린왕자는 질문을 멈추지 않았다.                    일단 질문하기 시작하면.

asked it. As for me, / I was upset over that bolt. And I
      나로 말하자면,     나사 때문에 화나 있었다.

answered with the first thing / that came into my head:
그래서 나는 첫 질문에 대답했다        머리에 떠오르는 대로:

"The thorns are of no use at all. Flowers have thorns / just for
"가시는 아무 쓸모도 없어.              꽃들은 가시를 가지고 있는 거야      그저 심술 부

spite!"
리려고!"

"Oh!"
"오!"

There was a moment of / complete silence. Then / the little
순간이 있었다              완전한 침묵의.        그리고 나서

prince flashed back at me, / with a kind of resentfulness:
어린왕자는 나를 쏘아봤다,        분개하여:

"I don't believe you! Flowers are weak creatures. They are
"믿을 수 없어!              꽃은 약한 창조물이야.              꽃은 순진하다고.

naive. They reassure themselves / as best they can. They
      그들은 자신들을 안심시키는 거야        할 수 있는 한 최선을 다해서.   그들은 믿고 있어

believe / that their thorns are terrible weapons…"
      자신들의 가시가 무서운 무기라고…"

upset 당황한, 걱정한 | spite 심술 | flash back 되쏘아보다 | resentfulness 분개, 성남 | naive 순진한 |
eassure 안심시키다, 기운을 돋우다

I did not answer. At that instant / I was saying to myself: / "If
나는 대답하지 않았다.        그 순간              나는 생각하는 중이었다:

this bolt still won't turn, / I am going to knock it out / with the
"이 나사가 돌아가지 않으면,          때려서 부숴야겠어              망치로"

hammer." Again the little prince disturbed / my thoughts:
다시 한 번 어린왕자는 방해했다              내 생각을:

"And you actually believe / that the flowers—— "
"아저씨는 정말로 믿고 있어        꽃들이 —"

"Oh, no!" / I cried. / "No, no, no! I don't believe anything.
"그만해, 그만!"    나는 소리쳤다.    "그만, 그만, 그만!   난 아무 것도 믿지 않아 .

I answered you with the first thing / that came into my
네 첫 질문에 대답했던 거야              머리에 떠오르는 대로.

head. Don't you see / —— I am very busy / with matters of
넌 안 보이는 거야        — 지금 바쁘다고        중요한 일로!"

consequence!"

He stared at me, / thunderstruck.
그는 나를 쳐다봤다.          너무 놀란 모습으로.

"Matters of consequence!"
"중요한 일이라고!"

He looked at me there, / with my hammer in my hand, / my
그는 나를 바라봤다,          손에 망치를 들고,

fingers black with engine-grease, / bending down over an
손가락은 엔진 오일로 검게 변한 채,          비행기 밑에 엎드려 있는 나를

object / which seemed to him extremely ugly...
그것이 그에게는 아주 이상해 보인 것 같았다…

"You talk / just like the grown-ups!"
"아저씨는 말하네    어른처럼 !"

That made me a little ashamed. But he went on, / relentlessly:
그 말은 나를 부끄럽게 만들었다.              그러나 그는 계속했다,          인정사정 없이:

disturb 혼란 시키다, 방해하다 | thunderstruck 벼락은 맞은 듯한, 극도로 놀란 | grease 기름, 윤활유 | go on (
이야기 등을) 계속하다 | relentlessly 집요하게, 사정없이

"You mix everything up together... / You confuse
"아저씨는 모든 것을 뒤죽박죽 섞어 놨어…          모든 것을 혼란스럽게 했어…"

everything..."

He was really very angry. He tossed his golden curls / in the
그는 정말 화를 냈다.          곱슬머리를 흩날리면서          바람에.

breeze.

"I know a planet / where there is a certain red-faced
"나는 별을 알고 있어          붉은 얼굴의 신사가 살고 있는.

gentleman. He has never smelled a flower. He has never looked
그는 꽃 향기를 맡아 본 적이 없어.          그는 별을 바라본 적도 없어.

at a star. He has never loved any one. He has never done
그는 누군가를 사랑해 본 적도 없어.          그는 아무 것도 한 적이 없어

anything / in his life / but add up figures. And all day / he
평생동안          숫자를 더하는 것 외에는.          그리고 하루종일          그는 끊임없이 말해,

says over and over, / just like you: / 'I am busy with matters of
아저씨처럼:          '나는 중요한 일로 바쁘다고!'라고

consequence!' And that makes him / swell up with pride. But
그리고 그것은 그를 만들었어          자신감에 넘치도록.          그러나 그는 사람이 아니야

he is not a man / —— he is a mushroom!"
— 그는 버섯이야!"

---

**Key Expression** 🔍

### 관계부사 where
관계부사 where는 '전치사 + 관계대명사'의 의미로 명사인 선행사를 수식하는
형용사절을 이끕니다. 선행사에는 장소를 나타내는 명사가 와요.

ex) I know a planet / where there is a certain red-faced gentleman.
　　　　　　　　　　　(=in which)
　　나는 붉은 얼굴의 신사가 있는 별을 알고 있어.

---

over and over 반복하여 | swell up 뽐내다 | mushroom 버섯

"A what?"
"뭐라고?"

"A mushroom!"
"버섯이라고!"

The little prince was now white / with rage.
어린왕자는 이제 창백해졌다          화가 나서 .

"The flowers have been growing thorns / for millions of years.
"꽃들은 가시를 키워왔어          수백만 년 동안.

For millions of years / the sheep have been eating them / just
수백만 년 동안          양들은 꽃들을 먹어왔어

the same. And is it not a matter of consequence / to try to
마찬가지로.     그런데 그게 중요한 문제가 아니라고          이해하려고 하는 것이

understand / why the flowers go to so much trouble / to grow
          왜 꽃들이 그런 수고를 하는지          가시를 키우는

thorns / which are never of any use to them? Is the warfare
          아무 쓸모도 없는?          전쟁이

/ between the sheep and the flowers / not important? Is this
          양과 꽃 사이의          중요하지 않아? 

not of more consequence / than a fat red-faced gentleman's
이건 중요한 문제가 아니야          붉은 얼굴 신사의 덧셈보다?

sums? And if I know —— I, myself —— one flower / which is
그리고 내가 알고 있다면     — 나, 내 자신이 —          한 송이 꽃을

unique in the world, / which grows nowhere but on my planet,
세계에서 유일한,          내 별에서만 자라는,

/ but which one little sheep can destroy / in a single bite some
그러나 양 한 마리가 파괴해 버릴 수도 있는          하루 아침에 한 입에,

morning, / without even noticing / what he is doing —— / Oh!
          알아차리지도 못한 채          자신이 무슨 짓을 하는지도 —

You think that is not important!"
오! 아저씨는 이게 중요하지 않은 거야!"

His face turned / from white to red / as he continued:
그의 얼굴은 변했다　　　흰색에서 붉은 색으로　　　애기를 계속함에 따라:

"If someone loves a flower, / of which just one single blossom
"누군가 한 송이 꽃을 사랑한다면,　　　단 한 그루 밖에 없는

grows / in all the millions and millions of stars, / it is enough
수억 개의 별 중에서,　　　그건 그를 행복하게 하

to make him happy / just to look at the stars. He can say
기에 충분해　　　그 별을 바라보는 것만으로.　　　그는 생각할 수 있어:

to himself: / 'Somewhere, my flower is there…' But if the
'어딘가에 내 꽃이 있어…'라고.　　　그러나 양이 그 꽃을 먹어

sheep eats the flower, / in one moment / all his stars will be
버린다면,　　　한순간에　　　그의 모든 별이 꺼져버리는 거야…

darkened… And you think that is not important!"
그런데 아저씨는 그게 중요하지 않다는 거야!"

He could not say / anything more. His words were choked / by
그는 말할 수 없었다　　　더 이상 아무것도.　　　그의 말은 막혀버렸다

sobbing.
흐느낌으로.

blossom 꽃 | choked 숨이 막히다 | sob 흐느껴 울다

The night had fallen. I had let my tools drop / from my hands.
그날 밤이 되었다.                              나는 내 도구를 내려 놓았다          내 손에서.

Of what moment now / was my hammer, my bolt, or thirst,
지금 이 순간에 뭐란 말인가          망치나 나사, 목마름이나 죽음이?

or death? On one star, one planet, my planet, the Earth / there
            하나의 별이자, 행성, 나의 행성인, 지구에

was a little prince / to be comforted. I took him in my arms, /
어린왕자가 있다        위로받아야 하는.          나는 그를 팔에 껴안고,

and rocked him. I said to him:
흔들어줬다.          나는 그에게 말했다:

"The flower that you love / is not in danger. I will draw you
"네가 사랑하는 꽃은                    위험하지 않아.          내가 입 마개를 그려 줄게

a muzzle / for your sheep. I will draw you a railing / to put
          네 양에게.          내가 울타리를 그려 줄게

around your flower. I will —— "
네 꽃 주위에 칠.          내가 — "

I did not know / what to say to him. I felt awkward / and
나는 알지 못했다          그에게 뭐라고 말해야 할지.          나는 어색했고

blundering. I did not know / how I could reach him, / where I
서툴렀다.          나는 알지 못했다          그에게 다가갈 수 있는 방법을.

could overtake him / and go on hand in hand with him / once
어디까지 그를 쫓아갈 수 있을지를          그래서 그의 손을 잡았다

more.
다시 한 번.

It is such a secret place, / the land of tears.
알 수 없는 곳이다.          눈물의 세계란.

comfort 돌보다, 위로하다 | rock 흔들다 | muzzle 입 마개, 재갈 | awkward 어색한, 서투른 | blundering
실수하는, 서투른

# 👑 8 👑

I / soon / learned to know this flower better. On the little
나는 곧 이 꽃에 대하여 더 잘 알게 되었다. 어린왕자의 별에는

prince's planet / the flowers had always been / very simple.
꽃들은 언제나 매우 간단했다.

They had only one ring of petals; / they took up no room at
그것들은 오직 한 개의 꽃잎만을 가지고 있다; 그것들은 자리를 전혀 차지하지 않았다;

all; / they were a trouble to nobody. One morning / they would
그것들은 누구에게도 문제가 되지 않는다. 어느 날 아침

appear in the grass, / and by night / they would have faded
꽃들은 풀밭에 피어나곤 했다, 그리고 밤이 되면 그들은 조용히 시들곤 했다.

peacefully away. But one day, / from a seed blown / from no
그러나 어느 날, 바람에 날려온 씨앗으로부터 어디로부터 왔는지

one knew where, / a new flower had come up; / and the little
아무도 모르는, 새로운 꽃이 피어나고 있었다;

prince had watched very closely / over this small sprout /
그리고 어린왕자는 매우 유심히 관찰하고 있었다 이 작은 싹에 대해

which was not like / any other small sprouts / on his planet. It
달라 보이는 여느 다른 작은 싹들과는 그의 별에 있는.

might, / you see, / have been a new kind of baobab.
이것은 어쩌면, 알다시피, 새로운 바오밥 나무일지도 모른다.

---

**Key Expression** 🎗

### would have+p.p ~ 했을 것이다
would have+p.p : ~했을 것이다 (주어에 의지가 있는 문장)
should have+p.p : ~했어야 했다 (과거에 하지 못한 행동에 대한 후회)
might have+p.p : ~했을지도 모른다 (추측)
could have+p.p : ~했을수도 있다 (가능성)

ex) One morning they would appear in the grass, and by night they would have
faded peacefully away.
어느 날 아침 그들은 풀밭에 피었다가, 밤이 되면 그들은 조용히 시들곤 한다.
If he had been honest, I would have employed him.
그가 정직했다면, 나는 그를 고용했을 것이다.

---

petal 꽃잎 | take up 차지하다 | fade away 죽다, 시들다 | blow 바람에 날리다, (바람이) 불다 | sprout 싹이
나다

55

But the shrub soon stopped growing, / and began to get ready
그러나 그 작은 나무는 곧 자라는 것을 멈추고,    준비하기 시작했다

/ to produce a flower. The little prince, / who was present / at
꽃을 피우기 위해.    어린왕자는,    그 자리에 있었던

the first appearance of a huge bud, / felt at once / that some
큰 꽃봉오리가 처음 피어나는 순간에.    즉시 느꼈다    어떠한 신비스러운 출

sort of miraculous apparition / must emerge from it. But the
현이    그것으로부터 반드시 일어날 것임을.

flower was not satisfied / to complete the preparations / for
그러나 그 꽃은 만족하지 않았다    준비를 마치는 것을

her beauty / in the shelter of her green chamber. She chose
아름다움을 위한    그녀의 초록색 방의 쉼터에서.    그녀는 색상을 골랐다

her colors / with the greatest care. She dressed herself slowly.
매우 조심스럽게.    그녀는 천천히 옷을 입었다.

She adjusted her petals / one by one. She did not wish to go
그녀는 꽃잎을 매만졌다    하나 하나씩.    그녀는 나가기를 원하지 않았다

out / into the world / all rumpled, / like the field poppies. It
세상에    헝클어진 모습으로,    양귀비꽃처럼.

was only in the full radiance of her beauty / that she wished
눈부실 만큼의 아름다움으로    그녀는 나타나기를 원했다.

to appear. Oh, yes! / She was a coquettish creature! And her
아, 정말!    그녀는 요염했다!

mysterious adornment / lasted for days and days.
그리고 이렇게 그녀의 신비한 치장은    수 일 동안 지속되었다.

Then one morning, / exactly at sunrise, / she suddenly showed
그러던 어느 날 아침,    해가 뜨자 마자,    그녀가 갑자기 모습을 드러냈다.

herself.

---

shrub 키 작은 나무, 관목 | huge bud 큰 봉오리 | miraculous 기적적인 | apparition 경이적인 것, 출현 |
emerge 나오다, 나타나다 | preparation 준비 | shelter 은신처 | chamber 방, 회의실 | adjusted 매만지다
| rumple (머리를) 헝클어뜨리다 | poppy 양귀비 | radiance 광채, 빛남 | coquettish 요염한, 교태 있는 |
adornment 꾸밈

And, after working / with all this painstaking precision, / she
그리고, 작업 후에　　　　　이 모든 수고를 꼼꼼하게 들인,

yawned and said:
그 꽃은 하품을 하며 말했다:

"Ah! I am scarcely awake. I beg that you will excuse me. My
"아!　　겨우 깨어났네요.　　　　　　용서해 주길 바래요.

petals are still all disarranged…"
내 꽃잎들이 아직도 헝클어져 있어서…"

But the little prince / could not restrain his admiration:
그러나 어린왕자는　　　　　　감탄을 금치 못했다:

"Oh! How beautiful you are!"
"오!　너무나도 아름다워요!"

"Am I not?" / the flower responded, / sweetly. "And I was
"그렇죠?"　　　꽃이 대답했다,　　　　　사랑스럽게.　"그리고 나는 태어났어요

born / at the same moment / as the sun…"
동시에　　　　　태양과 함께…"

## stop to+동사 vs. stop+동사ing

stop+~ing : ~하는 것을 멈추다(과거의 일)
stop to+동사 : ~을 하기 위하여 멈추다(미래의 일)

ex) But the shrub / soon stopped growing, / and began to / get ready to pro
duce / a flower.
그러나 그 관목나무는 곧 자라는 것을 멈추고, 꽃을 피울 준비를 시작했다.
Tom stopped to drink water
톰은 물을 마시기 위하여 멈추었다.
Tom stopped drinking water.
톰은 물마시는 것을 멈추었다.

painstaking 수고를 아끼지 않는, 공들인 | precision 꼼꼼함, 정확 | yawn 하품하다 | disarranged 헝클어지다
restrain 억누르다 | admiration 감탄, 칭찬

The little prince could guess easily enough / that she was not
어린왕자는 쉽게 생각할 수 있었다                          그 꽃이 그다지 겸손하지 않다고 —

any too modest —— / but how moving —— / and exciting —— /
                       그러나 얼마나 생동감 있고 —        신비한가 —

she was!
그 꽃이!

"I think it is time for breakfast," / she added an instant later. "If
"나는 생각한다   지금 아침 먹을 시간이라고,"          꽃은 곧 말을 이었다.

you would have the kindness / to think of my needs ——"
"친절을 베풀어 줄래요?                내가 필요한것을 생각하는 —"

And the little prince, / completely abashed, / went to look for a
어린왕자는,                 매우 당황하여,         물뿌리개를 찾으러 갔다.

sprinkling-can of fresh water. So, he tended the flower.
                            그리고, 그는 꽃을 돌보았다.

---

modest 겸손한 | instant 즉각적인 | abashed 당황한, 겸연쩍은 | sprinkling-can 물뿌리개 | tend 돌보다 |
torment 괴롭히다 | vanity 허영(심) | claw 발톱 | object 항의하다, 반박하다 | weed 잡초, 풀

So, too, / she began very quickly / to torment him / with her
그렇게, 또,　　꽃은 이내　　　　　　　　　그를 괴롭히기 시작했다　　허영심으로

vanity —— which was, if the truth be known, / a little difficult
— 사실상,　　　　　　　　　　　　　　　　　　꽤 다루기 힘든.

to deal with. One day, / for instance, / when she was speaking
어느 날,　　　　예를 들어,　　　자신의 네 개의 가시에 대해 이야기를 할 때,

of her four thorns, / she said to the little prince:
꽃은 어린왕자에게 말했다:

"Let the tigers come / with their claws!"
"호랑이들을 다 오라고 해요　　발톱을 세우고!"

"There are no tigers on my planet," / the little prince objected.
"내 별에는 호랑이들은 없어요."　　　　어린왕자가 반박했다.

"And, anyway, / tigers do not eat weeds."
"그리고, 어쨌든,　　호랑이는 잡초를 먹지 않아요."

"I am not a weed," / the flower replied, sweetly.
"나는 잡초가 아니에요."　　꽃이 대답했다.　　　상냥하게.

59

"Please excuse me..."
"미안해요..."

"I am not at all afraid of tigers," / she went on, / "but I have
"나는 호랑이를 전혀 무서워하지 않아요."          꽃은 계속했다.

a horror of drafts. I suppose / you wouldn't have a screen for
"그러나 나는 바람이 두려워요.   혹시   나를 위한 바람막이가 있을까요?"

me?"

"A horror of drafts —— / that is bad luck, / for a plant," /
"바람을 무서워하다니 —   운이 없네요.   식물치고는."

remarked the little prince, / and added to himself, "This
어린왕자가 말했다.          그리고 덧붙였다.

flower is a very complex creature..."
"이 꽃은 정말 까다로운 식물이야..."

"At night / I want you to put me / under a glass globe. It is
"밤이 되면   나를 넣어 주세요   유리 덮개 아래에 .

very cold / where you live. In the place where I came from
너무 추워요   당신이 사는 곳은.   내가 온 그곳은 —"

____,"

But she interrupted herself / at that point. She had come in the
그러나 꽃은 스스로 멈추었다   그 시점에서.   꽃은 씨앗의 형태로 여기에 왔다.

form of a seed. She could not have known / anything of any
꽃은 알 수 없었다   다른 세상의 어떠한 것도.

other worlds. Embarrassed over having let herself / be caught
스스로 당황했는지

on the verge of such a naive untruth, / she coughed two three
너무 뻔한 거짓말이 들통나서.   꽃은 두세 번 헛기침을 했다.

times, / in order to put the little prince in the wrong.
어린왕자에게 잘못을 돌리기 위해.

---

draft 통풍, 바람 I screen 바람막이 I complex 문제가 많은, 어려운 I glass globe 유리덮개 I embarrass
당황하다, 쩔쩔매다 I on the verge (파멸 등에) 직면하다

"The screen?"
"바람막이는?"

"I was just going to look for it / when you spoke to me…"
"지금 막 찾아보려고 했는데                            네가 계속 말을 해서…"

Then she forced her cough a little more / so that he should
그러자 꽃은 몇 번 더 억지로 기침했다                            어린왕자가 느끼도록

suffer from / remorse just the same.
똑같이 양심의 가책을.

So the little prince, / in spite of all the good will / that was
그래서 어린왕자는,                    선의에도 불구하고

inseparable from his love, / had soon come to doubt her. He
사랑에서 우러나온,                            곧 꽃을 의심하게 되었다.

had taken seriously words / which were without importance, /
그는 그 말을 심각하게 받아들였다                            대수롭지 않게 한 말을,

and it made him very unhappy.
그래서 그것이 그를 불행하게 만들었다.

"I ought not to have listened to her," / he confided to me /
"나는 꽃이 하는 말을 듣지 말 걸 그랬어,"                            그는 내게 털어놓았다

one day. "One never ought to listen / to the flowers. One
어느 날.        "누구도 들어서는 안 돼                            꽃의 이야기를.

should simply look at them / and breathe their fragrance.
단순히 그것들을 쳐다보기만 해야 해                            그리고 향기를 맡는 거야.

Key Expression

in spite of ~ 에도 불구하고, 무릅쓰고
여기에서 'in spite of~'는 'despite'와 같은 의미로 쓰였습니다.

ex) …~, in spite of all the good will that was inseparable from his love, ~…
모든 좋은 뜻에도 불구하고 그의 사랑으로부터 그것을 분리할 수는 없었다.
They went for a walk despite the rain.
그들은 비가 오는 데도 불구하고 산책을 나갔다.

remorse 동정, 불쌍히 여김 | inseparable 불가분한 | confide ~에게 (비밀을) 털어놓다 | fragrance 향기

61

Mine perfumed / all my planet. But I did not know / how to
내 꽃은 향기를 냈어          내 별 모든 곳에.          그러나 나는 몰랐어

take pleasure / in all her grace. This tale of claws, / which
기쁨을 즐기는 법을          꽃의 우아함 속에서.          이 호랑이 발톱 얘기도,

disturbed me so much, / should only have filled my heart / with
나를 짜증나게 했지만,          생각했어야 했어

tenderness and pity."
다정하고 측은하게."

And he continued / his confidences:
그리고 그는 계속했다          비밀 이야기를:

"The fact is that / I did not know / how to understand anything!
"사실은          난 아무것도 몰랐어          어떻게 이해를 해야 하는지!

/ I ought to have judged / by deeds and not by words. She cast
나는 판단했어야 하는데          말이 아니라 행동으로.          그 꽃은 줬어

/ her fragrance and her radiance / over me. I ought never to
향기와 광채를          나를 향해.          나는 도망치지 말았어야 했어

have run away / from her... I ought to have guessed / all the
꽃으로부터…          나는 깨달았어야 했어          그 모든 애정표현을

affecting / that lay behind / her poor little stratagems. Flowers
뒤에 숨겨진          꽃의 서툰 꾀의.

are so inconsistent! But I was too young / to know how to love
꽃은 정말 모순덩어리야!          그러나 나는 너무 어렸어          그 꽃을 사랑하는 방법을 알기엔…"

her..."

♛ 9 ♛

I believe / that for his escape / he took advantage of / the
나는 믿는다          그의 별을 떠나오기 위해서          그가 이용했다고

migration of a flock of wild birds. / On the morning of his
철새 무리의 이동을.          출발하던 날 아침에

disturb 방해하다 | tenderness 부드러움, 다정스러움 | confidence 신뢰, 확신, 비밀 | deed 행위, 행동 | cast (
축복, 시선 따위를) 주다 | affect 영향을 미치다 | stratagem 꾀, 계략, 책략 | inconsistent 앞뒤가 맞지 않은,
모순된 | advantage 이점, 장점 | migration 이동 | flock 무리, 떼

departure / he put his planet in perfect order. He carefully
그는 그의 별을 정돈했다.                     그는 조심스럽게 청소했다

cleaned out / his active volcanoes. He possessed two active
그의 활화산들을.                      그는 두 개의 활화산을 가지고 있었다;

volcanoes; / and they were very convenient / for heating his
그리고 그것들은 매우 편리했다                아침 식사를 데우는데

breakfast / in the morning. He also had one volcano / that was
아침에.                       그는 또한 화산 하나를 갖고 있었다        꺼져 버린.

extinct. But, as he said, / "One never knows!" So he cleaned
그러나, 그가 말했듯이,        "아무도 알 수 없는 일이다!"      그래서 그는 청소했다

out / the extinct volcano, too. If they are well cleaned out, /
불이 꺼진 화산도.               잘 청소되어 있으면,

volcanoes burn slowly and steadily, / without any eruptions.
화산들은 서서히 그리고 꾸준히 타오른다,              폭발 없이.

Volcanic eruptions / are like fires in a chimney.
화산 폭발은             굴뚝에서 뿜는 불과 같을 것이다.

On our earth / we are obviously much too small / to clean out
우리 지구에서는      인간들은 너무 작아서                      화산을 청소할 수가 없다.

our volcanoes. That is why / they bring no end of trouble /
그것이 ~한 이유이다    화산들이 끊임없이 문제를 일으키는

upon us.
우리에게.

**Key Expression**

### that is why 그것이 바로 ~한 이유이다
'that is why~'는 why 앞에 the reason 이라는 선행사가 생략된 관계부사 구문이에요. '그것이 바로 ~한 이유이다' 혹은 앞문장의 결과를 나타내는 의미로 '그래서 ~하는 것이다'로 해석할 수 있어요.

ex)  That is why / they bring no end of trouble upon us.
      그게 바로 그것들이 끊임없이 문제를 일으키는 이유이다.

put~in order 정돈하다 | volcano 화산 | possess 소유하다, 가지고 있다 | extinct (불이) 꺼진, (화산이) 활동을 그친 | steadily 꾸준히, 끊임없이 | eruption 폭발 | volcanic 화산의 | chimney 굴뚝

The little prince also pulled up, / with a certain sense of
어린왕자는 또한 뽑았다.                                                약간 낙담하는 기분으로

dejection, / the last little shoots of the baobabs. He believed
              바오밥 나무의 마지막 싹들을,                                    그는 믿었다

that / he would never want to return. But on this last morning
      다시 돌아오고 싶지 않을 거라고.                              하지만 마지막 날 아침에

/ all these familiar tasks / seemed very precious to him. And
  이런 모든 익숙한 일들이                      그에게 매우 소중해 보였다.

when he watered the flower / for the last time, / and prepared
그리고 꽃에 물을 주면서                            마지막으로,                       꽃을 놓으려고 준비할 때

to place her / under the shelter of her glass globe, / he realized
두기 위해                      유리 덮개 아래에,                                          그는 깨달았다

/ that he was very close to tears.
  금방 눈물이 날 것 같다고.

"Goodbye," / he said to the flower.
"잘 있어요,"            그는 꽃에게 말했다.

But she made no answer.
그러나 그녀는 대답하지 않았다.

"Goodbye," / he said again.
"잘 있어요,"            그는 다시 말했다.

The flower coughed. But it was not because she had a cold.
꽃은 기침을 했다.                      그러나 감기가 걸렸기 때문은 아니었다.

"I have been silly," / she said to him, / at last. "I ask your
"내가 어리석었어요,"            꽃이 그에게 말했다,            마침내.          "날 용서해 줘요,

forgiveness. Try to be happy…"
         행복해지도록 해요…"

He was surprised / by this absence of reproaches. He stood
그는 놀랐다                      이런 원망하지 않는 말투에.                      그는 그곳에 서 있었다

there / all bewildered, / holding the glass globe held arrested
        어리둥절해 하며,              유리 덮개를 공중에 든 채로.

in mid-air. He did not understand / this quiet sweetness.
                  그는 이해할 수 없었다                  이런 고요한 상냥함을.

dejection 실망, 낙담 | shoot 식물의 | precious 귀중한, 값비싼 | be close to 금방 ~할 것 같은
reproach 원망, 비난 | bewilder 어리둥절하게 하다, 당황케 하다

"Of course I love you," / the flower said to him. "It is my
"물론 나는 당신을 사랑해요."          꽃이 그에게 말했다.                    "내 잘못이에요

fault / that you have not known it / all the while. That is of
      당신이 그 사실을 몰랐던 것은                오랜 시간 동안.        그건 중요하지 않아요.

no importance. But you —— you have been just as foolish as
      그러나 당신은 —          당신도 나만큼이나 어리석었어요.

I. Try to be happy… / Let the glass globe be. I don't want it
행복해져요…            덮개는 내버려 둬요.          그건 더 이상 필요 없어요."

anymore."

"But the wind —— "
"하지만 바람이 —"

"My cold is not so bad as all that. / The cool night air will do
"내 감기는 그렇게 심하지 않아요.              서늘한 밤공기가 내게 좋아요.

me good. I am a flower."
      나는 꽃이니까요."

"But the animals —— "
"하지만 짐승들이 —"

"Well, I must endure / the presence of two or three
"난 견뎌야 해요            두세 마리 애벌레의 존재를

caterpillars / if I wish to become acquainted / with the
            알고 지내고 싶다면                          나비들과.

butterflies. It seems that they are very beautiful. And if not
나비들은 매우 아름다워 보이니까요.                          그리고 나비들과

the butterflies / and the caterpillars —— who will call upon
            애벌레들이 아니라면            — 누가 나에게 들르겠어요?

me? You will be far away…As for the large animals —— / I
당신은 멀리 가버릴 거니까요…      큰 동물에 대해서라면 —

am not at all afraid / of any of them. I have my claws."
나는 전혀 무섭지 않아요      그 어느 것도.      내게는 발톱이 있으니까요."

---

endure 견디다, 참다 | caterpillar 애벌레 | acquainted 알고 있는, 안면이 있는 | linger (우물쭈물) 오래
머무르다

**And naively, / she showed her four thorns. Then she added:**
그리고 천진난만하게,　꽃은 네 개의 가시를 보여 줬다.　　　　　그러고 나서 덧붙였다:

**"Don't linger like this. You have decided / to go away. Now**
'이렇게 우물쭈물 하지 말아요.　　당신은 결심했으니까요　　떠나기로.

**go!"**
이제 가요!'

**For she did not want / him to see her crying. She was such a**
꽃은 원하지 않았기 때문이다　　어린왕자가 그녀의 우는 모습을 보는 것을.

**proud flower…**
그토록 자존심 강한 꽃이었다…

### as~as 원급비교

'as +형용사·부사 원급 +as …'는 '…만큼 ~한'의 의미로 '원급비교' 혹은 '동등비교'라고 부릅니다.
그러나 첫번째 as 앞에 not을 붙여 'not as[so] +~ +as …'가 되면 '…만큼 ~하지 않은'라는 의미가 되므로 비교급과 같은 의미를 갖게 됩니다.

ex) You are as foolish as I.
　　당신은 나만큼이나 어리석었어. (you = I)
　　You are not as foolish as I.
　　당신은 나만큼 어리석지 않아. (you < I, 내가 더 어리석다)
　　My cold is not so bad as all that.
　　내 감기는 그렇게 심하지 않아.

## 👑 mini test 3

A. 다음 문장을 해석해 보세요.

(1) The little prince never let go a question, once he had asked it.
→

(2) At that moment I was very busy trying to unscrew a bolt that had got stuck in my engine.
→

(3) I was very much worried, for it was becoming clear to me that the breakdown of my plane was extremely serious.
→

(4) Embarrassed over having let herself be caught on the verge of such a naive untruth, she coughed two three times, in order to put the little prince in the wrong.
→

B. 다음 주어진 문장이 되도록 빈칸에 써 넣으세요.

(1) 나는 붉은 얼굴의 신사 한 명이 있는 별을 알고 있어.
[where / a certain / a planet / I know / red-faced / gentleman / there is]
→

(2) 나는 그에게 뭐라고 말해야 할 지 알지 못했다.
[did not / what / know / say to / to / him / I]
→

(3) 나는 너무 어려서 그녀를 사랑하는 법을 알지 못했다.
[how to / young / love / I was / to / know / her / too]
→

A. (1) 어린왕자는 일단 질문하기 시작하면 결코 질문을 멈추지 않았다. (2) 그 순간 나는 내 엔진에 끼어버린 나사를 푸느라 바빴다. (3) 나는 매우 걱정됐다. 왜냐하면 내 비행기의 고장이 매우 심각하다는 것이 분명해졌기 때문이었다. (4) 너무 뻔한 거짓말이 들통나서 스스로 당황했는지 어린왕자에게 잘못을 돌리기 위

(4) 내 감기는 그렇게 심하지 않아.
(is / not / My cold / as / so / all that / bad.)
→


C. 다음 주어진 문장이 본문의 내용과 맞으면 T, 틀리면 F에 동그라미 하세요.

(1) The secret of the little prince's life was revealed to me thanks to the sheep.
[ T / F ]

(2) He draw a rose for the little prince.
[ T / F ]

(3) The little prince made a fence for his rose.
[ T / F ]

(4) The little prince escaped from his planet leaving his rose behind.
[ T / F ]


D. 의미가 비슷한 것끼리 서로 연결해 보세요.

(1) abruptly ▶        ◀ ① blundering

(2) awkward ▶        ◀ ② embarrassed

(3) abashed ▶        ◀ ③ suddenly

(4) reproach ▶        ◀ ④ blame

He found / himself in the neighborhood / of the asteroids 325,
그는 알았다　　자신이 근처에 있음을　　　　　　　소행성 325, 326, 327, 328, 329, 그

326, 327, 328, 329, and 330. He began, therefore, / by visiting
리고 330호의.　　　　　　　　　그래서 그는 시작했다.　　　그들을 방문하기로,

them, / in order to add to his knowledge.
　　　전문을 넓히기 위해.

The first of them / was inhabited by a king. Clad in royal
그 첫 번째 별에는　　　왕이 살고 있었다.　　　　　자주빛의 담비모피 옷을 입고,

purple and ermine, / he was seated / upon a throne / which
　　　　　　　　　그는 앉아 있었다　　왕좌에　　　　동시에

was at the same time / both simple and majestic.
　　　　　　　　간소하면서도 위엄 있는.

"Ah! Here is a subject," / exclaimed the king, / when he saw
"아! 신하가 한 명 왔구나."　　　왕이 소리쳤다.

the little prince coming.
어린왕자가 오는 것을 봤을 때.

And the little prince asked himself:
그래서 그 어린왕자는 자문했다:

"How could he recognize me / when he had never seen me
"어떻게 그가 나를 알아보지　　　　이전에 나를 본 적이 없는데?"

before?"

He did not know / how the world is simplified / for kings. To
그는 알지 못했다　　　얼마나 세상이 단순한지를　　　왕들에게는.

them, / all men are subjects.
그들에게는,　모든 사람이 신하이다.

---

inhabit 살다 | clad ~(옷)을 입은 | royal purple 자주빛 | ermine 담비모피(북방 족제비의 흰색 겨울털, 왕들의 가운, 판사의 법복 등을 장식하는 데 쓰임) | throne 왕좌 | majestic 장엄한, 웅대한 | subject 신하 | exclaim 소리치다 | simplified 쉽게 한, 간소화 한

"Approach, / so that I may see you better," said the king, /
"가까이 오라,　　　내가 좀 더 잘 볼 수 있게."　　　왕이 말했다,

who felt consumingly proud / of being at last a king over
무척 자랑스럽게 느끼는　　　마침내 누군가의 왕이 된 것이.

somebody.

The little prince looked everywhere / to find a place to sit
어린왕자는 주변을 둘러보았다　　　앉을 자리를 찾기 위하여;

down; but the entire planet was crammed / and obstructed
그러나 별 전체가 덮여 있었고　　　막혀 있었다

/ by the king's magnificent ermine robe. So he remained
왕의 거대한 담비 망토로.　　　그래서 어린왕자는 똑바로 선 채였다,

standing upright, / and, / since he was tired, / he yawned.
　　　그래서,　그는 피곤하여,　　　하품을 했다.

"It is contrary to etiquette / to yawn in the presence of a
"예의에 어긋난 행동이다　　　왕의 앞에서 하품하는 것은,'

king," / the monarch said to him. "I forbid you to do so."
왕이 그에게 말했다.　　　"그렇게 하는 것을 금지하노라."

"I can't help it. I can't stop myself," / replied the little prince,
"그러지 않을 수 없어요.　참을 수가 없어요,"　　　어린왕자가 대답했다,

/ thoroughly embarrassed. "I have come on a long journey, /
완전히 당황하며.　　　"나는 긴 여행을 해 와서,

and I have had no sleep…"
잠을 자지 못했어요…"

**Key Expression** 📍

### 접속사 Since
접속사로 쓰이는 Since는 시간과 이유를 나타냅니다.

▶ 시간의 접속사 Since : ~이래, ~한 때부터

ex) I have known her since she was a child.
그녀가 어린애였을 때부터 쭉 알고 있다.

▶ 이유의 접속사 Since : ~이므로, ~이니까

ex) Since he was tired, he yawned. 그는 피곤해서, 하품했다.
→ 보통은 because로 바꿔써도 무방하지만, Since는 직접적 인과관계를 나타내지 않으므로, 문맥에
따라 because로 바꿔 쓸 수 없는 경우도 있어요.

approach 가까이 가다, 접근하다 | consumingly 엄청나게, 강렬하게 | be crammed by ~로 채워져 있다, ~로
덮여 있다 | upright (자세가) 올바른, 똑바로 | monarch 군주 | thoroughly 완전히, 철저하게

71

"Ah, then," / the king said. "I order you to yawn. It is years /
"아, 그러면." 그 왕이 대답했다 "하품하도록 허락한다. 오래되었구나

since I have seen anyone yawning. Yawns, / to me, / are object
누군가가 하품하는 것을 본 지. 하품하는 것이, 내게는, 굉장히 신기해 보

of curiosity. Come, / now! / Yawn again! / It is an order."
이는 구나. 자, 지금! 다시 하품을 하거라! 명령이다."

"That frightens me… I cannot, any more…" murmured the
"그렇게 말하니 놀랐잖아요… 할 수 없어요, 더 이상은…" 어린왕자는 중얼거렸다,

little prince, / now completely abashed.
완전히 겸연쩍은 듯이.

"Hum! Hum!" replied the king. "Then I —— I order you
"이런! 이런!" 그는 대답했다, "그러면 내가 — 내가 명령하노라

sometimes to yawn / and sometimes to —— "
어떤 때는 하품하고 어떤 때는 — "

He sputtered a little, / and seemed vexed.
그는 조금 빠르게 지껄였고, 화가 난 것처럼 보였다.

For / what the king fundamentally insisted upon was / that his
왜냐하면 왕이 근본적으로 주장하는 것은

authority should be respected. He tolerated no disobedience.
그의 권위가 존중받아야 한다는 것이기 때문이다. 그는 어떤 불복종도 용서할 수 없었다.

He was an absolute monarch. But, because he was a very
그는 절대 군주였다. 그러나, 그는 매우 착한 사람이었으므로,

good man, / he made / his orders reasonable.
그는 만들었다 그의 명령을 합리적으로.

"If I ordered a general," he would say, / by way of example,
"내가 만일 장군에게 명령한다면." 그는 말하곤 했다. 예를 들어,

/ "if I ordered a general / to change himself into a sea bird,
"내가 장군에게 명령한다면 갈매기로 변하라고,

/ and if the general did not obey me, / that would not be the
그런데 만약 장군이 나에게 복종하지 않는다면, 그것은 장군의 잘못이 아니니라.

fault of the general. It would be my fault."
그것은 내 잘못이다."

---

murmur 중얼거리다, 불평을 말하다 | abashed 창피한, 겸연쩍은 | sputter 빠르게 지껄이다 | vex 짜증나게 하다 |
fundamentally 근본적으로 | tolerate 견디다 | reasonable 합리적인

"May I sit down?" came now a timid inquiry / from the little
"앉아도 되나요?" 주뼛거리며 물었다 어린왕자가.

prince.

"I order you to do so," / the king answered him, / and
"내가 그렇게 하라고 명령하노라." 왕이 그에게 대답했다.

majestically gathered / in a fold of his ermine mantle.
그리고 위엄 있게 걷어 올렸다 그의 담비 모피로 만든 긴 망토자락을.

But the little prince was wondering… The planet was tiny.
그러나 어린왕자는 의아하게 생각했다… 그 별은 너무 작았다.

Over what could this king really rule?
왕은 도대체 무엇을 통치할 수 있는 거지?

"Sire," he said to him, "I beg that / you will excuse my asking
"폐하," 어린왕자가 왕에게 말했다, "간청 드립니다 질문 하나 해도 괜찮을지 —"

you a question —— "

"I order you / to ask me a question," / the king hastened to
"네게 명하노니 내게 질문을 하라." 왕은 그를 안심시키기 위해 서둘러 말했다.

assure him.

Key Expression 🍯

**조동사 May**

'May I~?'는 'Can I~?'에 비해 정중한 인상을 주고, 더 정중한 표현으로는
'Might I~?'가 있습니다.
조동사 May는 여러 가지 뜻이 있지만, 아래 두 가지가 가장 많이 쓰인답니다.

▶ ~일지(할지)도 모른다

ex) It may be true. 사실일지도 모른다, 아마 사실일 것이다.
He may go, or he may not. 그는 갈지도 모르고 안 갈지도 모른다.

▶ (허가를 나타내어) ~해도 좋다, ~해도 괜찮다

ex) You may go there at any moment. 언제라도 그곳에 가도 좋다.
You may ask. 물어봐도 괜찮다. (가벼운 명령을 나타냄)

inquiry 질문, 조사 | mantle 외투 | wondering 의아하게 생각하는 | sire (왕에 대한 경칭) 폐하, 전하 | hasten
서두르다

"Sire —— over what do you rule?"
"폐하       — 도대체 무엇을 통치하십니까?"

"Over everything," / said the king, / with magnificent
"모든 것을 다 통치하지."        왕이 대답했다,        간단 명료하게.

simplicity.

"Over everything?"
"모든 것을요?"

The king made a gesture, / which took in his planet, / the
왕은 몸짓으로 가리켰다,                  자신의 별과,

other planets, / and all the stars.
다른 별과,           모든 별들을.

"Over all that?" asked the little prince.
"그 전부를요?"           어린왕자가 물어봤다.

"Over all that," / the king answered.
"그 전부를."           왕이 대답했다.

For his rule was / not only absolute: / it was also universal.
그의 지배는           절대적일 뿐만 아니라:        우주 전체에 해당하는 것이었다.

"And the stars obey you?"
"그러면 별들도 폐하를 따르고 있나요?"

"Certainly they do," / the king said. "They obey instantly. I do
"물론이지."           왕이 대답했다.        "그들은 즉시 복종하지.

not permit insubordination."
나는 불복종을 허락하지 않으니라."

Such power was a thing / for the little prince / to marvel at.
그러한 권력은 ~것이었다          어린왕자에게는           놀랄 만한.

If he had been master of such complete authority, / he would
만약 어린왕자가 그러한 완벽한 권력을 가졌다면,           그는 ~있었을지도 모른다

have been able to / watch the sunset, / not forty-four time in
그는 ~있었을지도 모른다     일몰을 볼 수,        하루에 44번이 아닌,

one day, / but seventy-two, / or even a hundred, / or even two
72번,           100번이라도,           200번이라도,

insubordination 불복종 I marvel 놀라다

hundred times, / without ever having to move his chair. And
의자를 움직일 필요도 없이.                                              그래서

/ because he felt a bit sad / as he remembered his little planet
그는 조금 슬펐기 때문에                    그의 작은 별을 떠올리면서

/ which he had forsaken, / he plucked up his courage / to ask
그가 버리고 온,                    그는 용기를 내어

the king a favor:
왕에게 간청했다:

"I should like to see a sunset... / Do me that kindness... /
"저는 일몰을 보고 싶어요…                    소원을 들어주세요…

Order the sun to set..."
해에게 지도록 명령해 주세요…"

"If I ordered a general / to fly from one flower to another / like
"만약 내가 어떤 장군에게 명령한다면    이 꽃에서 저 꽃으로 날아다니라고

a butterfly, / or to write a tragic drama, / or to change himself
나비처럼,          또는 비극적인 드라마를 쓰라고,          또는 그 자신을 갈매기로 바꾸라고,

into a sea bird, / and if the general did not carry out / the
그런데 만약 장군이 수행하지 못한다면

order that he had received, / which one of us would be in the
그가 받은 명령은,                    우리 중 누구의 잘못이겠는가?"

wrong?" the king demanded "The general, or myself?"
왕이 물었다                    "장군인가, 나인가?"

forsaken 버리다 | pluck up one's courage 용기를 내다 | general 장군 | tragic 비극적인

75

"You," / said the little prince firmly.
"폐하입니다." 어린왕자가 똑똑히 말했다.

"Exactly. One must require from each one / the duty which
"바로 그거다. 누구에게든 요구해야 하는 법이니라 각자에게

each one can perform," / the king went on. "Accepted
수행 가능한 임무를," 왕은 계속했다. "권력은 기초해야 하느니라

authority rests / first of all / on reason. If you ordered your
무엇보다 사리에. 만약 네가 너의 백성들에게 명령한다면

people / to go and throw themselves into the sea, / they would
바다에 몸을 던지라고.

rise up in revolution. I have the right / to require obedience /
그들은 혁명을 일으킬 것이니라. 나는 권리를 갖는 것이다 복종에 요구할

because my orders are reasonable."
왜냐하면 내 명령은 사리에 맞기 때문에."

"Then my sunset? The little prince reminded him: / for he
"그러면 제가 일몰을 보고 싶다고 한 건요? 어린왕자가 그에게 상기시켰다:

never forgot a question once / he had asked it.
왜냐하면 그는 결코 그 질문을 잊는 법이 없었다 그가 물어 봤던.

"You shall have your sunset. I shall command it. But,
"넌 일몰을 보게 될 것이다. 내가 명령을 내리겠노라. 그러나,

according to my science of government, / I shall wait until
나의 통치 철학에 따라서,

conditions are favorable."
조건이 갖추어 질 때까지 기다려야 하노라."

"When will that be?" inquired the little prince.
"그럼 언제쯤이 될까요?" 어린왕자가 물어봤다.

"Hum! Hum!" replied the king; / and before saying anything
"에헴! 에헴!" 왕이 대답했다; 그리고 다른 것을 이야기 하기 이전에

else / he consulted a bulky almanac. "Hum! Hum! That will
그는 커다란 달력을 뒤적였다. "흠! 흠! 그때쯤이니라

be about —— about —— that will be this evening / about
— 대략 — 오늘 저녁 7시 40분쯤.

---

firmly 단호하게 | rest on ~에 의존하다 | revolution 혁명 | consult 상담하다, 찾다, 뒤적이다 | bulky 부피가
큰 | almanac 달력, 역서

twenty minutes to eight. And you will see / how well I am
그러면 너는 보게 될 것이다   얼마나 내 명령에 잘 복종하는지를!"

obeyed!"

The little prince yawned. He was regretting / his lost sunset.
그 어린왕자는 하품했다.          그는 아쉬워했다          일몰을 볼 수 없어서.

And then, too, / he was already beginning / to be a little
그리고, 그때, 또한,    그는 벌써 시작했다          조금씩 지루해지기.

bored.

"I have nothing more / to do here," / he said to the king. "So I
"제게 더 이상 없네요          여기에서 할 일이,"    어린왕자는 왕에게 말했다.

shall set out on my way again."
"그래서 가던 길을 다시 떠나겠습니다."

"Do not go," / said the king, / who was very proud of / having
"가지 마라."          왕이 대답했다.          매우 자랑스럽게 느끼던          신하가 생긴

a subject. "Do not go. I will make you a Minister!"
것을.          "가지 마라.    내가 널 대신으로 삼겠노라!"

"Minister of what?"
"어떤 대신을요?"

"Minister of —— of Justice!"
"대신          — 법무!"

regret 후회하다, 아쉬워하다 | set out 떠나다, 출발하다, 착수하다 | justice 법무

"But there is nobody here / to judge!"
그러나 여기에 아무도 없는 걸요        재판할!"

"We do not know that," / the king said to him. "I have not yet
"그건 모르지."                왕이 그에게 말했다.              "나는 아직 못했느니라

made / a complete tour of my kingdom. I am very old. There
나의 왕국을 완벽히 다 둘러보지도.              나는 매우 늙었다.

is no room here / for a carriage. And it tires me to walk."
여기에는 자리가 없다    마차를 위한.        그리고 나는 걷는 것이 피곤하다."

"Oh, but I have looked already!" said the little prince, /
"오, 그런데 나는 이미 둘러 보았어요!"              어린왕자가 대답했다.

turning around to give one more glance / to the other side of
한번 힐끗 보며 돌면서                              별의 반대편을.

the planet. On that side, / as on this, / there was nobody at
              저쪽에는,            여기처럼,        아무도 없어요…

all...

"Then you shall judge yourself," / the king answered. "That
"그러면 너는 네 자신을 심판하라."              왕이 말했다.

is the most difficult thing of all. It is much more difficult / to
"그것은 가장 어려운 것이다.              그건 훨씬 더 어려운 법이니라

judge oneself / than to judge others. If you succeed in judging
스스로를 심판하는 것은    남을 판단하는 것보다.        만약 네 스스로를 공정하게 판단하는 것에 성

yourself rightly, / then you are indeed a man of true wisdom."
공한다면,              그러면 너는 참으로 지혜로운 사람이니라."

"Yes," / said the little prince, / "but I can judge myself
"알겠어요."    어린왕자가 말했다.        "그러나 저는 제 자신을 어디에서나 심판할 수 있어요.

anywhere. I do not need to live / on this planet."
              저는 살 필요가 없어요        이 별에서."

carriage 마차 | turn around 주위를 둘러보다

"Hum! Hum!" said the king. "I have good reason to believe
"이런! 이런!"    왕이 대답했다.    "나는 ~이라고 믿노라

that / somewhere on my planet / there is an old rat. I hear him
내 별 어딘가에    늙은 쥐들이 있다고.    나는 밤에 그들의 소

at night. You can judge this old rat. From time to time / you
리가 들린다.    넌 이 늙은 쥐를 재판하거라.    때로는

will condemn him to death. Thus his life will depend on /
너는 그들을 사형에 처하거라.    그러면 그의 삶은 달려 있게 될 것이다

your justice. But you will pardon him / on each occasion; for
네 심판에.    그러나 너는 그를 용서해 주어라    매번;

he must be treated thriftily. He is the only one / we have."
그를 아껴서 다뤄야 하느니라.    그는 오직 하나이기 때문이다    우리가 가지고 있는."

"I," / replied the little prince, / "do not like to condemn
"저는요," 어린왕자가 대답했다,    "누구에게도 사형 선고를 내리고 싶지 않아요.

anyone to death. And now I think / I will go on my way."
그리고 저는 생각이 듭니다    이제 제 갈 길을 가야겠다고."

"No," said the king.
"그럴 수 없다." 왕이 대답했다.

## 최상급 vs. 비교급

▶ 단음절어와 흔히 쓰는 2음절어는 다음과 같은 패턴으로 변해요.

형용사+~er=비교급

ex) big +~er = bigger / easy+~er=easier

형용사+~est=최상급

ex) big+~est=biggest / easy+~est=easiest

▶more, most를 사용할 때: 대부분의 2음절어와 3음절어 이상의 말

ex) the most difficult thing 가장 어려운 것 / much more difficult thing 더 어려운 것

▶불규칙으로 변화하는 것들도 있어요.

ex) good-better-best / bad-worse-worst / little-less-least

condemn ~에 형을 선고하다 | thriftily 저축하여

But the little prince, / having now completed / his preparations
그러나 어린왕자는,　　　　　　모두 마친　　　　　　　　그의 준비를

/ for departure, / had no wish / to grieve the old monarch.
출발을 위한,　　　~하고 싶지 않았다　늙은 왕을 고통스럽게.

"If Your Majesty wishes / to be promptly obeyed," / he said, /
"폐하가 원하신다면　　　명령에 즉각 복종하기를,"　　　그가 말했다.

"he should be able to / give me / a reasonable order. He should
"폐하가 ~하실 수 있어야 합니다　내게 주시기를　합당한 명령을.　　폐하는 ~할 수 있

be able, / for example, / to order me / to be gone / by the end of
습니다,　　예를 들어,　　제게 명령할　　떠나라고　　1분 내에.

one minute. It seems to me / that conditions are favorable…"
　　　제 눈에는 ~ 해 보입니다　여건이 마련되어 있는 듯이…"

As the king made no answer, / the little prince hesitated / a
왕이 대답을 하지 않자,　　　　　어린왕자는 머뭇거렸다

moment. Then, / with a sigh, / he took his leave.
잠시.　　그리고,　　한숨을 쉬며,　　그는 떠났다.

"I make you my Ambassador," / the king called out, / hastily.
"너를 외교사절로 삼겠다."　　　왕이 소리쳤다　　　조급히.

He had a magnificent air of authority.
그는 엄청난 권위를 가지고 있다.

"The grown-ups are very strange," / the little prince said to
"어른들은 정말 이상해."　　　　어린왕자가 자신에게 말했다.

himself, / as he continued on his journey.
그리고 그는 그의 여행을 계속했다.

---

grieve 슬프게 하다 | Your Majesty 폐하 | hesitate 머뭇거리다 | ambassador 대사 | hastily 조급히

## 11

The second planet / was inhabited by a conceited man.
두 번째 별에는 　　　　　　허영심 많은 남자가 살고 있었다.

"Ah! Ah! / I am about to receive / a visit from an admirer!"
"아! 아! 　　　곧 받겠는걸 　　　　　숭배자의 방문을"

he exclaimed from afar, / as soon as he saw the little prince
그는 멀리서부터 소리쳤다, 　　　　어린왕자가 다가오는 것을 보자마자.

coming.

For, to conceited men, / all other men are admirers.
왜냐하면, 허영심 많은 남자에게, 　다른 모든 사람은 숭배자이기 때문이다.

"Good morning," / said the little prince. / "That is a queer hat
"안녕하세요." 　　　　　어린왕자가 말했다 　　　　　"이상한 모자네요

/ you are wearing."
아저씨가 쓰고 있는 것은"

"It is a hat for salutes," / the
"그건 인사를 하기 위한 모자야."

conceited man replied. / "It is
허영심 많은 남자가 대답했다 　　답례 인

to rise in salute / when people
사로 들어올리는 것이지 　사람들이 내게 환호를

acclaim me. Unfortunately, /
보낼 때. 　　　　불행히도,

nobody at all ever passes this
아무도 이 길을 지나가지 않지만."

way."

---

conceited 자만에 빠진, 우울한 | admirer 찬미자, 숭배자 | salute 인사 | acclaim 칭송하다, 환호를 보내다

"Yes?" / said the little prince, / who did not understand / what
"그래요?" 어린왕자가 말했다. 이해할 수 없었지만

the conceited man was talking about.
허영심 많은 남자가 말하고 있는 것을.

"Clap your hands, / one against the other," / the conceited man
"손뼉을 쳐 봐, 한쪽 손으로 다른 손을."

now directed him.
허영심 많은 남자는 이제 그에게 지시했다.

The little prince clapped his hands. The conceited man raised
어린왕자는 손뼉을 쳤다. 허영심 많은 남자는 모자를 들어

his hat / in a modest salute.
공손하게 인사했다.

"This is more entertaining / than the visit to the king," / the
"이번이 더 재미있는데 왕을 만났을 때보다."

little prince said to himself. And he began again / to clap his
어린왕자는 생각했다. 그리고 나서 그는 다시 시작했다 손뼉치기를,

hands, one against the other. The conceited man again / raised
이어서. 허영심 많은 남자는 또 다시

his hat in salute.
모자를 들어 인사했다.

After five minutes of this exercise, / the little prince grew tired
5분 동안 이러고 나니, 어린왕자는 싫증이 났다

/ of the game's monotony.
이 게임의 단조로움에.

"And what should one do / to make the hat come down?" / he
"그러면 무엇을 해야 하나요 모자를 내려놓게 하려면?"

asked.
그는 물었다.

But the conceited man did not hear him. Conceited people
그러나 허영심 많은 남자는 그 말을 듣지 못했다. 허영심 많은 사람들은 듣지 못하는 법

never hear anything / but praise.
이다 칭찬 외에는.

clap 박수를 치다 | entertaining 재미있는, 즐거운 | monotony 단조로운

"Do you really admire me very much?" / he demanded of the
"너는 정말로 나를 숭배하니?"                                    그가 어린왕자에게 물었다.

little prince.

"What does that mean —— 'admire'?"
"무슨 뜻인데요                        — '숭배'라는 게 ?'"

"To admire means / that you regard me / as the handsomest, /
"숭배한다는 건 의미해      네가 나를 인정하는 것을      제일 잘생겼다고,

the best-dressed, / the richest, / and the most intelligent man /
제일 옷을 잘 입는다고,      제일 부자라고,      그리고 제일 똑똑한 사람이라고

on this planet."
이 별에서.'

"But you are the only man / on your planet!"
"하지만 아저씨는 유일한 사람이잖아요      이 별에 사는!'"

"Do me this kindness. Admire me just the same."
"친절을 베풀어 줘.      나를 숭배해 줘"

"I admire you," / said the little prince, / shrugging his
"나는 아저씨를 숭배해요."      어린왕자는 말했다.      어깨를 약간 으쓱거리면서

shoulders slightly, / "but what is there / in that to interest you
"하지만 뭐가 있는 거죠      아저씨를 그렇게 즐겁게 만드는?'"

so much?"

And the little prince went away.
그리고 어린왕자는 가 버렸다.

"The grown-ups are certainly very odd," / he said to himself,
"어른들이란 정말 이상해."      그는 생각했다.

/ as he continued on his journey.
그의 여행을 계속하면서.

The next planet / was inhabited / on by a tippler. This was a
다음 별에는          살고 있었다          술꾼이.          이것은 매우 짧은 방문

very short visit, / but it plunged the little prince / into deep
이었지만,          그러나 이것은 어린왕자를 빠뜨렸다          깊은 우울에.

dejection.

"What are you doing there?" he said to the tippler, / whom he
"거기에서 뭘 하고 있어요?"          어린왕자는 술꾼에게 말했다.          말 없이 앉아 있는

found settled down in silence / before a collection of empty
빈 병 한 무더기를 앞에 놓고

bottles / and also a collection of full bottles.
그리고 또한 술이 가득 채워져 있는 병 한 무더기와.

"I am drinking," / replied the tippler, / with a lugubrious air.
"술 마시고 있지."          술꾼이 대답했다.          침울한 분위기로.

"Why are you drinking?" demanded the little prince.
"왜 술을 마셔요?"          어린왕자가 물었다.

"So that I may forget," / replied the tippler.
"잊기 위해서."          술꾼이 대답했다.

"Forget what?" inquired the little prince, / who already was
"무엇을 잊어요?"          어린왕자가 물었다          이미 그를 측은하게 생각하면서.

sorry for him.

"Forget that I am ashamed," / the tippler confessed, / hanging
"내가 부끄럽다는 것을 잊으려고."          술꾼은 고백했다.          고개를 떨구며.

his head.

"Ashamed of what?" / insisted the little prince, / who wanted
"뭐가 부끄러운데요?"          어린왕자는 계속했다.          그를 도와주고 싶어서.

to help him.

---

tippler 술꾼, 술고래 | plunge 빠지게 하다, 던져 넣다 | dejection 실의, 낙담 | lugubrious 애처로운, 우울한 | confess
고백하다

"Ashamed of drinking!" / The
"술 마시는 게 부끄러워!"

tippler brought his speech / to an
술꾼은 말을 마치고                          끝까지,

end, / and shut himself up / in an
입을 다물었다

impregnable silence.
영원한 침묵 속으로.

And the little prince went away,
그리고 어린왕자는 가던 길을 갔다,

/ puzzled.
난처해하며.

"The grown-ups are certainly
"어른들은 정말 매우, 매우 이상해,"

very, very odd,"

he said to himself, / as he
그는 생각하며,

continued on his journey.
그의 여행을 계속했다.

bring~to an end ~을 마치다, 끝내다 | impregnable (신념 따위가) 확고부동한, 난공불락의 | puzzle 당황케 하다,
난처하게 만들다

## ♔ mini test 4

### A. 다음 문장을 해석해 보세요.

(1) He did not know how the world is simplified for kings.
→

(2) How could he recognize me when he had never seen me before?
→

(3) The little prince looked everywhere to find a place to sit down.
→

(4) I order you to ask me a question.
→

### B. 다음 주어진 문장이 되도록 빈칸에 써 넣으세요.

(1) 그는 아주 좋은 사람이기 때문에, 그는 합리적인 명령을 만들었다.

Because he was a very good man, he made his orders
_____.

(2) 나는 복종을 요구할 권리를 가지고 있다 왜냐하면 나의 명령은 합리적이기 때문이다.

I have the right to _____ because my orders are reasonable.

(3) 나는 내 별 어딘가에 늙은 쥐가 있다고 믿고 있는 그럴만한 이유를 가지고 있다.

I have good reason to believe that _____ there is an old rat.

A. (1) 그는 왕들에게 세상이 얼마나 간단하다는 것을 몰랐다. (2) 그가 나를 전에 본 적이 없는데 어떻게 그가 나를 알아 볼 수가 있죠? (3) 어린왕자는 앉을 만한 곳을 찾으려 여기저기를 둘러보았다.

86   The Little Prince

(4) 불행히도, 아무도 전혀 <u>이 길을 지나가지 않는다</u>.

Unfortunately, nobody at all                .


**C. 의미가 비슷한 것끼리 서로 연결해 보세요.**

(1) Fundamentally  ▶        ◀ ① respect

(2) magnificent    ▶        ◀ ② cry, shout

(3) Exclaim        ▶        ◀ ③ basically

(4) Admire         ▶        ◀ ④ grand, majestic, superb


**D. 다음 주어진 문장이 본문의 내용과 맞으면 T, 틀리면 F에 동그라미 하세요.**

(1) The king was a reasonable commander.
[ T / F ]

(2) The tippler who lived in the next planet didn't feel ashamed of drinking.
[ T / F ]

(3) The tippler kept drinking to forget that he was ashamed.
[ T / F ]

(4) The king's rule was not only relative, but also limited.
[ T / F ]

## 13

The fourth planet / belonged to a businessman. This man was
네 번째 별은　　　　　상인의 별이었다.　　　　　　　　이 사람은 너무 바빠서

so much occupied / that he did not even raise his head / at the
고개조차 들지 않았다

little prince's arrival.
어린왕자가 도착했을 때.

"Good morning," / the little prince said to him. "Your cigarette
"안녕하세요."　　　　　어린왕자가 그에게 말했다.

has gone out."
"담뱃불이 꺼졌는데요"

"Three and two make five. Five and seven make twelve. Twelve
"3 더하기 2는 5.　　　　　5 더하기 7은 12.

and three make fifteen. Good morning. Fifteen and seven make
12 더하기 3은 15.　　　　안녕.　　　　15 더하기 7은 22.

twenty-two. Twenty-two and six make twenty-eight. I haven't
22 더하기 6은 28.

time to light it again. Twenty-six and five make thirty-one.
새로 불을 붙일 시간도 없구나.　　26 더하기 5는 31.

Phew! Then that makes five-hundred-and one million, six-
휴우!　　그러니까 모두 5억 162만 2,731이 되는군"

hundred-twenty-two thousand, seven-hundred-thirty-one."

"Five hundred million what?" / asked the little prince.
"무엇이 5억이에요?"　　　　　어린왕자가 물었다.

"Eh? Are you still there? Five-hundred-and-one million —— / I
"응?　　아직 거기 있었니?　　　　5억 100만—

can't stop… I have so much to do! I am concerned with matters
멈출 수가 없어…　할 일이 너무 많아서!　　　나는 중요한 일을 하고 있어.

of consequence. I don't amuse myself with balderdash. Two
쓸데없는 일로 낭비하지 않아.

---

go out (불이) 꺼지다 | consequence 결과, 중요함 | amuse ~를 즐겁게 하다 | balderdash 쓸데없는 일 | giddy
현기증 나는, 아찔한 | goodness knows 아무도 모름, 누가 알겠는가 | frightful 지독한, 요란한 | resound (소리가)
울리다, 울려 퍼지다 | attack 공격하다 | rheumatism 류머티즘 | loaf 빈둥거리다, 빈둥빈둥 돌아다니다

and five make seven..."
2 더하기 5는 7..."

"Five-hundred-and-one million what?" / repeated the little
"무엇이 5억 100만인데요?"                                      어린왕자가 다시 물었다,

prince, / who never in his life had let go of a question / once he
              그는 절대 질문을 그만두지 않는다

had asked it.
일단 묻기 시작하면.

The businessman raised his head.
상인은 고개를 들었다.

"During the fifty-four years / that I have inhabited this planet,
"54년 동안                              내가 이 별에 살아온,

/ I have been disturbed only three times. The first time was
    나는 딱 세 번 방해받았어.                          첫 번째는 22년 전,

twenty-two years ago, / when some giddy goose fell from
                      어디선가 정신없는 거위 떼가 떨어졌을 때야

goodness knows where. He made the most frightful noise / that
                                      지독한 소음을 내서

resounded all over the place, / and I made four mistakes in my
이곳 전체에 울려 퍼져서.                    계산에 4번이나 실수를 했어.

addition. The second time, / eleven years ago, / I was disturbed
        두 번째는,                      11년 전,

by an attack of rheumatism. I don't get enough exercise. I have
신경통이 발병했을 때지.                    나는 운동을 거의 못 해.

no time for loafing. The third time —— well, / this is it! I was
빈둥거릴 시간이 없어.            세 번째는 말이지    — 음,      지금이야!      내가 말하고

saying, / then, five-hundred-and-one millions —— "
있던 게.        그러니까, 5억 100만이었지 —"

Key Expression

**so (much)~that··· 너무 ~해서 ···하다**
'So+형용사·부사+that~' 구문은 '너무 ~해서 ~하다'라는 의미로 결과를 나타냅니다.
~ 자리에 명사를 넣을 경우에는 'so' 대신 'such'를 사용하세요.

ex) This man was so much busy that he did not even raise his head at the little
prince's arrival.
이 사람은 너무 바빠서 어린왕자의 도착에도 고개조차 들지 않았다.

"Millions of what?"
"무엇이 수백 만이냐고요?"

The businessman suddenly realized / that there was no hope
상인은 갑자기 깨달았다                           평온해질 가망이 없다는 사실을

of being left in peace / until he answered this question.
                        질문에 대답하기 전에는.

"Millions of those little objects," / he said, / "which one
"수백 만의 저기 작은 물체들."                그는 말했다.

sometimes sees in the sky."
"하늘에서 가끔 보는 것 말이야"

"Flies?"
"파리 말인가요?"

"Oh, no. Little glittering objects."
"오, 아니.     반짝반짝 빛나는 작은 것들 말이야."

"Bees?"
"벌이요?"

"Oh, no. Little golden objects / that set lazy men to idle
"오, 아니.    조그만 금빛 물체 말이야        게으름뱅이에게 허황된 공상을 하게 만드는.

dreaming. As for me, / I am concerned with matters of
             나로 말하자면,        중요한 일에 관계된 사람이야.

consequence. There is no time / for idle dreaming / in my
             시간이 없단다          허황된 꿈으로 빈둥거릴        내 인생에서."

life."

"Ah! You mean the stars?"
"아!    별 말인가요?"

"Yes, that's it. The stars."
"그래, 그거야.        별들을 말이야."

"And what do you do / with five-hundred millions of stars?"
"뭘 하는데요              5억 개의 별들로?"

---

glittering 반짝반짝 빛나는 | idle 빈둥거리다 | accurate 정확한 | reign over 군림하다, 통치하다

"Five-hundred-and-one million, / six-hundred-twenty-two
"5억                                                      62만 2천,

thousand, / seven-hundred-thirty-one. I am concerned with
      731개야,                                나는 중요한 일을 하는 사람이야:

matters of consequence: I am accurate."
                            정확한 사람이라고."

"And what do you do / with these stars?"
"그러니까 뭘 하느냐고요          이 별들을 가지고?"

"What do I do with them?"
"내가 그걸 가지고 뭘 하느냐고?"

"Yes."
"예."

"Nothing. I own them."
"아무것도.        나는 별들을 소유하는 거야."

"You own the stars?"
"별이 당신 것이라고요?"

"Yes."
"응."

"But I have already seen a king who —— "
"하지만 난 왕을 본 적이 있는데 그 사람은 ―"

"Kings do not own, / they reign over. It is a very different
"왕은 소유하는 게 아니야.          통치할 뿐이지.          그건 전혀 다른 문제라고."

matter."

---

**Key Expression** 🎯

**not ~ until···**
직역하면 '···할 때까지는 ~하지 않다'라는 뜻이지만, 의역하면 '···하고 나서야 비
로소 ~하다'라는 의미가 됩니다.

ex) There was no hope of being left in peace until he answered this question.
그가 이 질문에 대답하기 전에는 평온해질 희망이 없었다.

"And what good does it do you / to own the stars?"
"그러면 아저씨는 무엇을 할 건데요                        별을 가져서?"

"It does me the good / of making me rich."
"그건 내게 도움을 주지          내가 부자가 되도록."

"And what good does it / do you to be rich?"
"무슨 도움을 주는데요          당신이 부자가 되도록?"

"It makes it possible for me / to buy more stars, if any are
"그건 가능하게 해 주지          내가 더 많은 별을 사는 것을,

discovered."
별을 발견하기만 하면."

"This man," / the little prince said to himself, / "reasons a
"이 사람은,"          어린왕자는 생각했다.

little like my poor tippler…"
"그 술꾼이랑 비슷한 논리로군…"

Nevertheless, / he still had some more questions.
그럼에도 불구하고,          그는 계속 질문을 했다.

"How is it possible / for one to own the stars?"
"어떻게 가능한가요          사람이 별을 소유하는 게?"

"To whom do they belong?" / the businessman retorted, /
"별이 누구의 소유지?"          상인이 되물었다.

peevishly.
비위에 거슬린 듯이.

"I don't know. To nobody."
"모르죠.          누구의 것도 아니죠."

"Then they belong to me, / because I was the first person to
"그러니까 내 것이 되는 거야.          내가 제일 처음 생각했으니까."

think of it."

"Is that all that is necessary?"
"필요한 것은 그것 뿐인가요?"

---

nevertheless 그렇기는 하지만 | retort 되묻다, 반박하다 | peevishly 비위에 거슬린 듯이 | patent 특허(권) | administer
관리하다, 지배하다, 통치하다

"Certainly. When you find a diamond / that belongs to
"물론이지.　　　네가 다이아몬드를 발견했다면　　　　　주인이 없는,

nobody, it is yours. When you discover an island / that
그건 네 것이야.　　네가 섬을 발견했다면　　　　　　　주인이 없는,

belongs to nobody, / it is yours. When you get an idea / before
그것도 네 것이야.　네가 어떤 아이디어를 생각해 냈다면　　다른 누구보다 먼저,

any one else, / you take out a patent on it: / it is yours. So with
그것에 대해 특허를 내서:　　　　　　　네 것이 되는 거야.　나도 마찬가지지:

me: / I own the stars, / because nobody else before me / ever
나는 별을 소유하는 거야.　왜냐하면 나 이전에 어느 누구도　　　　　　별을 갖겠다는 생각을

thought of owning them."
하지 않았으니까."

"Yes, that is true," / said the little prince. "And what do you
"그래요, 그건 맞아요,"　　어린왕자는 말했다.　　　　　"그런데 그걸로 무엇을 할 건데요?"

do with them?"

"I administer them," / replied the businessman. "I count them
"난 그걸 관리하지,"　　　상인은 답변했다.　　　　　　　"별을 세고 또 세는 거야.

and recount them. It is difficult. But I am a man / who is
＊ 그건 어려운 일이지.　　　그러나 나는 사람이야

naturally interested / in matters of consequence."
관심을 갖는　　　　　　　중요한 일에."

Key Expression 📍

**make it possible (for…) to ~ : (…가) ~하는 것을 가능하게
하다**

make는 5형식에서 'make + ~목적어 + …목적보어'의 형태로 '~를 …로 만들
다'라는 의미로 쓰입니다. 이 구문에서는 목적어 자리에 가목적어 it을 놓고 진목
적어 to부정사 형태로 놓아 '(to부정사) 하는 것을 가능하게 만들다'라는 의미
가 됩니다.

ex) It makes it possible for me to buy more stars.
　　그것은 내가 더 많은 별을 사는 것을 가능하게 해 준다.
　→ to 부정사 앞에 의미상 주어 'for+목적격'을 넣어 '…가 ~하는 것을 가능하
게 하다'라는 의미가 완성됩니다.

93

The little prince was still not satisfied.
어린왕자는 그래도 만족하지 않았다.

"If I owned a silk scarf," / he said, / "I could put it around my
"만약 나한테 실크 스카프가 있다면요." 그는 말했다. "그걸 목에 둘러서

neck / and take it away with me. If I owned a flower, / I could
가져갈 수 있어요. 나한테 꽃이 있다면,

pluck that flower / and take it away with me. But you cannot
그 꽃을 꺾어서 가지고 갈 수 있어요. 하지만 당신은 딸 수 없잖아요

pluck / the stars from heaven…"
하늘에 있는 별을…"

"No. But I can put them in the bank."
"못 하지. 하지만 나는 그것을 은행에 맡길 수 있어."

"Whatever does that mean?"
"그게 무슨 뜻이에요?"

"That means / that I write the number of my stars / on a little
"그건 말이지 별의 숫자를 적는 거야 작은 종이에.

paper. And then / I put this paper / in a drawer / and lock it
그리고 나서 나는 이 종이를 넣어 서랍에 그리고 열쇠로 잠그는 거지."

with a key."

"And that is all?"
"그게 끝이에요?"

"That is enough," / said the businessman.
"그것으로 충분해," 상인은 말했다.

"It is entertaining," / thought the little prince. "It is rather
"그거 재미있군." 어린왕자는 생각했다. "꽤 시적이기도 한데.

poetic. But it is of no great consequence."
그렇지만 중요한 일은 아닌 걸."

On matters of consequence, / the little prince had ideas /
중요한 일에 대해, 어린왕자의 생각은

which were very different from / those of the grown-ups.
매우 달랐다 어른들의 생각과.

pluck (꽃을) 꺾다

"I myself own a flower," / he continued his conversation /
"제게는 꽃이 하나 있는데," 　　　　어린왕자는 대화를 계속했다

with the businessman, / "which I water every day. I own three
상인과의, 　　　　　"매일 물을 주고 있어요. 　　　　　화산이 세 개 있는데,

volcanoes, / which I clean out every week / (for I also clean
　　　매주 그것들을 청소해요 　　　　　　　(꺼진 화산도 청소를 하죠;

out the one that is extinct; / one never knows) / It is of some
　　　　　　　어떻게 될지 아무도 모르니까요)　　그건 내 화산들에 도움이

use to my volcanoes, / and it is of some use to my flower, /
되죠, 　　　　　　그리고 내 꽃에도 도움이 되요,

that I own them. But you are of no use to the stars…"
내가 소유하고 있는.　　하지만 당신은 별한테 아무 쓸모가 없잖아요…"

The businessman opened his mouth, / but he found nothing to
상인은 입을 열었다, 　　　　　　　　그러나 대답할 말이 없었다.

say in answer. And the little prince went away.
　　　　　　그리고 어린왕자는 떠나버렸다.

"The grown-ups are certainly altogether extraordinary," /
"어른들은 정말로 이상해," 

he said simply, talking to himself / as he continued on his
그는 그렇게 생각했다, 　　　　　　　그의 여행을 계속하면서.

journey.

---

**Key Expression** 🔑

### of + 추상명사 = 형용사
영어에서 'of + 추상명사' 형태가 종종 형용사와 같은 역할를 합니다.
of use = useful / of importance = important / of interest =
interesting 등으로 응용해보세요.

ex) It is of some use to my flower
　　 그것은 내 꽃에게 약간 유용하다.
　　 It is of no great consequence.
　　 그것은 그다지 중요하지 않다.

# 14

The fifth planet / was very strange. It was the smallest of
다섯 번째 별은 아주 묘했다. 이것은 그 중에서 가장 작은 별이었다.

all. There was just enough room on it / for a street lamp and
이 별에는 작은 공간 밖에 없었다 오직 가로등과 그 점등원이 있을 만한.

a lamplighter. The little prince / was not able to reach / any
어린왕자는 이해되지 않았다

explanation of / the use of a street lamp and a lamplighter, /
도무지 어떤 설명도 가로등과 점등원이 왜 필요한지,

somewhere in the heavens, / on a planet which had no people, /
하늘 어딘가에서, 사람이 아무도 없는 어떤 별에,

and not one house. But he said to himself, / nevertheless:
그리고 어떤 집도 없는. 그러나 그는 생각했다, 그럼에도 불구하고:

"If may well be that / this man is absurd. But he is not so
"~할 수도 있어 이 사람도 어리석을 수 있어. 그러나 그는 그렇게 어리석지는 않아

absurd / as the king, / the conceited man, / the businessman,
왕이나, 허영심 많은 남자나, 사업가나,

/ and the tippler. For at least / his work has some meaning.
술꾼만큼. 적어도 그의 일은 어떤 의미가 있어.

When he lights his street lamp, / it is as if he brought one
그가 가로등을 켤 때는, 세상에 별이 하나 더 나타나는 것처럼,

more star to life, or one flower. When he puts out his lamp, /
또는 꽃 한 송이를. 그가 가로등을 끌 때는,

he sends the flower, or the star, / to sleep. That is a beautiful
그가 꽃 한 송이, 또는 별 하나를, 잠들게 하는 것이야. 이것은 정말 아름다운 직업이야.

occupation. And since it is beautiful / it is truly useful."
그리고 아름답기 때문에 정말 쓸모 있는 거야."

When he arrived / on the planet / he respectfully saluted the
그는 도착했을 때 별에 점등원에게 공손히 인사했다.

lamplighter.

lamplighter (가로등에) 불 켜는 사람 | explanation 해명, 설명 | put out (불을) 끄다 | respectfully 정중하게

"Good Morning. Why have you just put out your lamp?"
"안녕하세요. 　　　　　　왜 방금 가로등을 끄셨나요?"

"Those are the orders," / replied the lamplighter. "Good
"그것은 명령이었어." 　　　　　　점등원이 대답했다 　　　　　　"안녕?"

morning."

"What are the orders?"
"명령이 뭐였어요?"

"The orders are / that I put out my lamp. Good evening."
"명령은 　　　　　　나보고 등을 끄란 거였어. 　　　　　　안녕."

And he lighted his lamp again.
그리고 그는 가로등을 다시 켰다.

"But why have you just lighted it again?"
"그런데 왜 다시 불을 켰나요?"

"Those are the orders," / replied the lamplighter.
"명령이었어." 　　　　　　점등원이 대답했다.

"I do not understand," / said the little prince.
"이해할 수 없어요." 　　　　　　어린왕자가 대답했다.

"There is nothing to understand," / said the lamplighter.
"이해하고 말고 할 필요가 없어." 　　　　　　점등원이 말했다.

"Orders are orders. / Good morning."
"명령은 명령일 뿐이야. 　　　　　　안녕."

And he put out his lamp.
그리고 그는 불을 껐다.

---

Key Expression

### as if 마치 ~ 인 것처럼

보통 as if 절 안에서는 가정법을 쓰지만, 구어체에서는 보통 직설법으로도 사용해요.

ex) when he lights his street lamp, / it is as if he brought one more star to life, or one flower.
그가 가로등을 켰을 때, 그것은 마치 그가 그의 삶에 혹은 꽃에게 하나의 별을 가져다 준 것 같았다.

**Then he** mopped **his** forehead / **with a** handkerchief /
그리고 그는 그의 이마를 닦았다　　　　　　　그의 손수건으로

decorated **with red** squares.
빨간 정사각 무늬로 장식된.

"**I** follow **a terrible profession. In the old days** / **it was**
"나는 정말 이상한 직업에 종사해.　　　　옛날에는　　　　할 만 했어.

**reasonable. I put the lamp out** / **in the morning,** / **and in the**
나는 불을 끄고　　　　아침에는,　　　　밤에는

**evening** / **I lighted it again. I had the rest of the day** / **for**
다시 불을 켰어.　　　나는 여분의 시간이 있었어

**relaxation** / **and the rest of the night** / **for sleep.**"
휴식을 위한　　　그리고 나머지 밤 시간에는　　잠을 위한."

mop 닦다 | forehead 이마 | handkerchief 손수건 | decorated 장식된 | square 정사각형, (바둑판의) 눈 |
follow (직업에) 종사하다, ~을 직업으로 하다

"And the orders have been changed / since that time?"
"그런데 명령이 바뀌었나요                          그때 후로?"

"The orders have not been changed," / said the lamplighter.
"명령은 바뀌지 않았어."                          점등원이 말했다.

"That is the tragedy! / From year to year / the planet has
"그것이 비극이야!           그때부터 지금까지       별은 계속해서 빨리 돌고 있는데

turned more rapidly / and the orders have not been changed!"
그 명령은 아직도 바뀌지 않았어!"

"Then what?" asked the little prince.
"그래서요?"           어린왕자가 물었다

"Then —— / the planet now makes a complete turn every
"그래서—           그 별은 이제는 1분에 한번씩 돌고 있어.

minute, / and I no longer have a single second / for repose.
나는 1초도 시간이 없어                          휴식을 위한.

Once every minute / I have to light my lamp / and put it out!"
매 1분마다           나는 등을 켜야 하고           꺼야 돼!"

"That is very funny! / A day lasts only one minute, / here
"그거 너무 재미있어요!           하루가 오직 1분만 지속되다니,

where you live!"
여기 당신이 사는 곳에서는!"

"It is not funny at all!" said the lamplighter. "While we have
"전혀 재미있지 않아!"           점등원이 말했다.           "우리가 이렇게 이야기 하는 동

been talking together / a month has gone by."
안에           한 달이 지나갔어."

tragedy 비극 | repose 휴식

"A month?"
"한 달?"

"Yes, a month. Thirty minutes. Thirty days. Good evening."
"응, 한 달.    30분.    30일.    안녕."

And he lighted his lamp again.
점등원은 다시 등을 켰다.

As the little prince watched him, / he felt / that he loved
어린왕자는 그를 쳐다보면서,    그는 느꼈다    그가 그 점등원을 사랑한다는 것을

this lamplighter / who was so faithful to his orders. He
명령에 그토록 충실한.

remembered the sunsets / which he himself had gone to seek,
그는 일몰을 기억해냈다    자신이 찾아다녔던.

/ in other days, / merely by pulling up his chair; / and he
예전에,    의자를 조금씩 뒤로 물리면서;

wanted to help his friend.
그리고 그는 친구를 도와주고 싶어졌다.

"You know," / he said, / "I can tell you a way / you can rest /
"있잖아요."    어린왕자가 말했다,    "나는 방법을 말해 주고 싶어요    아저씨가 쉴 수 있는

whenever you want to…"
원할 때면 언제나…"

"I always want to rest," / said the lamplighter.
"나는 언제나 쉬고 싶어."    점등원이 말했다.

For it is possible for a man / to be faithful and lazy / at the
사람들에게는 가능한 것이다    성실하면서도 게으른 것이    동시에.

same time.

The little prince went on / with his explanation:
어린왕자는 계속했다    그의 설명을:

merely 단지, 다만

"Your planet is so small / that three strides will take you / all
"아저씨의 별은 너무도 작으니까          세 걸음이면 다 돌 수 있잖아요

the way around it. To be always in the sunshine, / you need
이 주변을 모두.          언제나 햇빛 속에 있으려면.

only walk along / rather slowly. When you want to rest, / you
걷기만 하면 되요          조금 더 천천히.          쉬고 싶을 때면.

will walk —— / and the day will last / as long as you like."
걸어 봐요 —          그러면 낮이 길어질 거예요          아저씨가 원하는 만큼."

"That doesn't do me much good," / said the lamplighter. "The
"그건 별로 도움이 안 되는 걸,"          점등원이 말했다.

one thing I love in life / is to sleep."
"내가 오직 내 삶에서 원하는 것은          잠을 자는 것이니까."

"Then you're unlucky," / said the little prince.
"그렇다면 안 되었네요,"          어린왕자가 말했다.

"I am unlucky," / said the lamplighter. "Good morning."
"나는 운이 없군,"          점등원이 말했다.          "안녕."

And he put out his lamp.
그리고는 그는 가로등을 껐다.

stride 큰 걸음, 한 걸음(의 폭) | all the way 내내

"That man," / said the little prince to himself, / as he
"저 사람은," 어린왕자는 생각했다.

continued farther on his journey, / "that man would be
계속 더 멀리 여행하며, "저 사람은 무시를 당하겠지:

scorned / by all the others: / by the king, by the conceited
다른 사람들로부터, 허영심이 많은 사람으로부터,

man, by the tippler, by the businessman. Nevertheless / he is
술꾼으로부터, 사업가로부터, 그럼에도 불구하고

the only one of them all / who does not seem to me ridiculous.
그는 그 중에 유일한 한 사람이다 내게 우스워 보이지 않는.

Perhaps that is because / he is thinking of something else /
아마도 그건 ~ 때문일 것이다 그가 다른 것을 생각하기

besides himself."
그 자신 외에."

He breathed a sigh of regret, / and said to himself again:
그는 한숨을 쉬며, 다시 생각했다:

"That man is the only one of them all / whom I could have
"저 사람은 그 중 유일한 한 사람이야 내가 친구로 사귀고 싶었던.

made my friend. But his planet is indeed too small. There is
그러나 그의 별은 참으로 너무 작아.

no room on it / for two people…"
그 곳엔 자리가 없어 두 사람을 위한 자리조차…"

What the little prince did not dare confess / was that he was
어린왕자가 감히 고백하지 못한 것은

sorry most of all to leave this planet, / because it was blest /
그가 그 별을 떠나기 가장 아쉬웠다는 점이었다. 신의 축복을 받았기 때문에

every day with 1440 sunsets!
매일 1,440번이나 해가 지는!

---

scorn 경멸하다, 모욕하다 | ridiculous 우스운, 어리석은 | bless 신의 축복을 빌다(blest는 bless의 과거분사)

## 15

**The sixth planet was / ten times larger / than the last one. It was**
여섯 번째 별은　　　　　　　10배나 컸다　　　　　　이전의 별보다.

**inhabited by an old gentleman / who wrote** voluminous **books.**
그 곳에는 노신사가 살고 있었다　　　　　　　　　팡장히 큰 책을 쓰고 있는.

**"Oh, look! Here is an explorer!" / he exclaimed to himself /**
"오, 보자!　　탐험가가 왔구나!"　　　그는 소리쳤다

**when he saw little prince coming.**
어린왕자가 오는 것을 보고.

**The little prince sat down on the table / and** panted **a little. He**
어린왕자는 책상에 앉아서　　　　　　　숨을 헐떡였다.

**had already traveled so much and so far!**
그는 지금까지 너무 많은 그리고 너무 멀리 여행을 한 것이다!

**"Where do you come from?" / the old gentleman said to him.**
"넌 어디에서 왔니?"　　　　　　　　　노신사가 그에게 물었다.

**"What is that big book?" / said the little prince. "What are you**
"그 큰 책은 무엇인가요?"　　　　어린왕자가 말했다.

**doing?"**
"할아버지는 뭘 하고 계신가요?"

Key Expression 🍗

**ten times larger than ~ : ~보다 10배 큰**

'~보다 몇 배, ~의 몇 배'를 나타내는 배수비교는 원급과 비교급 두 가지고 표현
할 수 있어요.

배수 + as + 형용사/부사 + as +비교할 대상
=배수 +비교급 + than +비교할 대상

여기서 배수의 자리에는 twice(2배), three times(3배) 등을 넣습니다.

ex) The sixth planet was ten times larger than the last one.
　　　　　　　　　 = ten times as large as
　여섯 번째 별은 지난번보다 10배 컸다.

voluminous 부피가 큰 | pant 헐떡거리다, 숨차다

"I am a geographer," / said the old gentleman.
"나는 지리학자란다."    노신사가 말했다.

"What is a geographer?" / asked the little prince.
"지리학자가 무엇인가요?"    어린왕자가 물었다.

"A geographer is a scholar / who knows the location / of all
"지리학자는 학자란다    위치를 알고 있는

the seas, rivers, towns, mountains, and deserts."
모든 바다, 강, 마을, 산, 그리고 사막의."

"That is very interesting," / said the little prince. "Here at
"그거 참 재미있네요."    어린왕자가 말했다.    "여기 드디어

last is a man / who has a real profession!" And he cast a look
진정한 직업인이 있군요!"    그리고 그는 주위를 둘러봤다

around him / at the planet of the geographer. It was the most
지리학자의 별을.    그것은 가장 멋지고 훌륭한 별이었다

magnificent and stately planet / that he had ever seen.
그가 지금까지 보았던.

"Your planet is very beautiful," / he said. "Has it any oceans?"
"할아버지 별은 정말 아름다워요."    그가 말했다.    "이 별에는 바다가 있나요?"

"I couldn't tell you," / said the geographer.
"말해 줄 수가 없단다."    지리학자가 말했다.

"Ah!" The little prince was disappointed. "Has it any
"아!"    어린왕자는 실망했다.    "산은 있나요?"

mountains?"

"I couldn't tell you," / said the geographer.
"그것도 모른다."    지리학자가 말했다.

"And towns, / and rivers, and deserts?"
"그럼 마을은요,    그리고 강이나 사막은요?"

"I couldn't tell you that, either."
"그것도 알 수 없지."

"But you are a geographer!"
"하지만 할아버지는 지리학자잖아요!"

geographer 지리학자 | stately 위엄 있는

"Exactly," / the geographer said. "But I am not an explorer. I
"맞아."          지리학자는 말했다.                    "하지만 나는 탐험가가 아니야.

haven't a single explorer on my planet. It is not the geographer
내 별에는 탐험가가 한 명도 없단다.                    지리학자는 밖으로 나가지 않아

who goes out / to count the towns, the rivers, the mountains,
                마을이나 강, 산, 바다를 헤아리기 위해서.

the seas, the oceans, and the deserts. The geographer is
                                        지리학자는 아주 중요한 사람이라서

much too important / to go loafing about. He does not leave
돌아다닐 수가 없어.          지리학자는 책상을 떠나지 않아.

his desk. But he receives the explorers in his study. He asks
그러나 연구를 통해 탐험가들을 만나지.                    탐험가들에게 질문을 하고,

them questions, / and he notes down / what they recall of
받아적는 거야                      그들이 여행에 대해 회상하는 것을.

their travels. And if the recollections of any one among them
                    그리고 그들 중 누군가의 회상이

/ seem interesting to him, / the geographer orders an inquiry
흥미롭게 보이면,                    지리학자는 조사해 보는 거야

into / that explorer's moral character."
그 탐험가의 도덕적인 인격에 대해서."

"Why is that?"
"그건 왜요?"

Key Expression

**관계대명사 what : ~한 것**
관계대명사 'what'은 선행사를 포함한 관계대명사로 '~한 것'이라 해석되며 명
사절을 이끕니다. 여기서 'what'은 'the thing which[that]'으로 바꿔 생
각할 수 있죠.

ex) He notes down what they recall of their travels.
그는 그들이 자신들의 여행에 대해 회상하는 것을 받아적는다.

study 연구실, 서재, 사무실 | recall 회상하다 | recollection 회상, 기억 | moral character 도덕적 성품

"Because / an explorer who told lies / would bring disaster /
"왜냐하면        거짓말을 하는 탐험가는            문제를 일으키거든

on the books of the geographer. So would an explorer / who
지리학자의 책에.                              탐험가도 마찬가지야

drank too much."
술을 너무 많이 마시는."

"Why is that?" / asked the little prince.
"그건 왜요?"            어린왕자는 물었다.

"Because intoxicated men see double. Then the geographer /
"왜냐하면        술에 취한 사람들은 사물을 두 개로 보거든.      그러면 지리학자는

would note down two mountains / in a place where there was
산이 두 개라고 적게 될 거야              산이 하나 밖에 없는 지역에."

only one."

"I know someone," / said the little prince, / "who would make
"저도 알고 있어요."          어린왕자는 말했다              "좋지 않은 탐험을 하는 사람을"

a bad explorer."

"That is possible. Then, / when the moral character of the
"그럴 수도 있지.          그래서,      탐험가의 도덕적 인격이

explorer / is shown to be good, / an inquiry is ordered / into
               좋아 보인다면,              조사가 이뤄지지           into

his discovery."
그의 발견에 대해."

"One goes to see it?"
"확인하기 위해 가나요?"

"No. That would be too complicated. But one requires the
"아니.      그건 너무 복잡해.                        하지만 탐험가에게 요구를 하지

explorer / to furnish proofs. For example, / if the discovery
               증거물을 제공하라고.      예를 들어,      만약 그 발견이

in question is / that of a large mountain, / one requires that /
큰 산에 관한 것이라면,                        요구하는 거야

large stones be brought back from it."
큰 돌을 가지고 오도록."

disaster 참사, 재난 | intoxicated 술에 취한 | furnish 비치하다, 제공하다

The geographer was suddenly / stirred to excitement.
지리학자는 갑자기                              흥분하여 움직였다.

"But you —— / you come from far away! You are an explorer!
"그런데 넌 ——    넌 멀리서 왔구나!              넌 탐험가구나!

You shall describe your planet to me!"
네 별에 대해 설명해 주렴!"

And, / having opened his big register, / the geographer
그러면서,    지리학자는 큰 장부를 펼치고,              연필을 깎았다.

sharpened his pencil. The recitals of explorers / are put down
                     탐험가들의 장황한 이야기는

first in pencil. One waits until the explorer has furnished
우선 연필로 적는다.    그리고 탐험가가 증거를 제시할 때까지 기다리는 것이다.

proofs, / before putting them down in ink.
              잉크로 옮겨 적기 전에.

"Well?" / said the geographer expectantly.
"그래서?"    지리학자는 기대하며 말했다.

"Oh, where I live," / said the little prince, / "it is not very
"음,    내가 사는 별은,"    어린왕자는 말했다.              "별로 흥미롭지 않아요.

interesting. It is all so small. I have three volcanoes. Two
             그건 아주 작아요.      나는 세 개의 화산을 가지고 있어요.

volcanoes are active / and the other is extinct. But one never
두 개는 활화산이고          다른 하나는 꺼졌어요.

knows."
하지만 어떻게 될지는 아무도 모르죠."

Key Expression 🔑

### 분사구문 해석하기
분사구문은 분사(현재분사,과거분사)를 사용해 부사절을 부사구로 간결하게 줄인 것을 말하며, '~때(as/when), ~하면서(while), ~한 후에(after), ~때문에(as/because), ~하면(if)' 등 다양한 의미를 가지고 있어요. 분사구문은 의미에 맞는 접속사 절로 바꿀 수 있습니다.

ex) Having opened his big register, / the geographer sharpened his pencil.
그의 커다란 기록부를 열고, 지리학자는 연필을 깎았다.
▶ After the geographer opened his big resister, he sharpened his pencil.

stir 움직이다, 휘젓다, 감동시키다 | excitement 흥분, 신남 | register 등록하다 | sharpen (연필 등을) 뾰족하게
하다, 깎다 | recital 이야기, 상세한 설명 | expectantly 기대감으로

"One never knows," / said the geographer.
"아무도 모르지."　　　　　　지리학자는 말했다.

"I have also a flower."
"제게는 꽃도 하나 있어요."

"We do not record flowers," / said the geographer.
"우리는 꽃을 기록하지 않아."　　　　　지리학자가 말했다.

"Why is that? The flower is the most beautiful thing / on my
"왜요?　　　　꽃은 가장 아름다운 것이라고요

planet!"
내 별에서!"

"We do not record them," / said the geographer, / "because they
"우리는 기록하지 않아."　　　　지리학자는 말했다.

are ephemeral."
"왜냐하면 꽃들은 수명이 짧으니까."

"What does that mean —— / 'ephemeral'?"
"무슨 뜻이죠 —　　　　　'수명이 짧다'는 게?"

"Geographies," / said the geographer, / "are the books which, /
"지리학이란."　　　　지리학자는 말했다.　　　"책이야.

of all books, / are most concerned with matters of consequence.
모든 책 중에서.　　가장 중요한 것들에 대한.

They never become old-fashioned. It is very rarely / that a
지리학은 시대에 뒤지는 일이 없어.　　　　아주 드물지

mountain changes its position. It is very rarely / that an ocean
산이 위치를 바꾸는 일은.　　　　　아주 드물지

empties itself of its waters. We write of eternal things."
바닷물이 말라버리는 일도.　　　우리는 변하지 않는 것만 기록한단다."

"But extinct volcanoes / may come to life again," / the little
"하지만 휴화산은　　　　다시 폭발할지도 모르잖아요."

prince interrupted. "What does that mean —— / 'ephemeral'?"
어린왕자는 말을 가로막았다.　"무슨 뜻이죠 —　　　'수명이 짧다'는 게?"

"Whether volcanoes are extinct or alive, / it comes to the same
"화산이 활화산이든 휴화산이든,　　　　우리에겐 마찬가지야."

thing for us," / said the geographer. "The thing that matters to
지리학자는 말했다.　　　"우리한테 중요한 것은

us / is the mountain. It does not change."
산이야.　　　　산은 변하지 않으니까."

"But what does that mean —— / 'ephemeral'?" / repeated the
"하지만 무슨 뜻이에요 —          '수명이 짧다는 건?'

little prince, / who never in his life / had let go of a question, /
어린왕자는 다시 물었다.   그는 평생동안          질문을 멈춘 적이 없다.

once he had asked it.
일단 질문하기 시작하면.

"It means, / 'which is in danger / of speedy disappearance'."
"그것은 의미해.   '위험에 처해 있는 것을   빠르게 사라져 버릴'."

"Is my flower in danger / of speedy disappearance?"
"내 꽃이 위험에 처해 있다는 것인가요   금방 사라져 버릴?"

"Certainly it is."
"분명히 그렇지."

"My flower is ephemeral," / the little prince said to himself, /
"내 꽃이 곧 사라진다고,"          어린왕자는 생각했다.

"and she has only four thorns / to defend herself / against the
"그런데 그녀에게는 네 개의 가시 밖에 없어   자신을 보호하기 위해   세상에 대항해서.

world. And I have left her on my planet, / all alone!"
          그런데 나는 그녀를 별에 두고 왔어.   홀로!"

That was his first moment of regret. But he took courage /
그는 처음으로 후회했다.          그러나 용기를 냈다

once more.
다시 한 번.

"What place would you advise me / to visit now?" he asked.
"제게 충고해 주시겠어요          이번에 방문할 곳을?"   그는 물었다.

"The planet Earth," / replied the geographer. "It has a good
"지구라는 별이야."          지리학자는 대답했다.          "평판이 좋더군."

reputation."

And the little prince went away, / thinking of his flower.
그리고 어린왕자는 떠났다.          그의 꽃을 생각하면서.

---

ephemeral 수명이 짧은, 덧없는 | rarely 좀처럼 ~않는 | eternal 영원한 | interrupt 끼어들다, 방해하다 |
defend 방어하다

109

## 16

So then / the seventh planet was the Earth.
그리하여　　일곱 번째 별은 지구였다.

The Earth is / not just an ordinary planet! One can count,
지구는　　　그냥 평범한 별이 아니었다!　　　그 곳에는,

there, / 111 kings (not forgetting, to be sure, the Negro kings
111명의 왕　（잊을 수 없는,　　확실한,　　아프리카 왕까지 포함하여),

among them), / 7,000 geographer, / 900,000 businessmen, /
7,000명의 지리학자,　　　900,000명의 사업가.

7,500,000 tipplers, / 311,000,000 conceited men / —— that is
7,500,000명의 술꾼,　　311,000,000명의 허영심이 많은 사람　—즉,

to say, / about 2,000,000,000 grown-ups.
약 20억 명의 어른들이 있다.

To give you an idea / of the size of the Earth, / I will tell you
네게 설명해 주기 위해서는　　지구의 크기에 대해.　　이야기를 하는 것이 좋겠다

that / before the invention of electricity / it was necessary to
전기가 발명되기 전에　　　유지하기 위해 필요했다는 것을,

maintain, / over the whole of the six continents, / a veritable
전 여섯 대륙을 통틀어.

army of 462,511 lamplighters / for the street lamps.
진정 462,511명이나 되는 점등원 무리가　　가로등을 위해.

Seen from a slight distance, / that would make a splendid
좀 떨어진 곳에서 보면,　　이 모습은 빛나는 광경을 이루었다.

spectacle. The movements of this army / would be regulated
이들 무리가 움직이는 모습은　　질서 정연했다

/ like those of the ballet / in the opera. First would come /
마치 무용단처럼　　오페라에서의.　　맨 처음은 나왔다

the turn of the lamplighters of New Zealand and Australia.
뉴질랜드와 호주의 점등원의 순서로.

Having set their lamps alight, / these would go off to sleep.
불을 켜고는,　　잠들기 위해 자리를 떴다.

ordinary 보통의, 통상의 | Negro (원래 아프리카 출신의) 흑인 | invention 발명, 발명품 | electricity 전기 |
continent 대륙 | veritable 진정한, 틀림없는 | splendid spectacle 빛나는 광경 | regulate 규정하다, 조절하다,
통제하다, 질서정연하게 하다 | ballet 무용극(단) | go off (~하러) 자리를 뜨다

Next, the lamplighters of China and Siberia / would enter for
다음으로는, 중국과 시베리아의 점등원이                          춤을 추며 들어왔고,

their steps in the dance, / and then they too would be waved
                              춤을 추며 사라진다

back / into the wings. After / that would come / the turn of the
     무대 뒤로.     그 다음으로는      나왔다

lamplighters of Russia and the Indies; / then those of Africa
러시아와 인도의 차례로;                          그리고 아프리카와 유럽;

and Europe; / then those of South America; / then those of
그리고 남아메리카와;                        그리고 북아메리카가.

North America. And never would they make a mistake / in the
              그리고 그들은 한 번도 실수를 하지 않았다

order of their entry / upon the stage. It would be magnificent.
무대에 등장하는 순서에서     무대 위에서.        장엄했다.

Only the man / who was in charge of the single lamp / at the
오직 한 사람      단 하나의 램프를 담당하고 있는

North Pole, / and his colleague / who was responsible for the
북극에서,      그리고 그의 동료들만      그 램프를 담당하고 있는

single lamp / at the South Pole —— / only these two would live
              남극에서 —              이 둘은 해방되었다

free / from toil and care: / they would be busy twice a year.
     그 수고스러운 일로부터:      그들은 일 년에 두 번만 바빴다.

Key Expression 

**in charge of ~을 맡고 있는, 담당하고 있는**
숙어 'in charge of'는 담당자를 표현할 때 사용되어요.

ex) A man who was in charge of the single lamp 등대를 담당하고 있는 한 사람
The nurse in charge of the patient 그 환자의 담당 간호사
The teacher in charge 담임교사

colleague 동료 | toil 고생, 수고

## ♛ mini test 5

### A. 다음 문장을 해석해 보세요.

(1) This man was so much busy / that he did not even raise his head / at the little prince's arrival.
→

(2) The businessman suddenly realized / that there was no hope of being left in peace / until he answered this question.
→

(3) The little prince was not able to reach / any explanation of the use of a street lamp and a lamplighter, / somewhere in the heavens, / on a planet which had no people, / and not one house.
→

(4) If the recollections of any one among them / seem interesting to him, / the geographer orders an inquiry into / that explorer's moral character.
→

### B. 다음 주어진 문장이 되도록 빈칸에 써 넣으세요.

(1) 매 1분마다 나는 램프를 켜고 꺼야 해.

⬜ I have to light my lamp and put it out.

(2) 사람은 동시에 성실하면서 게으른 것이 가능하다.

⬜ to be faithful and lazy at the same time.

(3) 6번째 별은 이전 것보다 10배 컸다.

The sixth planet was ⬜ the last one.

A. (1) 이 사람은 너무 바빠서 어린왕자의 도착에 고개조차 들지 않았다. (2) 상인은 이 질문에 대답하기 전까지는 평화롭게 될 희망이 없음을 갑자기 깨달았다. (3) 어린왕자는 하늘 어딘가 사람도 집도 없는 별에 가로등이나 점등원이 왜 필요한지 이해가 가지 않았다. (4) 만약 그들 중 누군가의 회상이 그의 관심을 끌

112    The Little Prince

(4) <u>화산이 꺼져 있든 살아 있든</u>, 그것 우리에게 똑같은 것이야.

                                          , it comes to the same thing for us.

## C. 다음 주어진 문구가 알맞은 문장이 되도록 순서를 맞추어 보세요.

(1) 사람이 별을 소유하는 게 어떻게 가능합니까?
(the stars / possible / How / for one / is it / to own)
→

(2) 우리가 함께 이야기하는 동안에 1달이 지나갔다.
(a month / together / we / talking / has gone / have been / While / by)
→

(3) 그것은 내가 더 많은 별을 소유하는 것을 가능하게 한다.
(to buy / for me / possible / It / makes / more stars / it)
→

(4) 조금 떨어진 곳에서 보면, 그것은 멋진 장관을 이루었다.
(distance, / from / make / splendid / would / Seen / a / a / that / slight / spectacle)
→

## D. 다음 단어에 대한 맞는 설명과 연결해 보세요.

(1) loaf    ►    ◄ ① showing contempt

(2) repose    ►    ◄ ② lying around or hanging around

(3) pant    ►    ◄ ③ resting and feeling calm

(4) scorn    ►    ◄ ④ breathe quickly and loudly

면, 지리학자는 그 탐험가의 도덕적 인격에 대해 조사한다. | B. (1) Once every minute (2) It is possible for a man (3) ten times larger than (4) ever passes this way | C. (1) How is it possible for one to own the stars? (2) While we have been talking together a month has gone by, (3) It makes it possible for me to buy more stars. (4) Seen from a slight distance, that would make a splendid spectacle. | D. (1) ② (2) ③ (3) ④ (4) ①

113

When one wishes / to play the wit, / he sometimes wanders
사람이 원할 때          재치를 부리려고.          때로는 약간 어긋날 수 있다

a little / from the truth. I have not been altogether honest / in
진실로부터.          내가 항상 정직했던 것은 아니었다

what I have told you / about the lamplighters. And I realize /
내가 여러분에게 말한 것에서          점등원에 대해 .          그리고 나는 깨달았다

that I run the risk of giving / a false idea of our planet / to those
내가 줄 위험이 있음을          우리별에 대해 잘못된 생각의

who do not know it. Men occupy / a very small place upon the
그것에 대해 모르는 사람들에게.    사람들은 차지한다          지구 위의 아주 작은 공간만.

Earth. If the two billion inhabitants / who people its surface
20억의 인구가          모두 지구 표면 위에 똑바로 서서

were all to stand upright / and somewhat crowded together, /
바짝 다가선다면,

as they do / for some big public assembly, / they could easily
그들이 그러하듯    어떤 큰 집회에서,          그들은 쉽게 들어갈 수 있을 것이다

be put / into one public square / twenty miles long and twenty
하나의 광장에          길이 20마일과 폭 20마일의.

miles wide. All humanity could be piled up / on a small Pacific
전 인류는 쌓아올려질 수도 있다          태평양의 작은 섬 안에.

islet.

The grown-ups, / to be sure, / will not believe you / when you
어른들은,          분명,          여러분을 믿지 않을 것이다          그 사실을 얘기한다면.

tell them that. They imagine / that they fill / a great deal of
어른들은 생각한다          자신들이 차지하고 있다고          거대한 공간을.

space. They fancy / themselves / as important as the baobabs.
어른들은 믿고 있다    자신들이          바오밥 나무만큼이나 중요하다고.

You should advise them, then, / to make their own calculations.
그럴 때 여러분은 그들에게 조언해야 한다.          그들 자신의 계산을 해 보라고.

---

wit 재치, 지혜 | wander 거닐다, 다른 데로 가다 | run the risk of 위험이 있다, 위험을 무릅쓰다 | false 틀린,
사실이 아닌 | inhabitant 주민 | surface 표면 | humanity 인류, 인간성 | pile up 쌓아 올리다 | islet 작은 섬 |
fancy oneself as (그렇지 않은데) ~이라고 믿다 | calculation 계산, 추정

They adore figures, / and that will please them. But do not
어른들은 숫자를 좋아한다.                그러나 그 충고는 그들을 만족시킬 것이다.            그러나 여러분은 시간을

waste your time / on this extra task. It is unnecessary. You
낭비하지는 말라            이 문제에 대해.            그럴 필요는 없다.            여러분은,

have, / I know, / confidence in me.
            내 생각에는,        나를 신뢰하면 된다.

When the little prince arrived / on the Earth, / he was very
어린왕자가 도착했을 때                지구에,            그는 매우 놀랐다

much surprised / not to see any people. He was beginning to
            아무도 만날 수 없었던 것에.        그는 겁이 나기 시작했다

be afraid / he had come to the wrong planet, / when a coil of
            잘못된 별에 온 것은 아닌지,                그때 금빛의 고리가,

gold, / the color of the moonlight, / flashed across the sand.
            달빛 색깔인,                        모래를 가로지르며 빛났다.

"Good evening," / said the little prince courteously.
"안녕."            어린왕자가 예의 바르게.

"Good evening," / said the snake.
"안녕."            뱀이 대답했다.

## Key Expression 🔑

### 재귀대명사 '~self'의 용법

'~self' 형태의 대명사를 재귀대명사라고 부릅니다. 재귀대명사의 쓰임에는 '~자신'이란 의미로 문장의 주어와 목적어가 같을 때 쓰이는 재귀 용법과 주어나 목적어의 의미를 강조하기 위해 쓰이는 강조 용법의 두 가지가 있습니다.

ex) They fancy themselves as important as the baobabs.
그들은 그들 자신을 바오밥나무 만큼이나 중요하다고 상상했다.
→ themselves를 지우면 문장이 성립 안됨(재귀 용법)

I myself did it.
내 자신이 그것을 했다.
→ myself를 지워도 문장이 성립됨(강조 용법)

adore 좋아하다, 숭배하다 | unnecessary 불필요한, 쓸데없는 | coil (여러 겹으로 둥글게 감아놓은) 고리 |
courteously 예의 바르게

"What planet is this / on which I have come down?" / asked
"이것은 무슨 별이지          내가 도착한?"

the little prince.
어린왕자가 물었다.

"This is the Earth; / this is Africa," / the snake answered.
"이곳은 지구야;          이곳은 아프리카야,"          뱀이 대답했다.

"Ah! / Then / there are no people / on the Earth?"
"아!          그러면          사람이 하나도 없니          지구에는?"

"This is the desert. There are no people in the desert. The
"여기는 사막이야.          사막에는 사람이 살지 않아.

Earth is large," / said the snake.
지구는 크거든,"          뱀이 말했다.

The little prince sat down on a stone, / and raised his eyes /
어린왕자는 바위 위에 앉아서,          눈을 들어

toward the sky.
하늘을 쳐다봤다.

"I wonder," / he said, / "Whether the stars are set alright in
"난 궁금해,"          그는 말했다.          "별들이 하늘에서 빛나는 건지

heaven / so that one day each one of us may find his own
모든 사람들이 언젠가는 자신의 별을 다시 찾아낼 수 있도록 하기 위해…

again… / Look at my planet. It is right there / above us. But
내 별을 봐.          바로 저기 있어          우리 머리 위에.

how far away it is!"
하지만 너무나 멀리 있구나!"

"It is beautiful," / the snake said. "What has brought you
"아름다운 별이구나,"          뱀이 말했다.          "넌 여기에 뭐 하러 온 거야?"

here?"

"I have been having some trouble / with a flower," / said the
"나는 갈등이 있었어          어느 꽃이랑,"

little prince.
어린왕자가 말했다.

"Ah!" / said the snake.
"그래!"          뱀이 말했다.

And they were both silent.
그리고 그들은 둘 다 말이 없었다.

"Where are the men?" / the little prince at last / took up the
"사람들은 어디에 있어?"　　　　　　　어린왕자가 마침내　　　　　　　대화를 다시 시작했다.

conversation again. "It is a little lonely / in the desert…"
　　　　　　　　　　　　"좀 외롭네　　　　　　　사막에서는…"

"It is also lonely / among men," / the snake said.
"마찬가지로 외로워　　　　사람들 사이에 있어도,"　　뱀이 대답했다.

The little prince gazed at him / for a long time.
어린왕자는 뱀을 빤히 바라봤다　　　　　　　　오랫동안.

"You are a funny animal," / he said at last. "You are no
"넌 재미있는 동물이구나,"　　　　　　　그는 마침내 말했다.　　"너는 가늘구나

thicker / than a finger…"
　　　손가락보다도…"

"But I am more powerful / than the finger of a king," / said
"하지만 난 힘이 훨씬 세단다　　　　　　왕의 손가락보다도,"

the snake.
뱀이 말했다.

The little prince smiled.
어린왕자는 미소 지었다.

"You are not very powerful. You haven't even any feet. You
"넌 힘이 세지 않은 걸.　　　　　　　　　넌 다리도 없잖아.

cannot even travel…"
여행할 수도 없고…"

---

Key Expression 🍋

**What brings you here?**

직역하면 '무엇이 널 여기로 데려 왔니?'라는 뜻이지만, '여기 무슨 일로 왔어?, 여
기는 어떤 일로 온 거야?'라는 의미로 쓰입니다. what은 바로 용무를 가리키는
말이 됩니다. here 대신 'to + 장소'를 넣어도 됩니다.

ex) What has brought you here?
　　 넌 여기에 뭐 하러 온 거야?

---

gaze at 빤히 바라보다

117

"I can carry you / farther than any ship could take you," / said
"난 널 데려갈 수 있어    어떤 배보다도 멀리,"

the snake.
뱀이 말했다.

He twined himself / around the little prince's ankle, / like a
뱀은 또아리를 틀었다    어린왕자의 발 주위에,

golden bracelet.
금팔찌처럼.

"Whomever I touch, / I send back to the earth / from whence
"내가 건드리는 사람은 누구든지,    땅으로 되돌려 보내지    그가 태어난 곳으로,"

he came," / the snake spoke again. "But you are innocent and
그는 말했다.    뱀은 다시 말했다.    "하지만 너는 순수하고 진실하니까

true, / and you come from a star…"
그리고 다른 별에서 왔으니…"

The little prince made no reply.
어린왕자는 대답하지 않았다.

"You move me to pity —— / you are so weak / on this Earth /
"넌 내게 가엾은 생각이 들게 하는 구나 —    넌 아주 연약하니까    지구에서

made of granite," / the snake said. "I can help you, / some day,
화강암 땅인,"    뱀은 말했다.    "난 널 도와줄 수 있어,    언젠가,

/ if you grow too homesick / for your own planet. I can —— "
그리움이 깊어지면    네가 떠나온 별에 대해.    내가 할 수 있어 —"

"Oh! I understand you very well," / said the little prince. "But
"그래! 잘 알았어,"    어린왕자가 말했다.    "그런데

/ why do you always speak / in riddles?"
넌 왜 항상 말만 하니    수수께끼 같은 ?"

"I solve them all," / said the snake.
"난 그걸 모두 풀 수 있거든,"    뱀이 말했다.

And they were both silent.
그리고 그들은 모두 입을 다물었다.

twine 감다 | ankle 발목 | bracelet 팔찌 | whence 어디서 | granite 화강암 | riddle 수수께끼

The little prince crossed the desert / and met with only one
어린왕자는 사막을 횡단하다가　　　　　　　　　꽃 한 송이를 만났다.

flower. It was a flower / with three petals, / a flower of no
그것은 꽃이었다　　　꽃잎이 세 장 있는,　　　시시한 꽃.

account at all.

"Good morning," / said the little prince.
"안녕하세요."　　　　어린왕자가 말했다.

"Good morning," / said the flower.
"안녕."　　　　꽃이 말했다.

"Where are the men?" the little prince asked, / politely.
"사람들은 어디 있어요?"　　　어린왕자가 물어봤다,　　　공손하게.

The flower had once seen / a caravan passing.
그 꽃은 한 번 본 적이 있었다　　　사막의 상인들이 지나가는 것을.

"Men?" she echoed. "I think / there are six or seven of them
"사람들?" 그녀가 말했다　　"내 생각에는　예닐곱 명 정도 있는 것 같아.

in existence. I saw them, / several years ago. But one never
내가 그들을 봤어,　　몇 년 전에.　　　그러나 아무도 몰라

knows / where to find them. The wind blows them away. They
어디에서 그들을 찾을지.　　바람이 그들을 몰고 다니거든.

have no roots, / and that makes their life very difficult."
그들은 뿌리가 없어서,　　그들의 삶은 꽤 힘들 거야."

"Goodbye," / said the little prince.
"안녕히 계세요."　　어린왕자가 말했다.

"Goodbye," / said the flower.
"잘 가."　　꽃이 말했다.

---

no account 시시한 | politely 공손히, 예의 바르게 | caravan (사막의) 대상 | existence 존재

After that, / the little prince climbed / a high mountain. The
그 후,　　　　어린왕자는 올라갔다　　　　　　높은 산으로.

only mountains / he had ever known / were the three volcanoes,
유일한 산은　　　　그가 알고 있는　　　　　세 개의 화산뿐이었다,

/ which came up to his knees. And / he used the extinct volcano
그리고 그것들은 그의 무릎밖에 안 찼다.　　　그래서　어린왕자는 불 꺼진 화산을 사용했다

/ as a footstool. "From a mountain / as high as this one," / he
발판으로 .　　　　"산에서라면　　　이렇게 높은,"

said to himself, / "I shall be able to see / the whole planet / at
그는 생각했다,　　　　"볼 수 있을 거야　　　별 전체를

one glance, / and all the people…"
한 눈에,　　　그리고 사람들도…"

But he saw nothing, / save peaks of rock / that were sharpened
그러나 그는 아무것도 보지 못했다,　산봉우리 밖에　　　바늘처럼 날카로운.

like needles.

"Good morning," / he said courteously.
"안녕,"　　　　그는 예의 바르게 말했다.

"Good morning —— Good morning —— Good morning," /
"안녕　　　　　— 안녕　　　　　—안녕,"

answered the echo.
메아리가 대답했다.

"Who are you?" / said the little prince.
"너는 누구니?"　　　어린왕자가 말했다.

"Who are you —— Who are you —— Who are you?" / answered
"너는 누구니　　　— 너는 누구니　　　— 너는 누구니?"

the echo.
메아리가 대답했다.

"Be my friends. I am all alone," / he said.
"내 친구가 되어 줘.　난 너무 외로워,"　　　그가 말했다.

---

footstool 발판 | save(=except) ~을 제외하고 | peak 절정, (산의) 봉우리 | sharpen 날카로워지다, 선명해지다
| harsh 거친

"I am all alone —— all alone —— all alone," / answered the
"난 너무 외로워          — 외로워          — 외로워,"          메아리가 대답했다.

echo.

"What a queer planet!" / he thought. "It is altogether dry, /
"정말 이상한 별이야!"          그는 생각했다.          "너무 메마르고,

and altogether pointed, / and altogether harsh and forbidding.
뾰족하고,          너무 거칠고 험악해.

And / the people have no imagination. They repeat / whatever
그리고     사람들은 상상력이 없어.          그들은 따라 해

one says to them… On my planet / I had a flower; / she always
남이 한 말은 뭐든지…          내 별에서는          꽃이 하나 있었는데;

was the first to speak…"
항상 먼저 말을 걸어 주었는데…"

Key Expression

**복합관계대명사 whatever**
whatever는 복합관계대명사로 선행사를 포함하며 명사절이나 부사절을 이끕
니다. 명사절일 때에는 '~하는 것은 무엇이든(=anything that)', 부사절일 때
에는 '무엇이 아무리 ~할지라도(=no matter what)'라는 의미입니다.

ex) They repeat whatever one says to them
    그들은 누군가가 그들에게 하는 말은 무엇이든 따라 한다.

forbidding 싫은, 험악한

## 20

But it happened / that after walking for a long time / through
그러나 그 일이 일어났다     한참을 걷고 난 후                    모래, 바위, 눈을

sand, and rocks, and snow, / the little prince at last came upon
지나,                          어린왕자는 마침내 길에 다다랐다.

a road. And all roads lead to the abodes of men.
           그리고 모든 길은 사람 사는 곳으로 연결되어 있는 것이다.

"Good morning," / he said.
"안녕하세요."              그가 말했다.

He was standing before a garden, / all a-bloom with roses.
그는 정원 앞에 서 있었다.                      활짝 핀 장미와 함께.

abode 주거(자), 사람 사는 곳 | a-bloom(=abloom) 꽃이 피어, 개화하여

**"Good morning,"** / said the roses.
"안녕." 그 장미가 말했다.

**The little prince gazed at them. They all looked like his**
그 어린왕자는 그들을 뚫어지게 보았다. 그들은 모두 그의 꽃과 닮아 보였다.

**flower.**

**"Who are you?"** he demanded, / thunderstruck.
"당신들은 누구세요?" 그가 물었다. 몹시 놀라며.

**"We are roses,"** / the roses said.
"우리는 장미꽃이야." 장미가 대답했다.

Key Expression

### 가정법 if절
가정법은 if 절의 시제에 따라 여러 가지 다른 용법으로 쓰일 수 있습니다.

▶ If +S+ V, S+ will+ V: '~라면 ..할 것이다'
**(가정법 현재 : 현재, 미래의 불확실한 일)**

ex) If it's sunny tomorrow, I will go hiking.
만약 내일 날씨가 맑으면, 하이킹을 갈 것이다.

▶ If +S+동사과거, S+would +V: '만일 (지금) ~한다면 … 할 텐데'
**(가정법 과거 : 현재 사실의 반대 가정)**

ex) If she should see that…. She would cough most dreadfully.
만약 그녀가 봐야만 했다면, 그녀는 더욱 심하게 기침을 했었을 텐데..

▶ If I had+p.p, S+would have+p.p: '만일 (그때) ~하고 있었다면, (그후)…했을 텐데.'
**(가정법 과거완료 : 과거 사실의 반대 가정)**

ex) If I had had enough money, I would have bought that car.
만약 내가 충분히 돈이 있었다면, 그 차를 샀을 텐데.

▶ If I had +p.p, S+would+V + now: '만일 (그때) ~하고 있었다면, 지금쯤 …할 텐데'
**(복합가정법 : 가정법 과거완료+가정법 과거)**

ex) If I hadn't bought that car, I would have more money now.
만약 내가 그때 차를 사지 않았다면, 지금쯤 돈이 좀 더 있을 텐데.

And he was overcome with sadness. His flower had told him /
그리고 그는 슬픔을 가누지 못했다.                          그의 꽃은 그에게 말했었다

that she was the only one of her kind / in all the universe. And
자기같은 꽃도 단 하나 뿐이라고                         온 지구에서.

here were five thousand of them, / all alike, / in one single
그런데 여기에는 5,000송이나 있다.              모두 비슷한 것이,    한 정원 안에만!

garden!

"She would be very much annoyed," / he said to himself, / "if
"그녀는 아주 짜증날 수도 있어."                            그가 자신에게 말했다.

she should see that... / She would cough most dreadfully, /
"만약 그녀가 이것을 본다면…        그녀는 심하게 기침을 했을 것이다.

and she would pretend / that she was dying, / to avoid being
그녀는 했을 것이다               죽어가는 척,              조롱 당하는 것을 피하게 위해.

laughed at. And I should be obliged to pretend / that I was
그리고 나는 연기를 해야만 할 거야

nursing her back to life —— for if I did not do that, / to humble
그녀를 위로해 주는 것처럼 —        만약 내가 그렇게 하지 않으면,

myself also, / she would really allow herself to die..."
내가 죄책감 느끼게 하려고,       그녀는 정말 죽을 수도 있을 거야..."

---

overcome 압도하다 | universe 우주, 세계, 만물 | alike (아주) 비슷한 | annoy 속태우다, 괴롭히다 |
dreadfully 몹시 | nursing 간호직 | reflection 모습, 반영

Then he went on with his reflections: / "I thought that I was
그리고 그는 또 생각했다:                                      "나는 내가 부자라고 생각했는데,

rich, / with a flower that was unique in all the world; / and
　　　세상에 단 하나뿐인 유일한 꽃을 가지고 있어서;

all I had was a common rose. A common rose, and three
그런데 내가 가진 것은 흔한 꽃이었어.　　　흔한 꽃 한 송이,　　　그리고 화산 세 개,

volcanoes / that come up to my knees —— /and one of them
내 무릎까지 오는 —

perhaps extinct forever... / That doesn't make me a very great
그것도 하나는 불이 영영 꺼질지도 몰라…　　　그걸로는 난 훌륭한 왕자가 되기는 힘들 거 같아…"

prince..."

And he lay down in the grass / and cried.
그는 풀밭에 누워서　　　　　울었다.

## ♔ mini test 6

### A. 다음 문장을 해석해 보세요.

(1) It was a flower with three petals, a flower of no account at all.
   →

(2) She would pretend that she was dying, to avoid being laughed at.
   →

(3) They have no roots, and that makes their life very difficult.
   →

(4) But it happened that after walking for a long time through sand, and rocks, and snow, the little prince at last came upon a road.
   →

### B. 다음 주어진 문장이 되도록 빈칸에 써 넣으세요.

(1) 어린왕자는 <u>사막을 횡단했고</u>, 꽃 하나를 만났다.

   The little prince ⬜⬜⬜⬜⬜⬜⬜ and met with only one flower.

(2) 그의 꽃은 그녀가 <u>온 우주에</u> 단 하나뿐이라고 그에게 말해왔다.

   His flower had told him that she was the only one of her kind ⬜⬜⬜⬜⬜⬜.

(3) 그 어린왕자는 돌 위에 앉았고, <u>하늘을 향하여 눈을 들었다.</u>

   The little prince sat down on a stone, and ⬜⬜⬜⬜⬜
   ⬜⬜⬜⬜⬜⬜.

(4) 그 어린왕자는 그를 오랫동안 <u>뚫어지게 보았다.</u>

   The little prince ⬜⬜⬜⬜⬜ him for a long time.

## C. 다음 주어진 문장이 본문의 내용과 맞으면 T, 틀리면 F에 동그라미 하세요.

(1) The little prince has raised various kinds of flowers.
(T / F)

(2) The little prince met a snake through his journey.
(T / F)

(3) The only mountains the little prince had ever known were the three volcanoes which is almost same as his height.
(T / F)

(4) The flower had once seen a caravan passing.
(T / F)

## D. 다음 빈칸에 알맞은 단어를 보기에서 골라 써 넣으세요.

[보기] at one glance    upon the earth    to be sure    to be afraid

(1) I shall be able to see the whole planet _____, and all the people.
나는 전체 별을 그냥 한 눈으로 볼 수 있었다. 그리고 사람들도.

(2) Men occupy a very small place _____.
사람들은 지구에서 매우 작은 부분을 차지한다.

(3) The grown-ups, _____, will not believe you when you tell them that.
어른들은, 분명히, 네가 그들에게 그 얘기를 할 때 널 믿지 않을 것이다.

(4) He was beginning _____ he had come to the wrong planet.
그는 그가 다른 별에 왔을까 봐 걱정하기 시작했다.

래, 바위, 눈 위를 한참이나 걸은 후에 도로에 다다를 수 있었다. | B. (1) crossed the desert (2) in all the universe (3) raised his eyes toward the sky. (4) gazed at | C. (1) F (2) T (3) F (4) T | D. (1) at one glance (2) upon the earth (3) to be sure (4) to be afraid

127

## 21

It was then / that the fox appeared.
바로 그때였다     여우가 나타난 것은.

"Good morning," / said the fox.
"안녕,"                      여우가 말했다.

"Good morning," / the little prince responded politely, /
"안녕하세요."                 어린왕자가 공손하게 대답하며,

although when he turned around / he saw nothing.
주위를 돌아보았지만                          그는 아무것도 보지 못했다.

"I am right here," / the voice said, / "under the apple tree."
"난 여기 있어."           목소리가 말했다.          "사과나무 아래야."

"Who are you?" / asked the little prince, / and added, / "You
"넌 누구니?"           어린왕자가 물었다.                      그리고 덧붙였다,

are very pretty to look at."
"넌 참 예쁘구나."

"I am a fox," / the fox said.
"난 여우야."          여우가 말했다.

"Come and play with me," / proposed the little prince. / "I am
"이리 와서 나랑 놀자."                                    어린왕자가 제안했다.

so unhappy."
"난 너무 쓸쓸해."

"I cannot play with you," / the fox said. "I am not tamed."
"난 너랑 놀 수 없어."                    여우가 말했다.            "난 길들여지지 않았거든."

"Ah! Please excuse me," / said the little prince.
"그래!   미안해,"                        어린왕자는 말했다.

But after some thought, / he added:
그러나 잠시 생각한 후에.                    다시 말했다:

"What does that mean —— 'tame'?"
"무슨 뜻이야                  — '길들인다'는 건?"

"You do not live here," / said the fox. "What is it / that you are
"넌 여기 살지 않는 구나."            여우가 말했다.         "도대체 뭐야        네가 찾고 있는 게?"

looking for?"

"I am looking for men," / said the little prince. "What does
"사람들을 찾고 있어."                  어린왕자가 말했다.

that mean —— 'tame'?"
"무슨 뜻이야                  — '길들인다'는 건?"

Key Expression 🍎

**It is~that… 강조구문**
It is와 that 사이에 강조하는 말(주어, 목적어, 부사구)를 넣어 강조하는 구문
을 만들 수 있습니다.
'~한 것은 바로 …이다'라고 해석하지요.

ex) It was then that the fox appeared. 여우가 나타난 것은 '그때'였다.
   What is it that you are looking for? 네가 찾고 있는 게 도대체 '무엇'인데?
   → It is ~ that 강조구문의 의문문 버전이에요.
   'What is it that~?'은 '~는 도대체 뭐야?'로 외워두시면 편해요.

propose 제안하다 | tame 길들이다, 따르게 하다

"Men," / said the fox. "They have guns, / and they hunt. It is
"사람들은," 여우가 말했다. "그들은 총을 가지고 있고, 사냥을 하지.

very disturbing. They also raise chickens. These are their only
그건 아주 성가신 일이야. 또 사람들은 닭도 키워. 이것들이 그들의 유일한 즐거움이야.

interests. Are you looking for chickens?"
너도 닭을 찾고 있니?"

"No," / said the little prince. "I am looking for friends. What
"아니," 어린왕자가 말했다. "난 친구를 찾고 있어.

does that mean —— 'tame'?"
"무슨 뜻이야 — '길들인다'는 건?"

"It is an act / too often neglected," / said the fox. "It means to
"그건 행동이지 너무 자주 잊혀지는," 여우가 말했다.

establish ties."
"인연을 맺는다는 뜻이야."

"'To establish ties'?"
"'인연을 맺는다'고?"

"Just that," / said the fox. / "To me, / you are still nothing more
"바로 그거야." 여우는 말했다. "내게 있어. 넌 아직 어린 소년일 뿐이야

than a little boy / who is just like a hundred thousand other
다른 수백 수천 명의 소년들과 같은.

little boys. And I have no need of you. And you, on your part,
그리고 넌 내게 필요가 없어. 네 입장에서도,

/ have no need of me. To you, / I am nothing more than a fox /
내가 필요 없지. 네게는, 난 한 마리 여우일 뿐이니까

like a hundred thousand other foxes. But if you tame me, / then
다른 수백 수천 마리의 여우들과 같은. 하지만 네가 나를 길들인다면,

we shall need each other. To me, / you will be unique / in all
그때 우리는 서로를 필요로 하는 거야. 내게는, 넌 하나 밖에 없는 사람이 되고

the world. To you, / I shall be unique / in all the world…"
세상에서. 네게는, 난 하나 뿐이 없는 여우가 되는 거야 세상에서…"

"I am beginning to understand," / said the little prince. "There
"나는 이해할 것 같아," 어린왕자가 말했다.

is a flower… I think that she has tamed me…"
"꽃이 하나 있었는데… 그 꽃이 나를 길들였나 봐…"

establish ties 인연을[관계를] 맺다 | nothing more than ~에 지나지 않는 | perplex 어찌할 바를 모르고 |
curious 궁금한

"It is possible," / said the fox. "On the Earth / one sees all sorts
"그럴 수도 있지,"        여우가 말했다.        "지구에는        별의별 것이 다 있으니까."

of things."

"Oh, but / this is not on the Earth!", / said the little prince.
"하지만        지구에 있는 게 아닌 걸!",        어린왕자가 말했다.

The fox seemed perplexed, / and very curious.
여우는 당황한 것 같았다.        그리고 궁금해했다.

"On another planet?"
"다른 별에 있다고?"

"Yes."
"응."

"Are there hunters / on that planet?"
"사냥꾼들이 있니        그 별에는?"

"No."
"아니."

"Ah, that is interesting! Are there chickens?"
"오, 그거 재미있는데!        닭은 있니?"

"No."
"아니."

"Nothing is perfect," / sighed the fox.
"완벽한 것은 없구나,"        여우는 한숨을 쉬었다.

---

Key Expression 📍

**nothing more than~ : ~에 지나지 않는**
nothing(no) more than은 '~ 이상은 아니다', 즉 '~에 지나지 않는, ~일뿐'
이라는 의미로, 'only'와 비슷한 뜻을 가지고 있어요.

ex) To me, you are still nothing more than a little boy.
    내게 있어서 넌 여전히 어린 꼬마일 뿐이다.

비슷한 표현을 몇개 더 알아볼까요?
▶ no more than : ~에 지나지 않는, 그저 ~일 뿐(=only)
▶ no less than : ~에 못지 않게, ~와 마찬가지로(=as much as)
▶ not more than : 많아야 ~이다, 기껏해야(=at most)
▶ not less than : 최소한, 적어도 ~이다(=at least)

131

But he came back to his idea.
그러나 자기 이야기를 계속했다.

"My life is very monotonous," / he said. "I hunt chickens; /
"내 삶은 매우 단조롭지."　　　　그는 말했다.　"난 닭을 사냥하고;

men hunt me. All the chickens are just alike, / and all the men
사람들은 나를 사냥하지.　모든 닭은 비슷하고,　　　　　모든 사람들도 비슷해.

are just alike. And, in consequence, / I am a little bored. But
　　　　　그래서, 결과적으로,　　　난 좀 심심해.　　　하지만 네

if you tame me, / it will be as if / the sun came to shine on my
가 날 길들인다면,　　그건 마치 ~같을 거야　태양이 내 삶을 비추게 된 것 같이.

life. I shall know the sound of a step / that will be different
난 네 발자국 소리를 알게 될 거야　　　　　다른 발자국들과 다른.

from all the others. Other steps / send me hurrying back /
다른 발자국 소리는　나를 서둘러 돌아가게 하지

underneath the ground. Yours will call me, / like music, /
땅 밑으로.　　　네 발자국 소리는 나를 불러낼 거야.　마치 음악처럼,

out of my burrow. And then look: / you see the grain-fields /
굴 밖으로.　　　그리고 저기를 봐:　들판이 보이지

down yonder? I do not eat bread. Wheat is of no use to me.
저 아래?　　난 빵을 먹지 않아.　　그래서 밀은 나에게 쓸모가 없어.

The wheat fields / have nothing to say to me. And that is
밀밭은　　　　내게 아무 말도 걸지 않아.　　　그래서 슬퍼.

sad. But you have hair / that is the color of gold. Think / how
하지만 네 머리는　　　　금빛이야.　　　　　생각해 봐

wonderful that will be / when you have tamed me! The grain,
얼마가 굉장할지　　　네가 나를 길들이게 되면!　　　금빛의 곡식은,

which also golden, / will bring me back / the thought of you.
　　　　　내게 떠올리게 할 거야　　네 생각을.

And I shall love to / listen to the wind / in the wheat…"
그리고 나는 좋아하게 될 거야　바람 소리 듣는 것을　밀밭에서 부는…"

The fox gazed at the little prince, / for a long time.
여우는 어린왕자를 쳐다보았다.　　　　　　오랫동안.

"Please —— tame me!" / he said.
"제발　　　— 나를 길들여 줘!"　그는 말했다.

---

underneath ~의 아래에, ~에 숨어서 | burrow 굴, 피난[은신]처 | grain-field 곡식 밭 | yonder 저쪽에 |
wheat 밀

132 The Little Prince

"I want to, very much," / the little prince replied. "But I have
"나도 정말 그러고 싶어."　　　　　　　어린왕자는 대답했다.

not much time. I have friends to discover, / and a great many
"그러나 시간이 없어.　　난 찾아야 할 친구가 있어.　　　　　그리고 많은 일들이 있어

things / to understand."
알아야 할."

"One only understands / the things that one tames," / said the
"사람이란 ~밖에 모르는 법이야　　자신이 길들인 것."　　　　　　여우는 말했다.

fox. "Men have no more time / to understand anything. They
"사람들은 시간조차 없어　　무엇인가를 알.　　　　　그들은 물

buy things / ready all made at the shops. But there is no shop
건을 사니까　　가게에서 다 만들어진.　　　　하지만 어디에도 가게는 없어

anywhere / where one can buy friendship, / and so men have
우정을 살 수 있는,　　　　　그래서 사람들은 친구가 없는 거야

no friends / any more. If you want a friend, / tame me…"
더 이상.　　네가 친구를 원한다면,　　　나를 길들여 줘…"

"What must I do, / to tame you?" / asked the little prince.
"무엇을 해야 하지, 너를 길들이려면?" 어린왕자가 물었다.

"You must be very patient," / replied the fox. "First / you
"참을성이 아주 많아야 해." 여우가 대답했다. "처음에는

will sit down / at a little distance from me —— / like that ——
너는 앉을 거야 내게서 약간 거리를 두고 — 그렇게 —

/ in the grass. I shall look at you / out of the corner of my
풀밭에서. 나는 널 보겠지 곁눈질로,

eye, / and you will say nothing. Words are the source / of
그러면 넌 아무 말도 하지 않을 거야. 말은 원인이니까

misunderstandings. But / you will sit / a little closer to me, /
오해를 일으키는. 그러나 너는 앉게 될 거야 조금씩 더 가까이 와서,

every day…"
매일 매일…"

The next day / the little prince came back.
다음 날 어린왕자가 돌아왔다.

"It would have been better / to come back / at the same hour,"
"~해 주면 좋겠어 돌아오도록 같은 시간에."

/ said the fox. "If, / for example, / you come / at four o'clock
여우가 말했다. "만약, 예를 들어, 네가 온다면 오후 4시에.

in the afternoon, / then at three o'clock / I shall begin to be
3시가 되면 난 행복해지기 시작할 거야.

happy. I shall feel happier / as the hour advances. At four
점점 더 행복해질 거야 시간이 흐름에 따라. 4시가 되면,

o'clock, / I shall already be worrying / and jumping about. I
난 이미 안절부절 못하고 뛰어다니겠지.

shall show you / how happy I am! But if you come / at just any
네게 보여 줄 거야 내가 얼마나 행복한지를! 그러나 네가 온다면 아무 때나,

time, / I shall never know / at what hour / my heart is to be
난 알지 못할 거야 몇 시에 내 심장이 준비를 해야 할지를

ready / to greet you… One must observe / the proper rites…"
너를 맞이할… 사람은 지켜야 해 적당한 의식을…"

---

worrying 애타는, 걱정되는 | jump about 뛰어 돌아다니다 | at just any time 아무 때나 | observe 지키다,
유지하다 | proper 적당한, 적절한 | rite 관례, 의식 | vineyard 포도밭

"What is a rite?" / asked the little prince.
"의식이 뭔데?"　　　　　어린왕자가 물었다.

"Those also are actions / too often neglected," / said the fox.
"그것은 행동이야　　　　　너무 자주 잊혀지는."　　　　여우가 말했다.

"They are / what make one day / different from other days,
"그것은　　　하루를 만들지　　다른 날들과 다르게.

/ one hour from other hours. There is a rite, / for example,
그리고 한 시간을 다른 시간과 다르게.　　의식이 있어,　　　예를 들면,

/ among my hunters. Every Thursday / they dance with the
내 사냥꾼들에게도.　　　매주 목요일마다　　　그들은 마을 소녀들과 춤을 추지.

village girls. So Thursday is / a wonderful day for me! I can
그래서 목요일은　　　내게 최고의 날이야!

take a walk / as far as the vineyards. But if the hunters danced
난 산책을 할 수 있지　멀리 포도밭까지.　　　　그러나 사냥꾼들이 춤을 춘다면

/ at just any day would be like every other day, / and I should
아무 날에나 다른 날처럼,　　　　　난 결코 가질 수 없을 거야

never have / any vacation at all."
영원히 어떤 휴식도."

So the little prince tamed the fox. And / when the hour of his
그래서 어린왕자는 여우를 길들였다.　　　그리고　떠날 시간이

departure / drew near ——
가까워졌을 때 —

"Ah," / said the fox, / "I shall cry."
"아," 여우가 말했다. "난 울어버릴 거야."

"It is your own fault," / said the little prince. "I never wished /
"그건 네 탓이야," 어린왕자가 말했다. "난 원하지 않았어

you any sort of harm; / but you wanted / me to tame you…"
네게 어떤 해를 끼치는 것을; 하지만 네가 원했으니까 내가 널 길들이는 것을…"

"Yes, that is so," / said the fox.
"응, 그건 그래," 여우가 말했다.

"But now / you are going to cry!" / said the little prince.
"그런데 지금 넌 울려고 하잖아!" 어린왕자가 말했다.

"Yes, that is so," / said the fox.
"응, 그것도 그래," 여우가 말했다.

"Then / it has done you / no good at all!"
"그러면 그게 네게는 아무 도움도 안 되었잖아!"

"It has done me good," / said the fox, / "because of the color /
"내가 얻은 게 있어." 여우가 말했다. "빛깔 때문에

of the wheat fields." And then he added:
밀밭의…" 그리고 나서 그는 덧붙였다:

"Go and look again / at the roses. You will understand now /
"다시 찾아가 봐 장미꽃들에게. 넌 이제 알 수 있을 거야

that yours is unique / in all the world. Then / come back to say
네 장미가 하나 뿐이라는 것을 세상에서. 그리고 나서 내게 작별 인사를 하러 돌아와,

goodbye to me, / and / I will make you / a present of a secret."
그러면 내가 네게 만들어 줄게 비밀스러운 선물을."

---

Key Expression ♥

**do good : 도움이 되다**

'do good'은 '(~에게) 도움이 되다, 혹은 이롭다'라는 의미로 쓰이는 숙어에요.
do 목적어 good, 혹은 do good to 목적어와 같이 4형식 동사처럼 활용되죠.
good 대신 harm를 넣으면 '해롭다'라는 뜻으로 쓰입니다.

ex) It has done you no good at all. 그건 네게 아무 도움도 안 됐잖아.
It has done me good. 그건 내게 도움이 돼.

---

as yet 아직까지

The little prince went away, / to look again at the roses.
어린왕자는 가버렸다.　　　　　　　　　장미를 다시 보러.

"You are not at all like my rose," / he said. "As yet / you are
"너희들은 내 장미와 전혀 달라."　　　　　　　　　그는 말했다.　"아직까지　너희들은 아무것도

nothing. No one has tamed you, / and you have tamed no one.
아니야.　　아무도 너희들을 길들이지 않았고,　　　너희들도 누군가를 길들이지 않았어.

You are like my fox / when I first knew him. He was only a
너희들은 내 여우와 같아          내가 그를 처음 만났을 때의.          그는 여우일 뿐이었지

fox / like a hundred thousand other foxes. But I have made
다른 수십 마리와 여우들과 같은.                      그러나 난 그를 친구로 만들었어.

him my friend, / and now / he is unique in all the world."
                그리고 이제     그는 세상에서 하나 밖에 없는 여우가 됐어."

And / the roses were very much embarrassed.
그러자     장미들은 매우 당황했다.

"You are beautiful, / but you are empty," / he went on. "One
"너희들은 아름다워.          하지만 너희들은 비어 있어."          그는 계속 말했다.

could not die for you. To be sure, / an ordinary passerby
"누구도 너희들을 위해 죽을 수 없어.     확실히,          지나가는 평범한 사람은 생각하겠지

would think / that my rose looked / just like you —— / the
                내 장미가 보인다고          너희들과 마찬가지로 —

rose that belongs to me. But in herself alone / she is more
내게 속한 장미 말이지.          하지만 그 한 송이 만으로도     내 장미는 훨씬 중요해

important / than all the hundreds of you other roses: / because
수백 송이의 다른 장미들보다:                      왜냐하면 꽃이

it is she / that I have watered; / because it is she / that I have
니까     내가 물을 준;          왜냐하면 꽃이니까     내가 보호해 준;

sheltered behind the screen; / because it is for her / that I have
                왜냐하면 그녀를 위해서이니까

killed the caterpillars / (except the two or three that we saved /
내가 벌레를 잡아 준 것은     (두세 마리는 제외하고);

to become butterflies); / because it is she / that I have listened
나비가 되도록          왜냐하면 그녀이니까     내가 이야기를 들어준 것은,

to, / when she grumbled, or boasted, / or even sometimes /
그녀가 투덜거리거나, 뽐낼 때.          혹은 때때로

when she said nothing. Because she is my rose."
아무 말도 하지 않을 때에도.          왜냐하면 그녀는 내 장미이니까."

passerby 통행인 | grumble 투덜대다 | boast 자랑하다, 떠벌리다

And he went back / to meet the fox.
그리고 그는 다시 돌아왔다        여우를 만나러.

"Goodbye," / he said.
"안녕."              그가 말했다.

"Goodbye," / said the fox. "And now / here is my secret, / a
"안녕."        여우가 말했다.      "그리고 이제      여기 내 비밀이 있어,

very simple secret: It is only with the heart / that one can see
아주 간단한 비밀이야:      바로 마음으로 봐야 한다는 거지      제대로 볼 수 있으려면;

rightly; / what is essential is / invisible to the eye."
             본질적인 것은              눈에 보이지 않거든."

"What is essential is / invisible to the eye," / the little prince
"본질적인 것은          눈에 보이지 않는다."        어린왕자가 따라 했다,

repeated, / so that he would be sure to remember.
             확실히 기억하기 위해서.

"It is the time / you have wasted for your rose / that makes
"바로 시간이야      네가 네 장미를 위해 쓴

your rose so important."
네 장미를 소중하게 만든 것은."

"It is the time / I have wasted for my rose —— " / said the little
"바로 시간이야          내가 내 장미를 위해 쓴 —"                              어린왕자가 말했다.

prince, / so that he would be sure to remember.
              확실히 기억하기 위해서.

"Men have forgotten / this truth," / said the fox. "But you
"사람들은 잊어버렸어          이 진리를 ."          여우가 말했다.

must not forget it. You become responsible, / forever, / for
"그러나 넌 잊으면 안 돼.          넌 책임지게 되는 거야.          영원히,

what you have tamed. You are responsible / for your rose…"
네가 길들인 것에 대해.          넌 책임이 있어          네 장미에…"

"I am responsible / for my rose," / the little prince repeated, /
"난 책임이 있다          내 장미에 ."          어린왕자가 반복했다.

so that he would be sure to remember.
확실히 기억하기 위해서.

## ☼ 22 ☼

"Good morning," / said the little prince.
"안녕하세요."          어린왕자가 말했다.

"Good morning," / said the railway switchman.
"안녕."          철도원이 말했다.

"What do you do here?" the little prince asked.
"여기에서 뭐하고 있어요?"          어린왕자가 물어봤다.

"I sort out travelers, / in bundles of a thousand," / said the
"나는 여행자들을 분류하지,          천 명 단위로."          철도원이 말했다.

switchman. "I send off the trains / that carry them: / now to
철도원이 말했다.          "나는 기차를 배웅했어          그들을 운반하는:          자 오른쪽으로,

the right, / now to the left."
              자 왼쪽으로."

---

railway 철로, 철길 | switchman 철도원 | sort out 분류하다, 가려내다 | bundle 묶음 | send off (길 떠나는
사람을) 배웅하다 | brilliantly 번쩍번쩍, 찬연히 | roar 으르렁거리는 소리, 굉음 | locomotive engineer 기관사

And a brilliantly lighted express train / shook the switchman's
그러자 불을 밝게 밝힌 급행열차가                    철도원의 조종실을 흔들었다

cabin / as it rushed by / with a roar like thunder.
            질주하면서      천둥과 같은 요란한 소리와 함께.

"They are in a great hurry," / said the little prince. "What are
"정말 바쁜가 봐요."                    어린왕자가 말했다.

they looking for?"
"저들은 뭘 찾고 있죠?"

"Not even the locomotive engineer / knows that," / said the
"기관사조차도                        그건 모르지."      철도원이 말했다.

switchman.

And a second brilliantly lighted express / thundered by, / in
그리고 불을 밝게 밝힌 또 다른 급행열차가              천둥소리를 내며 지나갔다.

the opposite direction.
반대 방향으로.

"Are they coming back already?" demanded the little prince.
"벌써 돌아오는 건가요?"                    어린왕자가 물었다.

"These are not the same ones," / said the switchman. "It is an
"같은 기차가 아니야,"                    철도원이 말했다.

exchange."
"엇갈려 가는 거야."

"Were they not satisfied / where they were?" asked the little
"마음에 안 들었나봐요            그들이 있던 곳이?"      어린왕자가 물었다.

prince.

"No one is ever satisfied / where he is," / said the switchman.
"아무도 만족하지 않아            자기가 있던 곳에 대해."    철도원이 대답했다.

## Key Expression 🔑

### 전치사 like
Like는 일반적으로 동사로는 '좋아하다'라는 의미를 지니고 있지만,
전치사로 사용될 때는 '~처럼, ~와 같이'라는 뜻으로 사용되어요.

ex) It sounds like thunder. 천둥번개 소리와 같았다.
    Susan swam like a fish 수잔은 물고기처럼 헤엄쳤다
    I cannot do it like you. 나는 자네처럼은 할 수 없어.

And they heard / the roaring thunder of / a third brilliantly
그리고 그들은 들었다        으르렁거리는 천둥 소리를

lighted express.
세 번째로 밝은 빛을 비추며 오는 급행열차의.

"Are they pursuing / the first travelers?" demanded the little
"저들은 쫓아가는 건가요        첫 번째 승객들을 ?"        어린왕자가 물어봤다.

prince.

They are pursuing / nothing at all," / said the switchman.
"그들은 뒤쫓고 있지 않아        아무도."        철도원이 말했다.

"They are asleep in there, / or if they are not asleep / they are
"그들은 거기에서 자고 있거나,        자고 있지 않다면        하품하고 있을

yawning. Only the children / are flattening their noses / against
거야.        오직 아이들만이        코를 비비고 있지

the windowpanes."
유리창에 대고."

"Only the children know / what they are looking for," / said
"오직 어린이들만 알고 있어요        그들이 무엇을 찾고 있는지,"

the little prince. "They waste their time / over a rag doll / and
어린왕자가 말했다.        "그들은 시간을 쏟죠        봉제 인형을 가지고 노는데

it becomes very important to them; / and if anybody takes it /
그리고 그것은 그들에게 매우 중요해요;        그리고 누군가가 그것을 빼앗으면,

away from them, / they cry…"
그들에게서,        그들은 울어버리죠…"

"They are lucky," the switchman said.
"그들은 운이 좋아,"        철도원이 말했다.

## Key Expression

**take away from~ : ~에게서 빼앗다**

'take away'는 'takeout'으로도 쓰이는데, '가져가다, 꺼내다, 데리고 가다'
라는 의미가 됩니다.
'take away from'은 '~에게서 빼앗다'라는 뜻으로 쓰입니다.

ex) …if anybody takes it away from them, they cry…
    …누군가가 그들에게서 그것을 빼앗으면, 그들은 울어버리죠…

---

pursue 뒤쫓다 | flatten 평평하게 하다 | windowpane (끼워 놓은) 창유리 | rag doll 봉제 인형

"Good morning," / said the little prince.
"안녕하세요,"　　　　　　　　어린왕자가 말했다.

"Good morning," / said the merchant.
"안녕,"　　　　　　　　장사꾼이 대답했다.

This was the merchant / who sold pills / that had been invented
이 사람은 장사꾼이었다　　약을 파는　　　　발명된.

/ to quench thirst. You need only swallow / one pill a week, /
갈증을 해소해 주기 위해.　삼키기만 하면 된다　　　일주일에 한 알씩,

and you would feel no need / of anything to drink.
그러면 아무 필요도 느끼지 않을 것이다　　뭔가 마셔야겠다는.

"Why are you selling those?" / asked the little prince.
"아저씨는 왜 그것을 팔고 있어요?"　　　어린왕자가 물었다.

"Because / they save / a tremendous amount of time," / said
"왜냐하면　그 약들은 절약해 주거든 엄청난 시간을."

the merchant. "Computations have been made / by experts.
장사꾼이 말했다.　　"계산이 된 적 있어　　　　전문가들에 의해.

With these pills, / you save fifty-three minutes / in every
이 약들이 있으면,　　53분을 절약할 수 있다고　　　　일주일에."

week."

"And what do I do / with those fifty-three minutes?"
"그러면 뭘 하는데요　　　그 53분으로?"

"Anything you like…"
"네가 하고 싶은 것이면 무엇이든…"

merchant 상인 | pill 알약 | quench (갈증을) 해소하다 | swallow 삼키다 | tremendous 엄청난, 광장한 |
computation 계산 | expert 전문가, 전문적인

"As for me," / said the little prince to himself, / "if I had fifty-
"나라면," 어린왕자는 생각했다.

three minutes / to spend as I liked, / I should walk at my leisure
"내게 53분이 있다면  마음대로 쓸 수 있는,  나는 천천히 걸어가겠어

/ toward a spring of fresh water."
맑은 물이 있는 샘을 향하여."

👑 24 👑

It was now the eighth day / since I had had my accident / in the
8일째 되는 날이었다  내가 사고를 당한지,  사막에서

desert, / and I had listened to / the story of the merchant / as I
그리고 나는 들었다  상인에 대한 이야기를

was drinking / the last drop of my water supply.
마시면서  마지막 남은 물 한 방울을.

"Ah," I said to the little prince, / "these memories of yours / are
"아," 나는 어린왕자에게 말했다.  "네 기억들은

very charming; / but I have not yet succeeded / in repairing my
매우 멋지지만;  그러나 난 아직 성공하지 못했어  내 비행기 수리하는 것을;

plane; / I have nothing more to drink; / and I, too, should be
나는 더 이상 마실 것이 없어;  그리고 난, 정말 기쁠 거야

very happy / if I could walk at my leisure / toward a spring of
만약 내가 천천히 걸어갈 수 있다면  맑은 물이 솟는 샘을 향하여!"

fresh water!"

---

Key Expression 🔑

**as for me : 나라면**
'as for'는 '~로 말하자면'이라는 뜻을 가지고 있어요.
'as for me'는 '나로 말하자면, 나라면, 나로서는'의 의미로 쓰인답니다.

ex) "As for me," said the little prince to himself, "if I had fifty-three minutes to
spend as I liked, I should walk at my leisure toward a spring of fresh water."
"나라면", 어린왕자는 생각했다. "내게 마음대로 쓸 수 있는 53분이 있다면, 맑은
물이 있는 샘을 향하여 천천히 걸어가겠어."

"My friend the fox —— " the little prince said to me.
"내 친구 여우는 —"　　　　　　　　어린왕자가 내게 말했다.

"My dear little man, / this is no longer a matter / that has
"꼬마 친구야,　　　　　　　이제는 더 이상 문제가 아니야

anything to do with the fox!"
여우와 상관 있는!"

"Why not?"
"왜 아니야?"

"Because I am about to die of thirst…"
"왜냐하면 나는 목이 말라서 죽을 것 같아…"

He did not follow my reasoning, / and he answered me:
그는 나의 이유를 듣지 않고,　　　　　　내게 대답했다:

"It is a good thing / to have had a friend, / even if one is about
"좋은 일이야　　　　　　친구가 있는 것은　　　　　설사 내가 죽는다고 하더라도,

to die. I, for instance, am very glad / to have had a fox as a
예를 들어, 나는, 매우 기뻐　　　　　여우랑 친구가 되어서…"

friend…"

"He has no way of guessing the danger," / I said to myself.
"그는 위험에 대해 전혀 생각치 못하는군,"　　　　　나는 생각했다.

"He has never been / either hungry or thirsty. A little sunshine
"그는 ~해 본 적이 없어　　　배고프거나 목이 말라본 적이.　　　약간의 햇빛만이

is / all that he needs…"
그가 필요한 전부야…"

Key Expression 🍋

**be about to 이제 막 ~ 하려고 있다**

미래 시제를 나타내는 'be going to'보다 더 가까운 시점에 닥친 일을 표현하는 말이에요.

ex) I am about to die of thirst…. 목이 말라 죽을 것 같아
　　The performance is about to begin. 공연이 막 시작하려고 한다.

leisure 여가 |charming 매력적인, 멋진 |thirst 갈증

145

But he looked at me steadily, / and replied to my thought:
그러나 그는 나를 계속해서 바라보았다.    그리고 나의 생각에 응답했다:

"I am thirsty, too. Let us look for a well…"
"나도 너무 목이 말라.    우리 우물을 찾자…"

I made a gesture of weariness. It is absurd / to look for a well,
나는 분통터진다는 듯한 몸짓을 했다.    터무니없었다    우물을 찾는다는 것은,

/ at random, / in the immensity of the desert. But nevertheless
뜬금없이,    광대한 사막에서.    그러나 그럼에도 불구하고

/ we started walking.
우리는 걷기 시작했다.

When we had trudged along / for several hours, / in silence, /
터벅터벅 걷다 보니    몇 시간 동안,    말없이,

the darkness fell, / and the stars began to come out. Thirst had
밤이 찾아와서,    별들이 나오기 시작했다.

made me a little feverish, / and I looked at them / as if I were
목마름은 나를 조금 열이 나게 했고,    나는 별들을 보았다    마치 꿈 속에 있는 것처럼.

in a dream. The little prince's last words / came reeling back /
어린왕자의 마지막 말이    가물가물 떠올랐다

into my memory:
기억 속에:

"Then you are thirsty, too?" I demanded.
"너도 목말라?"    나는 물었다.

But he did not reply / to my question. He merely said to me:
그러나 그는 대답하지 않았다    나의 질문에 .    그는 단지 내게 말했다:

"Water may also be good / for the heart…"
"물은 좋을 거야    마음에도…"

I did not understand this answer, / but I said nothing. I knew
나는 그의 대답을 이해하지 못했다.    그러나 나는 아무 대답도 하지 않았다.

very well / that it was impossible / to cross-examine him.
나는 잘 알고 있었다    불가능하다는 것을    그에게 되묻는 것이.

---

steadily 착실하게, 끊임없이 | weariness 권태 | immensity 무한(한 공간) | trudge along 터벅터벅 걷다 |
feverish 열이 있는 | reel (실 따위를) 감다 | cross-examine 힐문하다, 반대 심문하다

He was tired. He sat down. I sat down beside him. And, / after
그는 피곤했다.    그는 앉아 있었다.    나는 그의 옆에 앉았다.    그리고,

a little silence, / he spoke again:
잠시 말이 없다가,    그는 다시 말하기 시작했다.

"The stars are beautiful, / because of a flower / that cannot be
"별들이 아름다운 건,    꽃 한 송이 때문이야    보이지 않는."

seen."

I replied, / "Yes, that is so." And, without saying anything
내가 대답했다.    "그래, 맞아."    그리고, 아무 말도 하지 않은 채,

more, / I looked across the ridges of sand / that were stretched
나는 모래 언덕을 바라보았다    펼쳐져 있는

out / before us / in the moonlight.
우리 앞에    달빛 아래.

"The desert is beautiful," / the little prince added.
"사막은 아름다워,"    그 어린왕자가 말을 이었다.

And that was true. I have always loved the desert. One sits
그리고 그것은 사실이었다.    나는 항상 사막을 좋아했다.

down on a desert sand dune, / sees nothing, / hears nothing.
모래 언덕에 앉아 있으면,    아무것도 보이지 않는다,    아무것도 들리지 않는다.

Yet through the silence / something throbs and gleams…
그러나 고요함 속에서    뭔가가 고동치고, 반짝거린다…

"What makes the desert beautiful," / said the little prince, / "is
"사막을 아름답게 만드는 것은,"    어린왕자가 말했다,

that somewhere / it hides a well…"
"어딘가에    우물을 숨기고 있어서야…"

## Key Expression

### to be sure 확실히, 물론
뒤에 'but'을 동반하여 양보구를 나타내어 '과연, 정말'이라는 뜻으로 쓰이기도 하고요, 'well' 등과 함께 쓰여서 감탄사적으로 놀라움을 나타내어 '놀라겠는걸, 저런'이라는 뜻으로 쓰이기도 해요.

ex) Well, to be sure! = Well, I'm sure! 이런 원!

---

ridge 산마루, 이랑, 언덕 | dune (해변의) 모래 언덕 | throb 가슴이 고동치다 | hide 감추다, 숨기다

I was astonished / by a sudden understanding / of that
나는 깜짝 놀랐다                        갑자기 깨닫게 되어서

mysterious radiation of the sands. When I was a little boy / I
그 신비로운 사막의 광채에 대해.                  내가 어린 소년이었을 때

lived in an old house, / and legend told us / that a treasure was
나는 낡은 집에서 살았다.      그리고 전설이 우리에게 말해줬다    보물이 거기에 묻혀있다고.

buried there. To be sure, / no one had ever known / how to find
물론,                       아무도 알지 못했다                보물을 찾는 방법을;

it; / perhaps / no one had ever even looked for it. But it cast an
아마도     아무도 찾은 적이 없었을 것이다.              그러나 그 전설은 마법을

enchantment / over that house. My home was hiding a secret /
걸었다          집 전체에.                    내 집은 비밀을 숨기고 있던 것이다

in the depths of its heart...
깊숙한 곳에…

"Yes," I said to the little prince. "The house, the stars, the
"그래."  나는 어린왕자에게 말했다.              "집, 별, 사막

desert —— what gives them their beauty / is something that is
——그것을 아름답게 하는 건                    눈에 보이지 않는 법이야!"

invisible!"

"I am glad," / he said, / "that you agree with my fox."
"난 기쁘다."      그가 말했다,       "아저씨가 내 여우에게 동의해서."

As the little prince dropped off to sleep, / I took him in my
어린왕자가 잠이 들자,                          나는 그를 팔에 안고,

arms / and set out walking once more. I felt deeply moved,
한 번 더 걷기 시작했다.                       나는 마음 깊이 감동했고,

/ and stirred. It seemed to me / that I was carrying / a very
뭉클했다.       그것은 나에게 ~해 보였다    안고 가는 것처럼

fragile treasure. It seemed to me, / even, that there was nothing
매우 깨지기 쉬운 보물을.   그것은 나에게 ~해 보였다.            없는 것처럼

/ more fragile / on all the Earth. In the moonlight / I looked at /
더 연약한 존재는       온 지구상에.              달빛 아래에서            나는 바라보았다

astonish 놀라게 하다 |radiation 방사선 |enchantment 마술 |drop off(=fall asleep) 잠들다 | fragile
깨어지기 쉬운

148    The Little Prince

his pale forehead, his closed eye, his locks of hair that trembled
그의 창백한 이마와,                  감은 눈,                    바람에 흐트러진 머리카락을,

in the wind, / and I said to myself: / "What I see here is /
그리고는 생각했다:                        "내가 여기에서 보고 있는 것들은

nothing / but a shell. What is most important is / invisible…"
껍데기일 뿐이야.      가장 중요한 것은                    보이지 않아…"

As his lips opened slightly / with the suspicion of a half-smile,
그의 입술이 살짝 열리면서              어렴풋한 미소를 띨 때,

/ I said to myself, again: / "What moves me so deeply, / about
난 다시 생각했다:                        "날 이토록 감동시킨 것은,

this little prince / who is sleeping here, / is his loyalty to a
어린왕자에 대해              여기에서 자고 있는,          꽃에 대한 그의 성실성이야

flower —— the image of a rose / that shines through this whole
          — 장미에 대한 이미지              온몸에 비추이는,

being / like the flame of a lamp, / even when he is asleep…"
램프의 불꽃처럼,                        잠들어 있는 순간마저도…"

And I felt him / to be more fragile still. I felt the need of
그리고 나는 깨달았다      그가 더욱 약해졌다는 것을.          내가 그를 잘 보호해야 한다고 느꼈다.

protecting him, / as if he himself were a flame / that might be
마치 그는 불꽃 같아서                              쉽게 꺼져버릴 수 있으니까

extinguished / by a little puff of wind…
            한 줄기 바람에도…

And, as I walked on so, / I found the well, at daybreak.
그리고, 나는 계속 걸었고 그래서,          나는 우물을 발견했다,          새벽녘에.

---

### Key Expression 🍎

**자동사 seem**
'~처럼 보이다, ~처럼 생각되다'라는 의미를 가지고 있는 seem은 주로 말하는
사람의 주관적인 판단을 나타내고 있어요. 'It seems that 주어+동사' 혹은 '
주어 seem+형용사+to부정사' 형태로 사용합니다.

ex) It seemed to me that I was carrying a very fragile treasure.
매우 부서지기 쉬운 보물을 내가 운반하고 있는 것처럼 보였다.
He seems glad to see us. 그는 우리들을 만나 기뻐하는 것 같다.
It would seem that the weather is improving. 날씨가 좋아질 것 같다

locks 머리카락 | tremble (몸을) 떨다 | shell (달걀, 조개 등의) 껍데기 | suspicion 혐의, 의심 | loyalty 성실성 |
flame 불길 | puff of wind 한 번 휙 부는 바람 | daybreak 동틀녘

149

A. 다음 문장을 해석해 보세요.

(1) To me, / you are still nothing more than a little boy / who is just like a hundred thousand other little boys.
　→

(2) But if you tame me, / it will be as if the sun came to shine on my life.
　→

(3) There is no shop anywhere / where one can buy friendship, / and so men have no friends any more.
　→

(4) You need only swallow one pill a week, / and you would feel no need of anything to drink.
　→

B. 다음 주어진 문장이 되도록 빈칸에 써 넣으세요.

(1) 같은 시간에 돌아오는 게 좋을 거야.

　　　　　　　　　　 to come back at the same hour.

(2) 네 장미를 중요하게 만든 것은 바로 네가 장미에 쏟아온 시간이야.

　　　　　　　　　　 you have wasted for your rose 　　　　
makes your rose so important.

(3) 사막을 아름답게 만든 것은 어딘가에 우물을 감추고 있기 때문이야.

　　　　　　　　　　 is that somewhere it hides a well.

(4) 네가 나를 길들인다면, 그건 마치 태양이 내 삶을 비추게 되는 것처럼 될 거야.

　　If you tame me, it will be 　　　　　　　　　　.

A. (1) 내게 있어, 넌 아직 10만 명의 다른 소년들과 같은 작은 소년일 뿐이다. (2) 그러나 네가 나를 길들인다면, 그건 내 삶에 태양을 비추이는 것 같을 거야. (3) 우정을 살 수 있는 가게는 어디에도 없으니까 사람들은 더 이상 친구가 없어. (4) 일주일마다 한 알씩만 삼키면, 넌 갈증을 느끼지 않을 거야. | B. (1) It would

150　The Little Prince

C. 다음 주어진 문구가 알맞은 문장이 되도록 순서를 맞춰보세요.

(1) 네가 찾고 있는게 도대체 무엇이니?
(you are / it / looking for / is / What / that)
→

(2) 중요한 것은 눈에 보이지 않아.
(invisible / is / essential / What / to the eye / is
→

(3) 널 길들이려면 무엇을 해야 하지?
(do / must / What / I / you / to tame)
→

(4) 내가 얼마나 행복한지 네게 보여 줄게.
(how / happy / I / you / show / I / am / shall)
→

D. 다음 빈칸에 알맞은 단어를 보기에서 골라 써 넣으세요.

[보기]  perplexed  pursuing  enchantment  absurd

(1) The fox seemed ▢▢▢, and very curious.
여우는 당황하며 궁금해하는 것 같았다.

(2) Are they ▢▢▢ the first travelers?
저들은 첫 번째 승객들을 쫓아가는 건가요?

(3) It is ▢▢▢ to look for a well, at random, in the immensity of
the desert.
광대한 사막에서 뜬금없이 우물을 찾는다는 것은 터무니없다.

(4) But it cast an ▢▢▢ over that house. 그러나 그것은 집 전체에 마법을 걸었다.

have been better  (2) It is the time / that (3) What makes the desert beautiful (4) as if the sun came
to shine on my life | C. (1) What is it that you are looking for? (2) What is essential is invisible to the
eye. (3) What must I do to tame you? (4) I shall show you how happy I am! | D. (1) perplexed (2)
pursuing (3) absurd (4) enchantment

151

"Men," / said the little prince, / "set out on their way / in
"사람들은," 어린왕자가 말했다. "길을 떠나지

express trains, / but they do not know / what they are looking
특급열차를 타고 . 하지만 그들은 알지 못해 자신들이 무엇을 찾고 있는지를.

for. Then they rush about, / and get excited, / and turn round
그래서 그들은 급히 서두르고, 흥분하면서, 같은 곳을 빙빙 맴돌지…"

and round…"

And he added:
그리고 그는 덧붙였다:

"It is not worth the trouble…"
"그것은 쓸데없는 짓이야…"

The well that we had come to / was not like the wells / of the
우리가 도착한 우물은 우물과는 달랐다 사하라 사막

Sahara. The wells of the Sahara / are mere holes / dug in the
에 있던 . 사하라 사막의 우물은 구멍에 불과했다 모래에 뚫은 .

sand. This one was like a well / in a village. But / there was
이것은 우물 같았다 마을에 있는 . 그러나

no village here, / and I thought / I must be dreaming…
여기에는 마을이 없었다. 그래서 나는 생각했다 꿈을 꾸고 있는 것이라고…

"It is strange," / I said to the little prince. "Everything is ready
"이상한데," 나는 어린왕자에게 말했다. "모든 것이 준비되어 있어:

for use: / the pulley, the bucket, the rope…"
도르래, 물통, 그리고 로프까지…"

He laughed, / touched the rope, / and set the pulley to
그는 웃으면서, 로프를 만지고, 도르래를 움직였다.

working. And the pulley moaned, / like an old weathervane/
그러자 도르래가 삐걱거렸다, 낡은 풍차처럼

which the wind has long since forgotten.
바람이 오랫동안 잠들어 있던.

---

rush about 급히 서두르다 | pulley 도르래 | bucket 두레박, 물통 | moan 삐걱거리다 | weathervane 풍향계,
풍차, 바람개비 | hoist 끌어올리다 | edge 끝, 가장자리 | achievement 성취, 업적 | shimmer 희미하게 빛나다

"Do you hear?" / said the little prince. "We have wakened the
"들려?"　　　　　　어린왕자가 말했다.　　　　　　　"우리는 우물을 깨운 거야,

well, / and it is singing…"
　　　　　　그래서 우물이 노래하고 있는 거야…"

I did not want / him to tire himself / with the rope.
나는 원하지 않았다　　그가 지치는 것을　　　　　　로프를 당기다가.

"Leave it to me," / I said. "It is too heavy for you."
"내게 줘."　　　　　나는 말했다.　"네게는 너무 무거워."

I hoisted the bucket slowly / to the edge of the well / and set it
나는 천천히 물통을 끌어올렸다　　　　　우물 끝까지　　　　　그리고 그곳에 얹어놓았다 —

there —— / happy, tired as I was, / over my achievement. The
　　　　피곤했지만, 기뻤다　　　　　내가 해낸 것이.

song of the pulley / was still in my ears, / and I could see / the
도르래의 노래 소리가　　　아직도 귓가에서 울리고 있었다,　그리고 볼 수 있었다

sunlight shimmer / in the still trembling water.
희미하게 반짝이는 햇빛을　　일렁이는 물 속에서.

"I am thirsty for this water," / said the little prince. "Give me
"이 물을 먹고 싶어."　　　　　어린왕자가 말했다.

some of it to drink…"
"마시게 좀 줘…"

And I understood / what he had been looking for.
그래서 나는 알게 되었다　　그가 무엇을 찾고 있었는지를.

---

### Key Expression 🎯

#### 형용사 + as I was : ~라고 하더라도

'형용사 + as + 주어 + 동사'는 '~라고 하더라도'라는 의미의 양보구문이에요.
형용사 자리에는 부사, 명사, 동사원형이 들어가기도 해요. 문장 중간에 들어갈 때
에는 앞뒤에 ,를 넣어 삽입구로 사용합니다.

ex) I hoisted the bucket slowly to the edge of the well and set it there — happy,
　　tired as I was, over my achievement.
　　나는 물통을 천천히 우물 끝까지 끌어올려 그곳에 놓았다 —피곤했지만, 내가 해
　　낸 것에 기뻤다.

153

I raised the bucket / to his lips. He drank, / his eyes closed.
나는 물통을 들어줬다          그의 입술까지.     그는 물을 마셨다   눈을 감고.

It was as sweet / as some special festival treat. This water
그것은 달콤했다          특별한 축제의 만찬처럼.                    이 물은 정말로

was indeed / a different thing / from ordinary nourishment.
              다른 것이었다          보통 먹는 음식들과는.

Its sweetness was born / of the walk under the stars, / the
그 달콤함은 생겨난 것이었다          별빛 아래에서의 걷기와,

song of the pulley, / the effort of my arms. It was good for
도르래의 노랫소리,          내 팔의 수고로부터.          그것은 마음에 들었다,

the heart, / like a present. When I was a little boy, / the lights
선물처럼.          내가 어렸을 때,          the lights

of the Christmas tree, / the music of the Midnight Mass, /
크리스마스 트리의 불빛과.          자정 미사의 음악,

the tenderness of smiling faces, / used to make up, / so, the
그리고 웃는 얼굴의 부드러움이.          만들곤 했다.          그렇게 환한 빛을

radiance / of the gifts I received.
              내가 받은 선물들에.

"The men where you live," / said the little prince, / "raise five
"아저씨가 사는 지구의 사람들은,"          어린왕자는 말했다.          "5,000송이의 장미

thousand roses / in the same garden —— / and they do not find
를 가꾸고 있어          한 정원에서 —          그런데 그들은 찾지 못하지

/ in it / what they are looking for."
  거기서는   자신들이 찾고자 하는 것을.'

"They do not find it," / I replied.
"그들은 찾지 못해"          내가 대답했다.

"And yet / what they are looking for / could be found / in one
"하지만          그들이 찾고자 하는 것은          찾을 수도 있어          in one

single rose, / or in a little water."
한 송이 장미에서,          혹은 한 잔의 물에서도.'

treat 한턱(냄) l indeed 정말(강조) l nourishment 음식물 l effort 수고, 노력 l Midnight Mass 자정 미사 l
tenderness 유연함, 친절 l radiance 빛, 광채 l breathe 숨을 쉬다

"Yes, that is true," / I said.
"그래, 네 말이 맞아."　　　　　나는 말했다.

And the little prince added:
그리고 어린왕자는 덧붙였다:

"But / the eyes are blind. One must look with the heart…"
"그러나　눈은 보지 못해.　　마음으로 찾아야 해…"

I had drunk the water. I breathed easily. At sunrise / the sand
나는 물을 마셨다.　　　　　그래서 쉽게 숨을 쉬었다.　태양이 떠오르자

is the color of honey. And that honey color / was making me
모래는 꿀빛을 띄었다.　　　그리고 그 꿀 빛깔은　　　　나를 행복하게 해 주었다.

happy, / too. What brought me, then, / this sense of grief?
　　　또한.　그러면 무엇이 내게 준 건지,　　이런 슬픔을?

"You must keep / your promise," / said the little prince, /
"아저씨는 지켜야 해　　약속을."　　　　　어린왕자는 말했다,

softly, / as he sat down / beside me once more.
부드럽게,　다가와 앉으면서　　다시 한 번 내 옆에.

"What promise?"
"무슨 약속?"

### used to : ~하곤 했었다

'used to'는 '~하곤 했었다'라는 의미로 과거의 습관을 말할 때 쓰는 표현입니다. 여기에는 지금은 하지 않는 습관이라는 의미가 함축되어 있어요. used to은 일종의 조동사처럼 취급하며 뒤에는 동사원형이 옵니다.

ex) When I was a little boy, the lights of the Christmas tree used to make up the radiance of the gifts I received.
내가 어렸을 때, 크리스마스 트리의 불빛이 내가 받은 선물에 광채를 만들어 내곤 했다.

"You know —— / a muzzle for my sheep... I am responsible /
"알잖아 — 　　　　　　내 양떼에 씌워 줄 입 마개 말이야… 　　나는 책임이 있거든

for this flower..."
꽃에 대해…"

I took / my rough drafts of drawings / out of my pocket. The
나는 꺼냈다 　스케치를 　　　　　　　호주머니로부터.

little prince looked them over, / and laughed as he said:
어린왕자는 그림들을 살펴보고, 　　　　　　웃으며 말했다:

"Your baobabs —— / they look a little like cabbages."
"아저씨의 바오밥 나무는 — 　좀 양배추처럼 생겼어."

"Oh!"
"저런!"

I had been so proud / of my baobabs!
나는 자부심이 있었는데 　　내 바오밥 나무에!

"Your fox —— / his ears look a little like horns; / and they are
"아저씨의 여우는 — 　귀가 뿔 같아; 　　　　　그리고 너무 길어."

too long."

And he laughed again.
그리고 그는 다시 웃었다.

"You are not fair, / little prince," / I said. "I don't know / how
"너무 심하구나, 　　어린왕자," 　　나는 말했다. "난 모르거든

to draw anything / except boa constrictors from the outside /
그리는 법을 　　　　보아뱀의 바깥쪽 뿐

and boa constrictors from the inside."
보아뱀의 안쪽과."

"Oh, that will be all right," / he said, / "children understand."
"아, 그건 괜찮아," 　　　　그는 말했다, 　　"아이들은 이해할 테니까."

So then / I made a pencil sketch / of a muzzle. And as I gave it
그래서 　　나는 연필로 그렸다 　　　　입 마개를. 　그리고 그것을 그에게 줬다

to him / my heart was torn.
조마조마해 하며.

"You have plans / that I do not know about," / I said.
"넌 계획이 있구나    내가 알지 못하는."    나는 말했다.

But he did not answer me. He said to me, / instead:
그러나 그는 내 말에 대답하지 않았다.    그는 말했다    대신:

"You know —— / my descent to the earth… Tomorrow will be
"있잖아 —    내가 지구에 떨어진 거…    내일이면 1주년이야."

its anniversary."

Then, / after a silence, / he went on:
그리고 나서,  잠시 침묵하다가,    이야기를 계속했다:

"I came down / very near here."
"나는 떨어졌었어    여기에서 아주 가까운 곳에."

And he flushed.
그리고 얼굴을 붉혔다.

And once again, / without understanding why, / I had a queer
다시 한 번,    이유를 알지 못한 채,

sense of sorrow. One question, however, / occurred to me:
나는 묘한 슬픔을 느꼈다.    그런데 질문이    떠올랐다:

"Then / it was not by chance / that on the morning / when I
"그러면    우연이 아니었구나    그 아침의 일이

first met you —— / a week ago —— / you were strolling along
내가 너를 처음 만났던 —    일주일 전에 —    네가 그렇게 어슬렁거리던 게,

like that, / all alone, / a thousand miles from any inhabited
혼자서,    사람들이 사는 곳에서 1,000마일이나 떨어진 곳을?

region? You were on your way back / to the place where you
너는 돌아가던 길이었니    네가 살던 곳으로?"

landed?"

The little prince flushed again.
어린왕자는 또 얼굴을 붉혔다.

---

descent 하강, 내리막 | anniversary (해마다의) 기념일 | flush (얼굴이) 붉어지다, 홍조를 띠다 | stroll
어슬렁거리다, 산책하다 | hesitancy 망설임 | weep 눈물을 흘리다, 울다

And I added, / with some hesitancy:
그리고 나는 말을 이었다,   잠시 망설이다가:

"Perhaps / it was because of the anniversary?"
"어쩌면   1주년이기 때문이야?"

The little prince flushed / once more. He never answered
어린왕자는 얼굴을 붉혔다      또 다시.       그는 묻는 말에 대답한 적이 없었다 —

questions —— / but when one flushed / does that not mean
           그러나 사람이 얼굴을 붉힐 때는      그건 "응"이라는 뜻이 아닌가?

"Yes"?

"Ah," / I said to him, / "I am a little frightened —— "
"아."      나는 그에게 말했다      "난 좀 겁이 나 —"

But he interrupted me.
그러나 그는 이렇게 대답했다.

"Now you must work. You must return / to your engine. I will
"아저씨는 이제 일을 해야지.       아저씨는 돌아가야 해      엔진이 있는 곳으로.

be waiting for you here. Come back tomorrow evening…"
나는 여기에서 기다릴게.       내일 저녁에 다시 와 줘…"

But I was not reassured. I remembered the fox. One runs the
그러나 나는 마음이 놓이지 않았다.       여우가 생각났다.

risk of weeping a little, / if one lets himself be tamed…
사람은 울 염려가 있는 것이다,      한 번 길들여지면…

## Key Expression 🏮

### 삽입된 however 해석하기

'however'가 '그러나'라는 의미를 갖는 접속부사가 된다는 것은 알고 계시죠?
'그러나'의 의미를 가질 때 however는 ,(쉼표)와함께 쓰이는데 문장 중간에 ,를
앞뒤에 두고 삽입되는 경우에는 해석을 하다가 갑자기 끊기고 말죠. 이럴 때에는
however를 문장 맨 앞에 놓고 '그러나~'로 시작해해석해 보세요.

ex) One question, however, occurred to me.
    그러나, 하나의 질문이 내게 떠올랐다.

159

Beside the well / there was the ruin / of an old stone wall .
우물가에는          무너진 잔해가 있었다          오래된 돌담의.

When I came back from my work, / the next evening, / I saw
내가 일을 마치고 돌아왔을 때,          그 다음 날 저녁,          나는 보았다

/ from some distance away / my little prince / sitting on top of
멀리서부터          어린왕자가          우물 위에 앉아서,

this wall, / with his feet dangling . And I heard him say:
발을 늘어뜨리고 있는 것을.          그리고 그가 말하는 것을 들었다:

"Then you don't remember. This is not the exact spot."
"넌 기억하지 못하잖아.          이곳은 정확한 지점이 아니야."

Another voice must have answered him, / for he replied to it:
다른 목소리가 그에게 대답한 것이 틀림없다.          그가 다시 대꾸했기 때문에:

"Yes, yes! It is the right day, / but this is not the place."
"그래, 그래! 날짜는 맞는데,          그러나 이곳은 그 장소가 아니야."

I continued my walk / toward the wall. At no time did I see / or
나는 계속해서 걸었다          돌담 쪽을 향하여.          나는 여전히 아무것도 보지 못했고

hear anyone. The little prince, / however, / replied once again:
아무것도 듣지 못했다. 어린왕자는,          그러나,          다시 대답했다:

"—— Exactly. You will see / where my track begins, / in the
"— 확실해.          넌 보게 될 거야          내 발자국이 시작한 곳을,          모래 위에서.

sand. You have nothing to do / but wait for me there. I shall be
넌 아무것도 안 해도 돼          그냥 나를 거기서 기다리기만 해.

there tonight."
오늘 밤 거기로 갈게."

I was only twenty meters / from the wall, / and I still saw
난 불과 20미터 떨어져 있었고          그 돌담으로부터,          여전히 아무것도 보지 못했다.

nothing.

After a silence / the little prince spoke again:
잠시 침묵 후에          어린왕자는 다시 말했다:

---

ruin 황폐, 무너진 잔해 |wall 돌담 |dangle (무엇이 달랑) 매달리다 |suffer 시달리다, 고통 받다 |asunder
조각조각으로 |leap 껑충 뛰다 |dig into one's pocket 자기 돈을 내(서 지불하)다 |fountain 샘(물) |apparent
명백한, 또렷한 |metallic sound 금속성의 소리

"You have good poison? You are sure / that it will not make me
"네 독은 좋은 거지?  확실하지  날 아프게 하지 않는 것이

suffer / too long?"
너무 오랫동안?"

I stopped in my tracks, / my heart torn asunder; / but still / I did
나는 멈춰 섰다.  가슴이 두근거려서:  그러나 여전히

not understand.
나는 이해되지 않았다.

"Now go away," said the little prince. "I want to get down / from
"이제 가 봐,"  어린왕자가 말했다.  "내려가고 싶어

the wall."
여기 돌담에서."

I dropped my eyes, / then, / to the foot of the wall —— and I
나는 시선을 내렸다.  그때,  돌담의 밑으로 —

leaped into the air. There before me, / facing the little prince,
그리고 공중으로 뛰어올랐다.  거기 내 앞에,  어린왕자와 마주하고 있는,

/ was one of those yellow snakes / that take thirty seconds / to
노란 뱀 하나가 있었다  30초 밖에 안 걸리는

bring your life to an end. Even as I was digging into my pocket
사람의 목숨을 빼앗는데.  나는 내 주머니 속을 뒤지면서

/ to get out my revolver / I made a running step back. But, at the
권총을 꺼내기 위하여  뒷걸음질 쳐서 달렸다.  그러나,

noise I made, / the snake let himself flow easily / across the sand
내가 내는 소리에,  그 뱀은 부드럽게 몸을 미끄러뜨려  모래를 가르며

/ like the dying spray of a fountain, / and, in no apparent hurry, /
꺼져가는 샘의 물방울처럼,  전혀 급하지 않게,

disappeared, / with a light metallic sound, / among the stones.
사라졌다.  희미한 금속 소리와 함께,  돌 사이로.

I reached the wall just in time / to catch my little man in my
나는 돌담에 아슬아슬하게 도착했다    어린왕자를 도와주기 위해;

arms; his face was white as snow.
그의 얼굴은 눈처럼 희었다.

"What does this mean?" I demanded. "Why are you talking
"그게 무슨 뜻이야?"    나는 물었다.    "지금 뱀이랑 이야기하고 있는 거야?"

with snakes?"

I had loosened the golden muffler / that he always wore. I had
나는 그 금빛 머플러를 풀어 주었다    그가 늘 메고 있던.

moistened his temples, / and had given him some water to
나는 그의 관자놀이를 촉촉하게 해 주었다.    그리고 마실 물을 좀 주었다.

drink. And now / I did not dare ask him / any more questions.
그리고 바로    나는 감히 그에게 묻지 않았다    더 이상의 질문은.

He looked at me very gravely, / and put his arms around my
그는 날 굉장히 심각한 표정으로 쳐다보다가,    그의 팔을 내 목에 둘렀다.

neck. I felt his heart beating / like the heart of a dying bird, /
나는 뛰고 있는 그의 심장 소리를 느꼈다    마치 죽어가는 새의 심장처럼.

shot with someone's rifle…
누군가의 총알을 맞고…

"I am glad / that you have found / what was the matter with
"나는 기쁘다    아저씨가 찾았다는 것에    네 엔진이 뭐가 문제였는지를."

your engine," he said. "Now you can go back home ―― "
그가 말했다.    "아저씨는 이제 집에 갈 수 있을 거야 ―"

"How do you know about that?"
"그것을 어떻게 알았니?"

I was just coming to tell him / that my work had been
"난 지금 막 네게 이야기해 주려고 온 거였어    일이 성공되었다고.

successful, / beyond anything that I had dared to hope.
거의 희망이 없었던 것.

He made no answer to my question, / but he added:
그는 내 질문에 대답하지 않았다.    그러나 그는 말을 이었다:

loosen 느슨하게 하다 ǀ moisten 적시다. 촉촉하게 하다 ǀ temple 관자놀이 ǀ gravely 침통하게 ǀ rifle 라이플,
소총 ǀ headlong 곧바로 ǀ abyss 심연, 나락 ǀ revive 활기를 되찾다

"I, too, am going back home today…"
"나도 오늘 집으로 돌아가…"

Then, sadly ——
그리고, 슬프게 —

"It is much farther… It is much more difficult…"
"훨씬 더 먼 곳으로….          훨씬 더 힘들 거야…"

I realized clearly / that something extraordinary was happening.
나는 명백하게 깨달았다    뭔가 심상치 않은 일이 벌어지고 있음을.

I was holding him close in my arms / as if he were a little child;
나는 그를 나의 팔에 꼭 안고 있었다          마치 그가 어린 아이인 것처럼;

/ and yet it seemed to me / that he was rushing headlong toward
그런데도 그렇게 보였다          그가 심연으로 빠져 들어가고 있는 것처럼

an abyss / from which I could do nothing / to restrain him…
내가 아무것도 할 수 없는 채로          그를 멈추기 위해…

His look was very serious, / like someone lost far away.
그의 안색은 매우 심각해 보였다.          길을 잃은 사람처럼.

"I have your sheep. And I have the sheep's box. And I have the
"나는 아저씨가 그려 준 양을 가지고 있어.   그리고 양을 넣을 상자도 있고.          입 마개도…"

muzzle…"

And he gave me a sad smile.
그리고 그는 내게 슬픈 미소를 지었다.

I waited a long time. I could see / that he was reviving / little by
나는 오랫동안 기다렸다.          나는 볼 수 있었다     그가 다시 기운을 차리는 것을          조금씩.

little.

"Dear little man," / I said to him, / "you are afraid…"
"오, 어린왕자야,"          내가 그에게 말했다.          "넌 두려워하고 있구나…"

He was afraid, / there was no doubt about that. But he laughed
그는 겁먹었었다.          그것에 대한 의심에 여지는 없다.          그러나 그는 희미하게 웃었다.

lightly.

"I shall be much more afraid / this evening…"
"훨씬 더 무서울 걸          오늘 밤에는…"

Once again / I felt myself frozen / by the sense of something
또 다시          온몸이 얼어붙는 것 같았다          돌이킬 수 없는 어떤 일에 대한 예감에.

irreparable. And I knew that / I could not bear / the thought of
                그리고 나는 알았다          견딜 수가 없다는 것을          다시는 들을 수가 없을 것이

never hearing / that laughter any more. For me, / it was like a
라는 생각이          더 이상은 그 웃음소리를.          나에게,          그것은 샘물 같은 것이었다

spring of fresh water / in the desert.
                사막에서의.

"Little man," / I said, / "I want to hear you laugh again."
"어린왕자야,"          내가 말했다.          "나는 네 웃음소리를 다시 듣고 싶어."

But he said to me:
그러나 그가 내게 말했다:

"Tonight, it will be a year... / My star, then, / can be found
"오늘 밤이면, 꼭 일 년이 돼···          내 별을, 그때,          찾을 수 있을 거야

/ right above the place / where I came to the Earth, / a year
바로 그곳 위에서          내가 지구에 왔던 그곳에.          일 년 전에···"

ago..."

"Little man," I said, "tell me that / it is only a bad dream ——
"어린왕자야,"          내가 말했다. "내게 말해 줘          그것은 단지 악몽이라고 ——

/ this affair of the snake, / and the meeting-place, / and the
뱀과 있었던 일,          만난 장소와          그 별에 대한 이야기가···"

star..."

But he did not answer my plea. He said to me, instead:
그러나 그는 내 부탁에 대답하지 않았다.          대신 그는 내게 말했다:

"The thing that is important / is the thing that is not seen..."
"중요한 것은          눈에 보이지 않는다는 것이야···"

"Yes, I know..."
"그래, 나도 알아···"

"It is just as it is / with the flower. If you love a flower / that
"그것은 마찬가지야          꽃의 경우도.          만약 아저씨가 꽃을 사랑한다면,

lives on a star, / it is sweet to look at the sky at night. All the
별에 살고 있는,          밤에 하늘을 보는 것이 즐거울 거야.

irreparable 돌이킬 수 없는 | bear 참다, 견디다 | plea 부탁, 청원

stars are / a-bloom with flowers…"
모든 별들이    꽃으로 활짝 피어나거든…"

"Yes, I know…"
"나도 알아…"

"It is just as it is / with the water. Because of the pulley, and
"그것은 마찬가지야    물의 경우와도.        도르래와 밧줄 때문에.

the rope, / what you gave me to drink was / like music. You
            아저씨가 내게 준 물은              음악 같았어.

remember —— how good it was."
기억나지    — 그게 얼마나 좋았는지."

"Yes, I know…"
"그래. 알아…"

"And at night / you will look up at the stars. Where I live /
"밤에            별들을 올려다 봐.            내가 사는 곳에는

everything is so small / that I cannot show you / where my
모든 것이 너무도 작아서        보여 줄 수 없어        내 별을 어디에서 찾을

star is to be found. It is better, like that. My star will just be
수 있는지.        그 편이 더 좋을지도 몰라.        내 별은 수많은 별들 중에 하나일 뿐이

one of the stars, / for you. And so you will love to / watch
니까        아저씨에게는. 그러면 아저씨는 좋아하게 될 거야        모든 별들을 보는

all the stars / in the heavens… They will all be your friends.
것을        하늘에 있는…        모두 친구가 되어 줄 거야.

## Key Expression

**afraid  ~을 무서워하는**

Frightened, terrified와 비슷한 뜻으로 쓰여요.

▶ Afraid for~

ex) He was afraid for the test. 그는 시험에 대하여 걱정을 했다

▶ Afraid of~

ex) The child was afraid of the dark. 그 아이는 어둠을 무서워했다

▶ Afraid to 부정사

ex) He was afraid to dive from the high board.
그는 높은 다이빙대에서 뛰어내리기가 무서웠다.

▶ Afraid that~

ex) We were afraid that he would find out. 우리는 그가 알게 될까 봐 불안했다.

165

And, besides, I am going to make you a present…"
그리고, 나는 아저씨한테 줄 선물이 있어…"

He laughed again.
그는 다시 웃었다.

"Ah, little prince, dear little prince! I love to hear that laughter!"
"아, 어린왕자야,     오, 어린왕자야!     나는 네 웃음소리가 너무 좋아!"

"That is my present. Just that. It will be as it was / when we
"그게 내 선물이야.     그것 뿐이야.     그건 마찬가지일 거야

drank the water…"
우리가 물을 마셨을 때랑…"

"What are you trying to say?"
"무슨 말을 하려는 거니?"

"All men have stars," / he answered, / "but they are not the same
"모든 사람은 별을 가지고 있어."     그가 대답했다,     "그러나 그것들은 같은 것들이 아니야

things / for different people. For some, / who are travelers, / the
다른 사람들에게.     어떤 사람들에게는, 여행자에게는,

stars are guides. For others / they are no more than little lights
별이 길잡이가 될 거야.     다른 사람에게는     작은 빛에 불과하지

/ in the sky. For others, / who are scholars, / they are problems.
하늘에 있는.     또 다른 사람들, 학자들에게는,     오히려 문제가 되지.

For my businessman / they are wealth. But all these stars / as no
사업가에게는     그것들은 재물이야.     그러나 이 모든 별들을

one else has them —— "
그 누구도 가지지는 못했어 —"

"What are you trying to say?"
"무슨 말을 하려는 거니?"

"In one of the stars / I shall be living. In one of them / I shall be
"그 별들 중의 하나에     내가 살고 있을 거야.     그것들 중의 하나에서     내가 웃고 있

laughing. And so it will be / as if all the stars were laughing, /
을 거야.     그러니까 그것은     마치 모든 별들이 웃고 있는 것과 같은 거야,

when you look at the sky at night… You —— only you —— will
아저씨가 밤에 하늘을 쳐다볼 때면…     아저씨는 — 단지 아저씨는 —     별을

have stars / that can laugh!"
가지고 있는 거야     웃을 수 있는!"

no more than(=only) 단지 | soothe 위로하다 | content 만족한 | properly 올바로, 실은 | shabby 시시한,
쓸데없는 | trick 장난, 농담

And he laughed again.
그리고 그는 다시 웃었다.

"And when your sorrow is comforted (time soothes all sorrows)
*아저씨의 슬픔이 가라 앉을 때가 되면                    (시간이 모든 슬픔을 달래니까)

/ you will be content that / you have known me. You will
만족하게 될 거야              아저씨가 날 알게 된 것을.

always be my friend. You will want to laugh with me. And you
아저씨는 언제나 내 친구일 거야.       나와 함께 웃고 싶을 거야.

sometimes open your window, / so, for that pleasure… And
그래서 때때로 창문을 열고,                    그리고는 기쁨으로…

your friends will be properly astonished / to see you laughing
그러면 아저씨의 친구들은 아마 깜짝 놀랄 거야              네가 웃는 것을 보고

/ as you look up at the sky! Then you will say to them, / 'Yes,
하늘을 쳐다보며!                    그럴 때는 그들에게 말할 거야.

the star always make me laugh!' And they will think you are
'그래, 별은 나를 웃게 만들어!'              그러면 그들은 아저씨가 미쳤다고 생각할 거야.

crazy. It will be a very shabby trick / that I shall have played on
그것은 매우 짓궂은 장난이 될 거야          내가 아저씨한테 하게 될…"

you…"

And he laughed again.
그는 또 다시 웃었다.

"It will be as if, / in place of the stars, / I had given you / a
'이것은 마치,          별 대신,                    아저씨에게 준 거야

great number of little bells / that knew how to laugh…"
수많은 작은 종들을                      웃을 줄 아는…"

And he laughed again. Then he quickly became serious:
그리고 그는 다시 웃었다.          그러더니 갑자기 심각해졌다:

"Tonight —— you know… Do not come."
"오늘 밤       — 알지…        오면 안 돼."

"I shall not leave you," / I said.
"오늘 밤에는 네 곁을 떠나지 않을 거야,"    나는 말했다.

"I shall look / as if I were suffering. I shall look a little / as if
'나는 보일 거야        몹시 괴로운 것처럼.              나는 보일 거야

I were dying. It is like that. Do not come to see that. It is not
죽어가는 것처럼.        그렇게 보일 거야.      보러 오지 마.

worth the trouble…"
그럴 필요가 없어…"

"I shall not leave you."
"네 곁을 떠나지 않을 거야…"

But he was worried.
그러나 그는 걱정했다.

---

### Key Expression 🎯

**부사 How : 어떻게, ..하는 방법, 어느 정도.**

How가 to부정사와 함께 쓰이거나 그 뒤에 절을 동반할 경우에는 '~하는 방법'
혹은 '어떻게 ~ 하는가'라고 해석됩니다.
지문에서 …'that knew how to laugh…'는 '웃는 법을 알고 있는…'이라
고 해석하면 되겠죠.

ex) He knows how to start a car. 그는 이 차를 출발시키는 방법을 알고 있었다.
   I don't know how to make a cake. 나는 케이크를 어떻게 만드는지 모른다.

---

malicious 악의 있는, 부당한(체포 등) | resolute 단호한

"I tell you —— it is also because of the snake. He must not bite
"내가 이 얘기를 하는 건 — 뱀 때문이기도 해.                        뱀이 아저씨를 물면 안 되니까.

you. Snakes —— they are malicious creatures. This one might
     뱀은 —               그것들은 심술궂은 생물이야.

bite you just for fun…"
재미 삼아 아저씨를 물 수도 있어…"

"I shall not leave you."
"나는 네 곁을 떠나지 않을 거야."

But a thought came to reassure him:
그러나 어떤 생각이 그를 안심시키는 것 같았다:

"It is true that / they have no more poison / for a second bite."
'사실은                뱀들은 더 이상 독이 없어              두 번째로 물 때에는.'

That night / I did not see him / set out on his way. He got
그날 밤              나는 그를 보지 못했다         길을 떠나는 것을.

away from me / without making a sound. When I succeeded
그는 나를 떠나버렸다      소리도 없이.                        내가 간신히 그를 따라 잡았을 때

in catching up with him / he was walking along / with a quick
                            그는 혼자 걷고 있었다

and resolute step. He said to me merely:
빠르고 단호한 걸음걸이로.       그는 내게 단지 이런 말만 했다:

"Ah! You are there…"
"아! 아저씨네…"

## Key Expression 🎗

### 전치사 without : ~없이, ~없으면

주로 without 다음에는 명사 형태로 나와서, '~가 없이' 이런 식으로 해석되지
만, 'without+동명사' 형태로 '~하지 않고, ~함이 없이'로도 잘 쓰입니다.
지문의 'He got away from me without making a sound.'는 '그는 소
리도 없이 나를 떠나버렸어요'라는 뜻이 됩니다.

ex) Tom spoke without thinking. 톰은 생각도 없이 말했다.
     She left without saying goodbye. 작별 인사도 없이 그녀는 떠났다.

And he took me by the hand. But he was still worrying
그리고 그는 내 손을 잡았다.　　　　　　　그러나 여전히 걱정하고 있었다.

"It was wrong of you to come. You will suffer. I shall look / as
"아저씨가 온 것은 잘못이야.　　　　아저씨는 괴로울 거야.　　나는 ~해 보일 텐데

if I were dead; and that will not be true…"
마치 내가 죽은 것처럼;　그렇지만 그것은 사실이 아닌데…"

I said nothing.
나는 아무 말도 하지 않았다.

"You understand… It is too far. I cannot carry this body with
"알잖아…　　　　너무도 멀어.　　이 몸을 가지고 갈수가 없어.

me. It is too heavy."
　　너무 무거워."

I said nothing.
나는 아무 말도 하지 않았다.

"But it will be like / an old abandoned shell. There is nothing
"하지만 이 몸은 ~같을 거야　낡고 버려진 껍데기.　　　슬퍼할 이유는 없어

sad / about old shells…"
　낡은 껍데기 때문에…"

I said nothing.
나는 아무 말도 하지 않았다.

He was a little discouraged. But he made one more effort:
그는 약간 풀이 죽어있었다.　　　하지만, 다시 한 번 노력했다:

"You know, it will be very nice. I, too, shall look at the stars.
"있잖아, 참 잘되었네.　　　　나도 별을 보게 될 거야.

All the stars will be wells / with a rusty pulley. All the stars
모든 별들은 우물이 될 거야　　　녹이 슨 도르래가 달린.　　모든 별이 부어주게 될 거야

will pour out / fresh water for me to drink…"
　　내가 마실 신선한 물을…"

I said nothing.
나는 아무 말도 하지 않았다.

abandoned 폐기된, 버림받은 | rusty 녹슨

"That will be so amusing! You will have five hundred million
"정말 엄청나겠지!                아저씨는 5억 개의 작은 종을 갖게 될 거고,

little bells, / and I shall have five hundred million springs of
                나는 5억 개의 맑은 샘을 갖게 되는 거야…"

fresh water…"

And he too said nothing more, / because he was crying…
그리고 그는 더 이상 아무 말을 하지 않았다.        그가 울고 있었기 때문에…

"Here it is. Let me go on / by myself."
"여기야.      가게 해 줘        나 혼자서."

And he sat down, / because he was afraid. Then he said, again:
그리고 그는 앉았다.      두려웠기 때문에.          그리고 그가 다시 말했다:

You know —— my flower… I am responsible for her. And she is
"있잖아 —        내 꽃 말이야…    난 그 꽃에 책임져야 해.          그녀는 너무 연

so weak! She is so naive! She has four thorns, / of no use at all,
약해!        그녀는 너무 순진해!      그녀는 네 개의 가시를 갖고 있을 뿐이야,   아무 쓸모 없는,

/ to protect herself / against all the world…"
스스로를 보호하기 위해서      세상에 맞서…"

I too sat down, / because I was not able to stand up / any longer.
나도 앉았다.      서 있을 수가 없어서                    더 이상 .

"There now —— that is all…"
"지금은 —        그게 다야…"

He still hesitated a little; / then he got up. He took one step. I
그는 조금 망설였다;        그리고 일어났다.      그는 한 발짝 내디뎠다.

could not move.
나는 움직일 수 없었다.

There was nothing there / but a flash of yellow close to his
거기에는 아무것도 없었다        단지 노란색 섬광이 그의 발목 가까이에 있을 뿐.

ankle. He remained motionless / for an instant. He did not cry
그는 움직임 없이 가만히 있었다      잠시 동안.          그는 울지 않았다.

out. He fell / as gently / as a tree falls. There was not even any
그는 쓰러졌다 부드럽게      나무가 쓰러지는 것처럼.    아무 소리도 나지 않았다.

sound, / because of the sand.
모래 때문에.

---

amusing 재미있는, 즐거운 | motionless 움직이지 않는 | gently 다정하게, 부드럽게

And now / six years have already gone by... I have never yet
이제 　　　　벌써 6년의 세월이 흘렀다…　　　　　　　나는 아직 이 이야기를 한 적이

told this story. The companions / who met me on my return /
없다.　　　　　동료는　　　　귀환 때 나를 만났던

were well content / to see me alive. I was sad, but I told them:
매우 기뻐했다　　　　내가 살아있다는 것을 보고.　나는 슬펐지만,　그들에게 말했다:

/ "I am tired."
"나는 너무 피곤해."

Now / my sorrow is comforted a little. That is to say —— /
이제 　내 슬픔은 조금 가라앉았다.　　　　　그러니까 —

not entirely. But I know that / he did go back to his planet, /
완전히는 아니다.　그러나 나는 알고 있다　그가 자신의 별로 돌아갔음을,

because I did not find his body / at daybreak. It was not such
왜냐하면 그의 몸을 찾을 수 없었으니까　해 뜰 무렵에.　그렇게 무거운 몸도 아니었는데…

a heavy body... And at night / I love to listen to the stars. It is
그래서 밤이면　　나는 별들의 소리를 듣는 것을 좋아한다.

like five hundred million little bells...
5억 개의 작은 종들이 울리는 소리와 같으니까…

But there is one extraordinary thing... When I drew the
그러나 이상한 일이 생겼다…　　　　　입 마개를 그려 주었을 때

muzzle / for the little prince, / I forgot to add / the leather strap
어린왕자에게,　　　그리는 것을 잊어버렸던 것이다　가죽 끈을 .

to it. He will never have been able to fasten it / on this sheep.
그는 그걸 묶을 수 없을 것이다　　　　　　　　　양에게.

companion 동료, 친구 | comfort 위로하다

So now I keep wondering: / what is happening on his planet?
그래서 지금 나는 궁금하다:                    그의 별에는 무슨 일이 일어났을까?

Perhaps the sheep has eaten the flower…
아마도 양이 꽃을 다 먹어버렸을 지도 몰라…

At one time / I say to myself: / "Surely not! The little prince shuts
한 번은              이런 생각도 했다:        "그럴 리가 없어!      어린왕자는 꽃을 보호할 거야

his flower / under her glass globe / every night, / and he watches
그의 꽃을          유리 덮개를 덮어서            매일 밤,

over his sheep / very carefully…" Then I am happy. And there is
그리고 양을 지켜보겠지   매우 주의 깊게…"         그러면 나는 행복해졌다.      그리고 행복이 보였다

sweetness / in the laughter of all the stars.
별들의 웃음 속에.

But at another time / I say to myself: "At some moment or other /
그러나 다른 순간에는       이렇게도 생각했다:       "어쩌다가

one is absent-minded, / and that is enough! On some one evening
방심하기라도 하면          그것으로 그만인데!        어느 날 저녁에

/ he forgot the glass globe, / or the sheep got out, / without
그가 유리 덮개를 잊어버리거나,        양이 뛰쳐나가기라도 한다면,

making any noise, / in the night…" And then / the little bells are
아무 소리도 내지 않고,        밤에…"        그러면

changed to tears…
작은 종들은 눈물로 변했다…

Here, then, / is a great mystery. For you / who also love the little
그러니, 이건,      정말 큰 미스테리이다.      여러분에게      어린왕자를 정말 사랑하는,

prince, / and for me, / nothing in the universe / can be the same /
그리고 내게,        우주상의 그 어떤 것도        같지가 않다

if somewhere, / we do not know where, / a sheep / that we never
만약 어딘가에,        우리가 알지 못하는 곳에,        양 한 마리가    우리가 본 적도 없는 —

## Key Expression 🎵

'Keep +ing'과 'keep on+ing'의 차이점
Keep+ing는 '계속해서 ~ 하다', keep on+ing은 '집요하게 계속 ~하다'라는
의미를 가지고 있어요.

ex) So now I keep wondering 나는 계속 궁금해한다.
How do you keep on doing that? 어떻게 너는 끈질기게 그것을 계속하니?

absent-minded 정신 나간, 방심한

174    The Little Prince

saw has —— / yes or no? —— / eaten a rose...
그랬는가 안 그랬는가? —      장미를 먹었는가를 따지는 것은…

Look up at the sky. Ask yourselves: Is it yes or no? Has the
하늘을 보라.              스스로에게 물어봐라:      그런가 아닌가?

sheep eaten the flower? And you will see / how everything
양이 꽃을 먹었을까 아닐까?            그러면 여러분은 알게 될 것이다  세상이 어떻게 변해가는지를…

changes...

And no grown-up will ever understand / that this is a matter of
그리고 어른들은 이해하지 못할 것이다              그것이 얼마나 중요한 일인지!

so much importance!


This is, to me, / the loveliest and saddest landscape / in the world. It is
이것은, 내게 있어,     가장 사랑스럽고 가장 슬픈 광경이다        세상에서.

the same as that / on the preceding page, / but I have drawn it again / to
이것은 똑같다      앞에 있는 장에 있는 것과,        그러나 나는 다시 한 번 그렸다

impress it on your memory. It is here / that the little prince appeared on
여러분 기억 속에 각인하기 위하여.      바로 그곳이다   어린왕자가 지구에 나타났다가,

Earth, / and disappeared.
       사라진 곳이.

Look at it carefully / so that you will be sure to recognize it / in case you
그림을 눈여겨보라        그것을 분명히 기억하도록              언젠가 여러분이

travel some day / to the African desert. And, if you should come upon
여행을 하게 된다면     아프리카 사막을.        그리고, 만약 이 장소를 지나게 된다면,

this spot, / please do not hurry on. Wait for a time, / exactly under the
이 곳을,     서둘러 가지 않기를 부탁한다.   잠시 기다려라,     바로 그 별 아래에서.

star. Then, / if a little man appears / who laughs, / who has golden hair /
그때,     만약 작은 사람이 나타난다면   웃고 있고,     머리가 금발인,

and who refuses to answer questions, / you will know who he is. If this
그리고 질문에 대답하기를 꺼려하는,      여러분은 그가 누구인지 알 것이다.   만약 이러한

should happen, / please comfort me. Send me word / that he has come
일이 벌어진다면,     내게 전해 달라.      내게 알려 달라      그가 돌아왔다고.

back.

landscape 풍경, 경치, 전망 | precede ~에 앞서다 | impress 기억하다, 인상 지우다

## A. 다음 문장을 해석해 보세요.

(1) I did not dare ask him any more questions.

→

(2) I had moistened his temples, and had given him some water to drink.

→

(3) The little prince looked everywhere to find a place to sit down.

→

(4) There was nothing there but a flash of yellow close to his ankle.

→

## B. 다음 주어진 문장이 되도록 빈칸에 써 넣으세요.

(1) 이것은 나에게 세상에서 <u>가장 사랑스러운</u> 그리고 <u>가장 슬픈</u> 광경이다.

This is, to me, the ⬚⬚⬚ and ⬚⬚⬚ landscape in the world.

(2) 언젠가 네가 <u>아프리카 사막</u>을 여행하게 될 때 네가 꼭 알아보기 위하여 조심히 잘 보아라.

Look it carefully so that you will be sure to recognize it in case you travel some day to the ⬚⬚⬚.

(3) 어른들은 <u>이것이 매우 중요한 것임</u>을 이해하지 못할 것이다!

No grown-up will ever understand that this ⬚⬚⬚!

(4) 그것은 <u>앞 페이지에 있는</u> 것과 같다. 그러나 나는 네 기억 속에 각인시키기 위해 다시 한 번 그렸다.

It is the same as that ⬚⬚⬚, but I have drawn it again to impress it on your memory.

C. 다음 주어진 문구가 알맞은 문장이 되도록 순서를 맞춰보세요.

(1) 나는 돌담쪽을 향해 계속하여 걸었다.
    (the wall / my walk / I / toward / continued)
    →

(2) 그의 얼굴은 눈처럼 희었다.
    (as / white / was / his face / snow )
    →

(3) 나는 뭔가 심상치 않은 일들이 벌어지고 있음을 분명하게 느꼈다.
    (something extraordinary / that / clearly / realized / I /
    happening / was)
    →

(4) 무슨 말을 하는 거니?
    (are / what / say / to / you / trying / ?)
    →

D. 다음 주어진 문구가 알맞은 문장이 되도록 순서를 맞춰 보세요.

(1) Impressive  ▶          ◀ ① a person's family origins

(2) interrupt  ▶           ◀ ② making you feel admiration, because they are
                              very large, good, skilful, etc.

(3) breathe  ▶             ◀ ③ stop what they are saying or doing

(4) descent  ▶             ◀ ④ take air into your lungs and send
                              it out again through your nose or mouth

〈The Little Prince〉를 다시 읽어 보세요.

# ♕ 1 ♕

Once when I was six years old I saw a magnificent picture in a book, called True Stories from Nature, about the primeval forest. It was a picture of a boa constrictor in the act of swallowing an animal. Here is a copy of the drawing.

In the book it said:

"Boa constrictors swallow their prey whole, without chewing it. After that they are not able to move, and they sleep through the six months that they need for digestion."

I pondered deeply, then, over the adventures of the jungle. And after some work with a colored pencil I succeeded in making my first drawing.

My Drawing Number One. It looked like this:

I showed my masterpiece to the grown-ups, and asked them whether the drawing frightened them.

But they answered:

"Frighten? Why should any one be frightened by a hat?"

My drawing was not a picture of a hat. It was a picture of a boa constrictor digesting an elephant.

But since the grown-ups were not able to understand it, I made another drawing: I drew the inside of the boa constrictor, so that the grown-ups could see it clearly. They always need to have things explained.

My Drawing Number Two looked like this:

The grown-ups' response, this time, was to advise me to lay aside my drawings of boa constrictors, whether from the inside or the outside, and devote myself instead to geography, history, arithmetic and grammar.

That is why, at the age of six, I gave up what might have been a magnificent career as a painter.

I had been disheartened by the failure of my Drawing Number One and my Drawing Number Two.

Grown-ups never understand anything by themselves, and it is tiresome for children to be always and forever explaining things to them.

So then I chose another profession, and learned to pilot airplanes. I have flown a little over all parts of the world; and it is true that geography has been very useful to me.

At a glance I can distinguish China from Arizona. If one gets lost in the night, such knowledge is valuable.

In the course of this life I have had a great many encounters with a great many people who have been concerned with matters of consequence.

I have lived a great deal among grown-ups. I have seen them intimately, close at hand. And that hasn't much improved my opinion of them.

Whenever I met one of them who seemed to me at all clear-sighted, I tried the experiment of showing him my Drawing Number One, which I have always kept.

I would try to find out, so, if this was a person of true understanding.

But, whoever it was, he, or she, would always say:

"That is a hat."

Then I would never talk to that person about boa constrictors, or primeval forests, or stars.

I would bring myself down to his level. I would talk to him about bridge, and golf, and politics, and neckties. And the grown-up would be greatly pleased to have met such a sensible man.

## ♚ 2 ♚

So I lived my life alone, without anyone that I could really talk to, until I had an accident with my plane in the Desert of Sahara, six years ago.

Something was broken in my engine. And as I had with me neither a mechanic nor any passengers, I set myself to attempt the difficult repairs all alone. It was a question of life or death for me: I had scarcely enough drinking water to last a week.

The first night, then, I went to sleep on the sand, a thousand miles from any human habitation. I was more isolated than a shipwrecked sailor on a raft in the middle of the ocean.

Thus you can imagine my amazement, at sunrise, when I was awakened by an odd little voice.

It said:

"If you please — draw me a sheep!"

"What!"

"Draw me a sheep!"

I jumped to my feet, completely thunderstruck. I blinked my eyes hard. I looked carefully all around me. And I saw a most extraordinary small person, who stood there examining me with great seriousness.

Here you may see the best portrait that, later, I was able to make of him. But my drawing is certainly very much less charming than its model.

That, however, is not my fault. The grownups discouraged me in my painter's career when I was six years old, and I never learned to draw anything, except boas from the outside and boas from the inside.

Now I stared at this sudden apparition with my eyes fairly starting out of my head in astonishment. Remember, I had crashed in the desert a thousand miles from any inhabited region. And yet my little man seemed neither to be straying uncertainly among the sands, nor to be fainting from fatigue or hunger or thirst or fear. Nothing about him gave any suggestion of a child lost in the middle of the desert, a thousand miles from any human habitation.

When at last I was able to speak, I said to him:

"But — what are you doing here?"

And in answer he repeated, very slowly, as if he were speaking of a matter of great consequence:

"If you please — draw me a sheep..."

When a mystery is too overpowering, one dare not disobey. Absurd as it might seem to me, a thousand miles from any human habitation and in danger of death, I took out of my pocket a sheet of paper and my fountain-pen. But then I remembered how my studies had been concentrated on geography, history, arithmetic and grammar, and I told the little chap (a little crossly, too) that I did not know how to draw.

He answered me:

"That doesn't matter. Draw me a sheep..."

But I had never drawn a sheep. So I drew for him one of the two pictures I had drawn so often. It was that of the boa constrictor from the outside. And I was astounded to hear the little fellow greet it with,

"No, no, no! I do not want an elephant inside a boa constrictor. A boa constrictor is a very dangerous creature, and an elephant is very cumbersome. Where I live, everything is very small. What I need is a sheep. Draw me a sheep."

So then I made a drawing.

He looked at it carefully, then he said "No. This sheep is already very sickly. Make me another."

So I made another drawing.

My friend smiled gently and indulgently.

"You see yourself," he said, "that this is not a sheep. This is a ram. It has horns."

So then I did my drawing over once more.

But it was rejected too, just like the others.

"This one is too old. I want a sheep that will live a long time."

By this time my patience was exhausted, because I was in a hurry to start taking my engine apart. So I tossed off this drawing.

And I threw out an explanation with it.

"This is only his box. The sheep you asked for is inside."

I was very surprised to see a light break over the face of my young judge:

"That is exactly the way I wanted it! Do you think that this sheep will have to have a great deal of grass?"

"Why?"

"Because where I live everything is very small…"

"There will surely be enough grass for him," I said. "It is a very small sheep that I have given you."

He bent his head over the drawing:

"Not so small that — Look! He has gone to sleep…"

And that is how I made the acquaintance of the little prince.

It took me a long time to learn where he came from.

The little prince, who asked me so many questions, never seemed to hear the ones I asked him. It was from words dropped by chance that, little by little everything was revealed to me.

The first time he saw my airplane, for instance (I shall not draw my airplane; that would be much too complicated for me), he asked me:

"What is that object?"

"That is not an object. It flies. It is an airplane. It is my airplane."

And I was proud to have him learn that I could fly.

He cried out, then:

"What! You dropped down from the sky?"

"Yes," I answered, modestly.

"Oh! That is funny!"

And the little prince broke into a lovely peal of laughter, which irritated me very much. I like my misfortunes to be taken seriously. Then he added:

"So you, too, come from the sky! Which is your planet?"

At that moment I caught a gleam of light in the impenetrable mystery of his presence; and I demanded, abruptly:

"Do you come from another planet?"

But he did not reply. He tossed his head gently, without taking his eyes from my plane:

"It is true that on that you can't have come from very far away…"

And he sank into a reverie, which lasted a long time. Then, taking my sheep out of his pocket, he buried himself in the contemplation of his treasure.

You can imagine how my curiosity was aroused by this half-confidence about the "other planets."

I made a great effort, therefore, to find out more on this subject.

"My little man, where do you come from? What is this 'where I live,' of which you speak? Where do you want to take your sheep?"

After a reflective silence he answered:

"The thing that is so good about the box you have given me is that at night he can use it as his house."

"That is so. And if you are good I will give you a string, too, so that you can tie him during the day, and a post to tie him to."

But the little prince seemed shocked by this offer:

"Tie him! What a queer idea!"

"But if you don't tie him", I said, "he will wander off somewhere, and get lost."

My friend broke into another peal of laughter:

"But where do you think he would go?"

"Anywhere. Straight ahead of him."

Then the little prince said, earnestly:

"That doesn't matter. Where I live, everything is so small!"

And, with a hint of sadness, he added:

"Straight ahead of him, nobody can go very far…"

## 👑 4 👑

I had thus learned a second fact of great importance: this was that the planet the little prince came from was scarcely any larger than a house! But that did not really surprise me much. I knew very well that in addition to the great planets — such as the Earth, Jupiter, Mars, Venus — to which we have given names, there are also hundreds of others, some of which are so small that one has a hard time seeing them through the telescope.

When an astronomer discovers one of these he does not give it a name,

but only a number. He might call it, for example, "Asteroid 325."
I have serious reason to believe that the planet from which the little
prince came is the asteroid known as B-612.

This asteroid has only once been seen through the telescope. That
was by a Turkish astronomer, in 1909. On making his discovery,
the astronomer had presented it to the International Astronomical
Congress, in a great demonstration. But he was in Turkish costume,
and so nobody would believe what he said.

Grown-ups are like that...

Fortunately, however, for the reputation of Asteroid B-612, a Turkish
dictator made a law that his subjects, under pain of death, should
change to European costume.

So in 1920 the astronomer gave his demonstration all over again,
dressed with impressive style and elegance. And this time everybody
accepted his report.

If I have told you these details about the asteroid, and made a note of
its number for you, it is on account of the grown-ups and their ways.
Grown-ups love figures. When you tell them that you have made a
new friend, they never ask you any questions about essential matters.
They never say to you, "What does his voice sound like? What games
does he love best? Does he collect butterflies?" Instead, they demand:
"How old is he? How many brothers has he? How much does he
weigh? How much money does his father make?" Only from these
figures do they think they have learned anything about him.

If you were to say to the grown-ups: "I saw a beautiful house made
of rosy brick, with geraniums in the windows and doves on the roof,"
they would not be able to get any idea of that house at all.

You would have to say to them: "I saw a house that cost $2,000."
Then they would exclaim: "Oh, what a pretty house that is!"

Just so, you might say to them:

"The proof that the little prince existed is that he was charming, that he laughed, and that he was looking for a sheep. If anybody wants a sheep, that is a proof that he exists."

And what good would it do to tell them that? They would shrug their shoulders, and treat you like a child.

But if you said to them: "The planet he came from is Asteroid B-612," then they would be convinced, and leave you in peace from their questions.

They are like that. One must not hold it against them. Children should always show great forbearance toward grown-up people.

But certainly, for us who understand life, figures are a matter of indifference.

I should have liked to begin this story in the fashion of the fairy-tales.

I should have liked to say: "Once upon a time there was a little prince who lived on a planet that was scarcely any bigger than himself, and who had need of a sheep......"

To those who understand life, that would have given a much greater air of truth to my story. For I do not want anyone to read my book carelessly.

I have suffered too much grief in setting down these memories. Six years have already passed since my friend went away from me, with his sheep. If I try to describe him here, it is to make sure that I shall not forget him.

To forget a friend is sad. Not everyone has had a friend. And if I forget him, I may become like the grown-ups who are no longer interested in anything but figures......

It is for that purpose, again, that I have bought a box of paints and some pencils. It is hard to take up drawing again at my age, when I have never made any pictures except those of the boa constrictor from the outside and the boa constrictor from the inside, since I was six.

I shall certainly try to make my portraits as true to life as possible. But I am not at all sure of success. One drawing goes along all right, and another has no resemblance to its subject. I make some errors, too, in the little prince's height: in one place he is too tall and in another too short. And I feel some doubts about the color of his costume. So I fumble along as best I can, now good, now bad, and I hope generally fair-to-middling.

In certain more important details I shall make mistakes, also. But that is something that will not be my fault.

My friend never explained anything to me. He thought, perhaps, that I was like himself. But I, alas, do not know how to see sheep through the walls of boxes.

Perhaps I am a little like the grown-ups. I have had to grow old.

## 5

As each day passed, I would learn, in our talk, something about the little prince's planet, his departure from it, his journey. The information would come very slowly, as it might chance to fall from his thoughts.

In this way, I heard, on the third day, about the catastrophe of the baobabs.

This time, once more, I had the sheep to thank for it.

The little prince asked me abruptly — as if seized by a grave doubt —

"It is true, isn't it, that sheep eat little bushes?"

"Yes, that is true."

"Ah! I am glad!"

I did not understand why it was so important that sheep should eat little bushes.

But the little prince added:

"Then it follows that they also eat baobabs?"

I pointed out to the little prince that baobabs were not little bushes, but, on the contrary, trees as big as castles; and that even if he brought a whole herd of elephants away with him, the herd would not able to eat up one single baobab. The idea of the herd of elephants made the little prince laugh.

"We would have to put them one on top of the other," he said.

But he made a wise comment:

"Before they grow so big, the baobabs start out by being little."

"That is strictly correct," I said.

"But why do you want the sheep to eat the little baobabs?"

He answered me at once, "Oh, come, come!" as if he were speaking of something that was self-evident.

And I was obliged to make a great mental effort to solve this problem, without any assistance.

Indeed, as I learned, there were on the planet where the little prince lived — as on all planets — good plants and bad plants. In consequence, there were good seeds from good plants, and bad seeds from bad plants.

But seeds are invisible. They sleep deep in the heart of the earth's darkness, until someone among them is seized with the desire to awaken.

Then this little seed will stretch itself and begin — timidly at first — to push a charming little sprig inoffensively upward toward the sun. If it is only a sprout of radish or a sprig of rosebush, one would let it grow wherever it might wish. But when it is a bad plant, one must destroy it as soon as possible, the very first instant that one recognizes it.

Now there were some terrible seeds on the planet that was the home of the little prince; and these were the seeds of the baobab. The soil of that planet was infested with them. A baobab is something you will never, never be able to get rid of if you attend to it too late. It spreads over the entire planet. It bores clear through it with its roots. And if the planet is too small, and the baobabs are too many, they would split it in pieces...

"It is a question of discipline," the little prince said to me later on. "When you've finished your own toilet in the morning, then it is time to attend to the toilet of your planet, just so, with the greatest care. You must see to it that you pull up regularly all the baobabs, at the very first moment when they can be distinguished from the rosebushes which they resemble so closely in their earliest youth. It is very tedious work," the little prince added, "but very easy."

And one day he said to me:

"You ought to make a beautiful drawing, so that the children where you live can see exactly how all this is. That would be very useful to them if they were to travel some day. Sometimes," he added, "there is no harm in putting off a piece of work until another day. But when it is a matter of baobabs, that always means a catastrophe. I knew a planet that was inhabited a lazy man. He neglected three little bushes..."

So, as the little prince described it to me, I have made a drawing of that planet.

I do not much like to take the tone of a moralist. But the danger of the baobabs is so little understood, and such considerable risks would be run by anyone who might get lost on an asteroid, that for once I am breaking through my reserve.

"Children", I say plainly, "watch out for the baobabs!"

My friends, like myself, have been skirting this danger for a long time, without ever knowing it; and so it is for them that I have worked so hard over this drawing. The lesson which I pass on by this means is worth all the trouble it has cost me.

Perhaps you will ask me, "Why are there no other drawings in this

book as magnificent and impressive as this drawing of the baobabs?"
The reply is simple. I have tried. But with the others I have not been
successful. When I made the drawing of the baobabs I was carried
beyond myself by the inspiring force of urgent necessity.

♕ 6 ♕

Oh, little prince! Bit by bit I came to understand the secrets of your
sad little life… For a long time you had found your only entertainment
in the quiet pleasure of looking at the sunset.
I learned that new detail on the morning of the fourth day, when you
said to me:
"I am very fond of sunsets. Come, let us go look at a sunset now."
"But we must wait," I said.
"Wait? For what?"
"For the sunset. We must wait until it is time."
At first you seemed to be very much surprised. And then you laughed
to yourself.
You said to me:
"I am always thinking that I am at home!"
Just so. Everybody knows that when it is noon in the United States the
sun is setting over France. If you could fly to France in one minute,
you could go straight into the sunset, right from noon. Unfortunately,
France is too far away for that.
But on your tiny planet, my little prince, all you need do is to move
your chair a few steps. You can see the day end and the twilight
falling whenever you like…
"One day," you said to me, "I saw the sunset forty-four times!"
And a little later you added:
"You know — one loves the sunset, when one is so sad…"

"Were you so sad, then?" I asked, "on the day of the forty-four sunsets?"

But the little prince made no reply.

## ♔ 7 ♔

On the fifth day, — again, as always, it was thanks to the sheep — the secret of the little prince's life was revealed to me.

Abruptly, without anything to lead up to it, and as if the question had been born of long and silent meditation on his problem, he demanded:

"A sheep — if it eats little bushes, does it eat flowers, too?"

"A sheep," I answered, "eats anything it finds in its reach."

"Even flowers that have thorns?"

"Yes, even flowers that have thorns."

"Then the thorns — what use are they?"

I did not know. At that moment I was very busy trying to unscrew a bolt that had got stuck in my engine. I was very much worried, for it was becoming clear to me that the breakdown of my plane was extremely serious. And I had so little drinking water left that I had to fear the worst.

"The thorns — what use are they?"

The little prince never let go of a question, once he had asked it. As for me, I was upset over that bolt. And I answered with the first thing that came into my head:

"The thorns are of no use at all. Flowers have thorns just for spite!"

"Oh!"

There was a moment of complete silence. Then the little prince flashed back at me, with a kind of resentfulness:

"I don't believe you! Flowers are weak creatures. They are naive. They reassure themselves as best they can. They believe that their thorns are terrible weapons..."

I did not answer. At that instant I was saying to myself:

"If this bolt still won't turn, I am going to knock it out with the hammer."

Again the little prince disturbed my thoughts:

"And you actually believe that the flowers — "

"Oh, no!" I cried.

"No, no, no! I don't believe anything. I answered you with the first thing that came into my head. Don't you see — I am very busy with matters of consequence!"

He stared at me, thunderstruck.

"Matters of consequence!"

He looked at me there, with my hammer in my hand, my fingers black with engine-grease, bending down over an object which seemed to him extremely ugly...

"You talk just like the grown-ups!"

That made me a little ashamed. But he went on, relentlessly:

"You mix everything up together... You confuse everything..."

He was really very angry. He tossed his golden curls in the breeze.

"I know a planet where there is a certain red-faced gentleman. He has never smelled a flower. He has never looked at a star. He has never loved any one. He has never done anything in his life but add up figures. And all day he says over and over, just like you: 'I am busy with matters of consequence!' And that makes him swell up with pride. But he is not a man — he is a mushroom!"

"A what?"

"A mushroom!"

The little prince was now white with rage.

"The flowers have been growing thorns for millions of years. For millions of years the sheep have been eating them just the same.

And is it not a matter of consequence to try to understand why the flowers go to so much trouble to grow thorns which are never of any use to them? Is the warfare between the sheep and the flowers not important? Is this not of more consequence than a fat red-faced gentleman's sums? And if I know — I, myself — one flower which is unique in the world, which grows nowhere but on my planet, but which one little sheep can destroy in a single bite some morning, without even noticing what he is doing — Oh! You think that is not important!"

His face turned from white to red as he continued:

"If someone loves a flower, of which just one single blossom grows in all the millions and millions of stars, it is enough to make him happy just to look at the stars. He can say to himself: 'Somewhere, my flower is there...' But if the sheep eats the flower, in one moment all his stars will be darkened... And you think that is not important!"

He could not say anything more. His words were choked by sobbing.

The night had fallen. I had let my tools drop from my hands. Of what moment now was my hammer, my bolt, or thirst, or death? On one star, one planet, my planet, the Earth there was a little prince to be comforted. I took him in my arms, and rocked him. I said to him:

"The flower that you love is not in danger. I will draw you a muzzle for your sheep. I will draw you a railing to put around your flower. I will — "

I did not know what to say to him. I felt awkward and blundering. I did not know how I could reach him, where I could overtake him and go on hand in hand with him once more.

It is such a secret place, the land of tears.

# ♔ 8 ♔

I soon learned to know this flower better. On the little prince's planet the flowers had always been very simple. They had only one ring of petals; they took up no room at all; they were a trouble to nobody. One morning they would appear in the grass, and by night they would have faded peacefully away.

But one day, from a seed blown from no one knew where, a new flower had come up; and the little prince had watched very closely over this small sprout which was not like any other small sprouts on his planet.

It might, you see, have been a new kind of baobab.

But the shrub soon stopped growing, and began to get ready to produce a flower. The little prince, who was present at the first appearance of a huge bud, felt at once that some sort of miraculous apparition must emerge from it.

But the flower was not satisfied to complete the preparations for her beauty in the shelter of her green chamber. She chose her colors with the greatest care. She dressed herself slowly. She adjusted her petals one by one. She did not wish to go out into the world all rumpled, like the field poppies. It was only in the full radiance of her beauty that she wished to appear. Oh, yes! She was a coquettish creature! And her mysterious adornment lasted for days and days.

Then one morning, exactly at sunrise, she suddenly showed herself. And, after working with all this painstaking precision, she yawned and said:

"Ah! I am scarcely awake. I beg that you will excuse me. My petals are still all disarranged…"

But the little prince could not restrain his admiration:

"Oh! How beautiful you are!"

"Am I not?" the flower responded, sweetly.

"And I was born at the same moment as the sun..."

The little prince could guess easily enough that she was not any too modest — but how moving and exciting she was!

"I think it is time for breakfast," she added an instant later.

"If you would have the kindness to think of my needs — "

And the little prince, completely abashed, went to look for a sprinkling-can of fresh water. So, he tended the flower.

So, too, she began very quickly to torment him with her vanity — which was, if the truth be known, a little difficult to deal with. One day, for instance, when she was speaking of her four thorns, she said to the little prince:

"Let the tigers come with their claws!"

"There are no tigers on my planet," the little prince objected.

"And, anyway, tigers do not eat weeds."

"I am not a weed," the flower replied, sweetly.

"Please excuse me..."

"I am not at all afraid of tigers," she went on, "but I have a horror of drafts. I suppose you wouldn't have a screen for me?"

"A horror of drafts — that is bad luck, for a plant," remarked the little prince, and added to himself, "This flower is a very complex creature..."

"At night I want you to put me under a glass globe. It is very cold where you live. In the place where I came from — "

But she interrupted herself at that point. She had come in the form of a seed. She could not have known anything of any other worlds. Embarrassed over having let herself be caught on the verge of such a naive untruth, she coughed two three times, in order to put the little prince in the wrong.

"The screen?"

"I was just going to look for it when you spoke to me…"

Then she forced her cough a little more so that he should suffer from remorse just the same.

So the little prince, in spite of all the good will that was inseparable from his love, had soon come to doubt her. He had taken seriously words which were without importance, and it made him very unhappy.

"I ought not to have listened to her," he confided to me one day.
"One never ought to listen to the flowers. One should simply look at them and breathe their fragrance. Mine perfumed all my planet. But I did not know how to take pleasure in all her grace. This tale of claws, which disturbed me so much, should only have filled my heart with tenderness and pity."

And he continued his confidences:

"The fact is that I did not know how to understand anything! I ought to have judged by deeds and not by words. She cast her fragrance and her radiance over me. I ought never to have run away from her… I ought to have guessed all the affecting that lay behind her poor little stratagems. Flowers are so inconsistent! But I was too young to know how to love her…"

## ♛ 9 ♛

I believe that for his escape he took advantage of the migration of a flock of wild birds. On the morning of his departure he put his planet in perfect order. He carefully cleaned out his active volcanoes.
He possessed two active volcanoes; and they were very convenient for heating his breakfast in the morning.
He also had one volcano that was extinct. But, as he said, "One never knows!"

So he cleaned out the extinct volcano, too. If they are well cleaned out, volcanoes burn slowly and steadily, without any eruptions. Volcanic eruptions are like fires in a chimney.

On our earth we are obviously much too small to clean out our volcanoes. That is why they bring no end of trouble upon us.

The little prince also pulled up, with a certain sense of dejection, the last little shoots of the baobabs. He believed that he would never want to return. But on this last morning all these familiar tasks seemed very precious to him. And when he watered the flower for the last time, and prepared to place her under the shelter of her glass globe, he realized that he was very close to tears.

"Goodbye," he said to the flower.

But she made no answer.

"Goodbye," he said again.

The flower coughed. But it was not because she had a cold.

"I have been silly," she said to him, at last.

"I ask your forgiveness. Try to be happy…"

He was surprised by this absence of reproaches. He stood there all bewildered, holding the glass globe held arrested in mid-air. He did not understand this quiet sweetness.

"Of course I love you," the flower said to him.

"It is my fault that you have not known it all the while. That is of no importance. But you — you have been just as foolish as I. Try to be happy… Let the glass globe be. I don't want it anymore."

"But the wind — "

"My cold is not so bad as all that. The cool night air will do me good. I am a flower."

"But the animals — "

"Well, I must endure the presence of two or three caterpillars if I wish to become acquainted with the butterflies. It seems that they are very beautiful.

And if not the butterflies and the caterpillars — who will call upon me? You will be far away... As for the large animals — I am not at all afraid of any of them. I have my claws."

And naively, she showed her four thorns.

Then she added:

"Don't linger like this. You have decided to go away. Now go!"

For she did not want him to see her crying. She was such a proud flower...

## ♕ 10 ♕

He found himself in the neighborhood of the asteroids 325, 326, 327, 328, 329, and 330. He began, therefore, by visiting them, in order to add to his knowledge.

The first of them was inhabited by a king. Clad in royal purple and ermine, he was seated upon a throne which was at the same time both simple and majestic.

"Ah! Here is a subject," exclaimed the king, when he saw the little prince coming.

And the little prince asked himself:

"How could he recognize me when he had never seen me before?"

He did not know how the world is simplified for kings. To them, all men are subjects.

"Approach, so that I may see you better," said the king, who felt consumingly proud of being at last a king over somebody.

The little prince looked everywhere to find a place to sit down; but the entire planet was crammed and obstructed by the king's magnificent ermine robe. So he remained standing upright, and, since he was tired, he yawned.

"It is contrary to etiquette to yawn in the presence of a king," the monarch said to him.

"I forbid you to do so."

"I can't help it. I can't stop myself," replied the little prince, thoroughly embarrassed.

"I have come on a long journey, and I have had no sleep…"

"Ah, then," the king said.

"I order you to yawn. It is years since I have seen anyone yawning. Yawns, to me, are object of curiosity. Come, now! Yawn again! It is an order."

"That frightens me… I cannot, any more…" murmured the little prince, now completely abashed.

"Hum! Hum!" replied the king.

"Then I — I order you sometimes to yawn and sometimes to — "
He sputtered a little, and seemed vexed.

For what the king fundamentally insisted upon was that his authority should be respected. He tolerated no disobedience. He was an absolute monarch. But, because he was a very good man, he made his orders reasonable.

"If I ordered a general," he would say, by way of example, "if I ordered a general to change himself into a sea bird, and if the general did not obey me, that would not be the fault of the general. It would be my fault."

"May I sit down?" came now a timid inquiry from the little prince.

"I order you to do so," the king answered him, and majestically gathered in a fold of his ermine mantle.

But the little prince was wondering… The planet was tiny. Over what could this king really rule?

"Sire," he said to him, "I beg that you will excuse my asking you a question — "

"I order you to ask me a question," the king hastened to assure him.

"Sire — over what do you rule?"

"Over everything," said the king, with magnificent simplicity.

"Over everything?"

The king made a gesture, which took in his planet, the other planets, and all the stars.

"Over all that?" asked the little prince.

"Over all that," the king answered.

For his rule was not only absolute: it was also universal.

"And the stars obey you?"

"Certainly they do," the king said.

"They obey instantly. I do not permit insubordination."

Such power was a thing for the little prince to marvel at.

If he had been master of such complete authority, he would have been able to watch the sunset, not forty-four time in one day, but seventy-two, or even a hundred, or even two hundred times, without ever having to move his chair.

And because he felt a bit sad as he remembered his little planet which he had forsaken, he plucked up his courage to ask the king a favor:

"I should like to see a sunset... Do me that kindness... Order the sun to set..."

"If I ordered a general to fly from one flower to another like a butterfly, or to write a tragic drama, or to change himself into a sea bird, and if the general did not carry out the order that he had received, which one of us would be in the wrong?" the king demanded "The general, or myself?"

"You," said the little prince firmly.

"Exactly. One must require from each one the duty which each one can perform," the king went on.

"Accepted authority rests first of all on reason. If you ordered your people to go and throw themselves into the sea, they would rise up in revolution. I have the right to require obedience because my orders are reasonable."

"Then my sunset?"

The little prince reminded him: for he never forgot a question once he had asked it.

"You shall have your sunset. I shall command it. But, according to my science of government, I shall wait until conditions are favorable."

"When will that be?" inquired the little prince.

"Hum! Hum!" replied the king; and before saying anything else he consulted a bulky almanac.

"Hum! Hum! That will be about — about — that will be this evening about twenty minutes to eight. And you will see how well I am obeyed!"

The little prince yawned. He was regretting his lost sunset.

And then, too, he was already beginning to be a little bored.

"I have nothing more to do here," he said to the king. "So I shall set out on my way again."

"Do not go," said the king, who was very proud of having a subject.

"Do not go. I will make you a Minister!"

"Minister of what?"

"Minister of — of Justice!"

"But there is nobody here to judge!"

"We do not know that," the king said to him.

"I have not yet made a complete tour of my kingdom. I am very old. There is no room here for a carriage. And it tires me to walk."

"Oh, but I have looked already!" said the little prince, turning around to give one more glance to the other side of the planet.

"On that side, as on this, there was nobody at all..."

"Then you shall judge yourself," the king answered.

"That is the most difficult thing of all. It is much more difficult to judge oneself than to judge others. If you succeed in judging yourself rightly, then you are indeed a man of true wisdom."

"Yes," said the little prince, "but I can judge myself anywhere. I do not need to live on this planet."

"Hum! Hum!" said the king.

"I have good reason to believe that somewhere on my planet there is an old rat. I hear him at night. You can judge this old rat. From time to time you will condemn him to death. Thus his life will depend on your justice. But you will pardon him on each occasion; for he must be treated thriftily. He is the only one we have."

"I," replied the little prince, "do not like to condemn anyone to death. And now I think I will go on my way."

"No," said the king.

But the little prince, having now completed his preparations for departure, had no wish to grieve the old monarch.

"If Your Majesty wishes to be promptly obeyed," he said, "he should be able to give me a reasonable order. He should be able, for example, to order me to be gone by the end of one minute. It seems to me that conditions are favorable..."

As the king made no answer, the little prince hesitated a moment. Then, with a sigh, he took his leave.

"I make you my Ambassador," the king called out, hastily.

He had a magnificent air of authority.

"The grown-ups are very strange," the little prince said to himself, as he continued on his journey.

The second planet was inhabited by a conceited man.

"Ah! Ah! I am about to receive a visit from an admirer!" he exclaimed from afar, as soon as he saw the little prince coming. For, to conceited men, all other men are admirers.

"Good morning," said the little prince.

"That is a queer hat you are wearing."

"It is a hat for salutes," the conceited man replied.

"It is to rise in salute when people acclaim me. Unfortunately, nobody at all ever passes this way."

"Yes?" said the little prince, who did not understand what the conceited man was talking about.

"Clap your hands, one against the other," the conceited man now directed him.

The little prince clapped his hands. The conceited man raised his hat in a modest salute.

"This is more entertaining than the visit to the king," the little prince said to himself. And he began again to clap his hands, one against the other. The conceited man again raised his hat in salute. After five minutes of this exercise, the little prince grew tired of the game's monotony.

"And what should one do to make the hat come down?" he asked. But the conceited man did not hear him. Conceited people never hear anything but praise.

"Do you really admire me very much?" he demanded of the little prince.

"What does that mean — 'admire'?"

"To admire means that you regard me as the handsomest, the best-dressed, the richest, and the most intelligent man on this planet."

"But you are the only man on your planet!"

"Do me this kindness. Admire me just the same."

"I admire you," said the little prince, shrugging his shoulders slightly,

"but what is there in that to interest you so much?"

And the little prince went away.

"The grown-ups are certainly very odd," he said to himself, as he
continued on his journey.

## ♔ 12 ♔

The next planet was inhabited on by a tippler. This was a very short
visit, but it plunged the little prince into deep dejection.

"What are you doing there?" he said to the tippler, whom he found
settled down in silence before a collection of empty bottles and also a
collection of full bottles.

"I am drinking," replied the tippler, with a lugubrious air.

"Why are you drinking?" demanded the little prince.

"So that I may forget," replied the tippler.

"Forget what?" inquired the little prince, who already was sorry for
him.

"Forget that I am ashamed," the tippler confessed, hanging his head.

"Ashamed of what?" insisted the little prince, who wanted to help
him.

"Ashamed of drinking!" The tippler brought his speech to an end, and
shut himself up in an impregnable silence.

And the little prince went away, puzzled.

"The grown-ups are certainly very, very odd,"

he said to himself, as he continued on his journey.

# ♔ 13 ♔

The fourth planet belonged to a businessman. This man was so much occupied that he did not even raise his head at the little prince's arrival.

"Good morning," the little prince said to him.

"Your cigarette has gone out."

"Three and two make five. Five and seven make twelve. Twelve and three make fifteen. Good morning. Fifteen and seven make twenty-two. Twenty-two and six make twenty-eight. I haven't time to light it again. Twenty-six and five make thirty-one. Phew! Then that makes five-hundred-and one million, six-hundred-twenty-two thousand, seven-hundred-thirty-one."

"Five hundred million what?" asked the little prince.

"Eh? Are you still there? Five-hundred-and-one million — I can't stop… I have so much to do! I am concerned with matters of consequence. I don't amuse myself with balderdash. Two and five make seven…"

"Five-hundred-and-one million what?" repeated the little prince, who never in his life had let go of a question once he had asked it.

The businessman raised his head.

"During the fifty-four years that I have inhabited this planet, I have been disturbed only three times.

The first time was twenty-two years ago, when some giddy goose fell from goodness knows where. He made the most frightful noise that resounded all over the place, and I made four mistakes in my addition. The second time, eleven years ago, I was disturbed by an attack of rheumatism. I don't get enough exercise. I have no time for loafing. The third time — well, this is it! I was saying, then, five-hundred-and-one millions — "

"Millions of what?"

The businessman suddenly realized that there was no hope of being left in peace until he answered this question.

"Millions of those little objects," he said, "which one sometimes sees in the sky."

"Flies?"

"Oh, no. Little glittering objects."

"Bees?"

"Oh, no. Little golden objects that set lazy men to idle dreaming. As for me, I am concerned with matters of consequence. There is no time for idle dreaming in my life."

"Ah! You mean the stars?"

"Yes, that's it. The stars."

"And what do you do with five-hundred millions of stars?"

"Five-hundred-and-one million, six-hundred-twenty-two thousand, seven-hundred-thirty-one. I am concerned with matters of consequence: I am accurate."

"And what do you do with these stars?"

"What do I do with them?"

"Yes."

"Nothing. I own them."

"You own the stars?"

"Yes."

"But I have already seen a king who — "

"Kings do not own, they reign over. It is a very different matter."

"And what good does it do you to own the stars?"

"It does me the good of making me rich."

"And what good does it do you to be rich?"

"It makes it possible for me to buy more stars, if any are discovered."

"This man," the little prince said to himself, "reasons a little like my poor tippler…"

Nevertheless, he still had some more questions.

"How is it possible for one to own the stars?"

"To whom do they belong?" the businessman retorted, peevishly.

"I don't know. To nobody."

"Then they belong to me, because I was the first person to think of it."

"Is that all that is necessary?"

"Certainly. When you find a diamond that belongs to nobody, it is yours. When you discover an island that belongs to nobody, it is yours. When you get an idea before any one else, you take out a patent on it: it is yours. So with me: I own the stars, because nobody else before me ever thought of owning them."

"Yes, that is true," said the little prince.

"And what do you do with them?"

"I administer them," replied the businessman.

"I count them and recount them. It is difficult. But I am a man who is naturally interested in matters of consequence."

The little prince was still not satisfied.

"If I owned a silk scarf," he said, "I could put it around my neck and take it away with me. If I owned a flower, I could pluck that flower and take it away with me. But you cannot pluck the stars from heaven…"

"No. But I can put them in the bank."

"Whatever does that mean?"

"That means that I write the number of my stars on a little paper. And then I put this paper in a drawer and lock it with a key."

"And that is all?"

"That is enough," said the businessman.

"It is entertaining," thought the little prince.

"It is rather poetic. But it is of no great consequence."

On matters of consequence, the little prince had ideas which were very different from those of the grown-ups.

"I myself own a flower," he continued his conversation with the businessman, "which I water every day. I own three volcanoes, which I clean out every week (for I also clean out the one that is extinct; one never knows) It is of some use to my volcanoes, and it is of some use to my flower, that I own them. But you are of no use to the stars…"

The businessman opened his mouth, but he found nothing to say in answer.

And the little prince went away.

"The grown-ups are certainly altogether extraordinary," he said simply, talking to himself as he continued on his journey.

## ♕ 14 ♕

The fifth planet was very strange. It was the smallest of all. There was just enough room on it for a street lamp and a lamplighter.

The little prince was not able to reach any explanation of the use of a street lamp and a lamplighter, somewhere in the heavens, on a planet which had no people, and not one house.

But he said to himself, nevertheless:

"If may well be that this man is absurd. But he is not so absurd as the king, the conceited man, the businessman, and the tippler. For at least his work has some meaning. When he lights his street lamp, it is as if he brought one more star to life, or one flower. When he puts out his lamp, he sends the flower, or the star, to sleep. That is a beautiful occupation. And since it is beautiful it is truly useful."

When he arrived on the planet he respectfully saluted the lamplighter.

"Good Morning. Why have you just put out your lamp?"

"Those are the orders," replied the lamplighter.

"Good morning."

"What are the orders?"

"The orders are that I put out my lamp. Good evening."

And he lighted his lamp again.

"But why have you just lighted it again?"

"Those are the orders," replied the lamplighter.

"I do not understand," said the little prince.

"There is nothing to understand," said the lamplighter.

"Orders are orders. Good morning."

And he put out his lamp.

Then he mopped his forehead with a handkerchief decorated with red squares.

"I follow a terrible profession. In the old days it was reasonable. I put the lamp out in the morning, and in the evening I lighted it again. I had the rest of the day for relaxation and the rest of the night for sleep."

"And the orders have been changed since that time?"

"The orders have not been changed," said the lamplighter.

"That is the tragedy! From year to year the planet has turned more rapidly and the orders have not been changed!"

"Then what?" asked the little prince.

"Then — the planet now makes a complete turn every minute, and I no longer have a single second for repose. Once every minute I have to light my lamp and put it out!"

"That is very funny! A day lasts only one minute, here where you live!"

"It is not funny at all!" said the lamplighter.

"While we have been talking together a month has gone by."

"A month?"

"Yes, a month. Thirty minutes. Thirty days. Good evening."

And he lighted his lamp again.

As the little prince watched him, he felt that he loved this lamplighter who was so faithful to his orders.

He remembered the sunsets which he himself had gone to seek, in other days, merely by pulling up his chair; and he wanted to help his friend.

"You know," he said, "I can tell you a way you can rest whenever you want to…"

"I always want to rest," said the lamplighter.

For it is possible for a man to be faithful and lazy at the same time.

The little prince went on with his explanation:

"Your planet is so small that three strides will take you all the way around it. To be always in the sunshine, you need only walk along rather slowly. When you want to rest, you will walk — and the day will last as long as you like."

"That doesn't do me much good," said the lamplighter. "The one thing I love in life is to sleep."

"Then you're unlucky," said the little prince.

"I am unlucky," said the lamplighter.

"Good morning."

And he put out his lamp.

"That man," said the little prince to himself, as he continued farther on his journey, "that man would be scorned by all the others: by the king, by the conceited man, by the tippler, by the businessman. Nevertheless he is the only one of them all who does not seem to me ridiculous. Perhaps that is because he is thinking of something else besides himself."

He breathed a sigh of regret, and said to himself again:

"That man is the only one of them all whom I could have made my friend. But his planet is indeed too small. There is no room on it for two people…"

What the little prince did not dare confess was that he was sorry most of all to leave this planet, because it was blest every day with 1440 sunsets!

The sixth planet was ten times larger than the last one. It was inhabited by an old gentleman who wrote voluminous books.

"Oh, look! Here is an explorer!" he exclaimed to himself when he saw little prince coming.

The little prince sat down on the table and panted a little. He had already traveled so much and so far!

"Where do you come from?" the old gentleman said to him.

"What is that big book?" said the little prince.

"What are you doing?"

"I am a geographer," said the old gentleman.

"What is a geographer?" asked the little prince.

"A geographer is a scholar who knows the location of all the seas, rivers, towns, mountains, and deserts."

"That is very interesting," said the little prince.

"Here at last is a man who has a real profession!"

And he cast a look around him at the planet of the geographer. It was the most magnificent and stately planet that he had ever seen.

"Your planet is very beautiful," he said.

"Has it any oceans?"

"I couldn't tell you," said the geographer.

"Ah!" The little prince was disappointed.

"Has it any mountains?"

"I couldn't tell you," said the geographer.

"And towns, and rivers, and deserts?"

"I couldn't tell you that, either."

"But you are a geographer!"

"Exactly," the geographer said.

"But I am not an explorer. I haven't a single explorer on my planet. It is not the geographer who goes out to count the towns, the rivers, the mountains, the seas, the oceans, and the deserts. The geographer is much too important to go loafing about. He does not leave his desk. But he receives the explorers in his study. He asks them questions, and he notes down what they recall of their travels. And if the recollections of any one among them seem interesting to him, the geographer orders an inquiry into that explorer's moral character."

"Why is that?"

"Because an explorer who told lies would bring disaster on the books of the geographer. So would an explorer who drank too much."

"Why is that?" asked the little prince.

"Because intoxicated men see double. Then the geographer would note down two mountains in a place where there was only one."

"I know someone," said the little prince, "who would make a bad explorer."

"That is possible. Then, when the moral character of the explorer is shown to be good, an inquiry is ordered into his discovery."

"One goes to see it?"

"No. That would be too complicated. But one requires the explorer to furnish proofs. For example, if the discovery in question is that of a large mountain, one requires that large stones be brought back from it."

The geographer was suddenly stirred to excitement.

"But you — you come from far away! You are an explorer! You shall describe your planet to me!"

And, having opened his big register, the geographer sharpened his pencil. The recitals of explorers are put down first in pencil. One waits until the explorer has furnished proofs, before putting them down in ink.

"Well?" said the geographer expectantly.

"Oh, where I live," said the little prince, "it is not very interesting. It is all so small. I have three volcanoes. Two volcanoes are active and the other is extinct. But one never knows."

"One never knows," said the geographer.

"I have also a flower."

"We do not record flowers," said the geographer.

"Why is that? The flower is the most beautiful thing on my planet!"

"We do not record them," said the geographer, "because they are ephemeral."

"What does that mean — 'ephemeral'?"

"Geographies," said the geographer, "are the books which, of all books, are most concerned with matters of consequence. They never become old-fashioned. It is very rarely that a mountain changes its position. It is very rarely that an ocean empties itself of its waters. We write of eternal things."

"But extinct volcanoes may come to life again," the little prince interrupted.

"What does that mean — 'ephemeral'?"

"Whether volcanoes are extinct or alive, it comes to the same thing for us," said the geographer.

"The thing that matters to us is the mountain. It does not change."

"But what does that mean — 'ephemeral'?" repeated the little prince, who never in his life had let go of a question, once he had asked it.

"It means, 'which is in danger of speedy disappearance'."

"Is my flower in danger of speedy disappearance?"

"Certainly it is."

"My flower is ephemeral," the little prince said to himself, "and she has only four thorns to defend herself against the world. And I have left her on my planet, all alone!"

That was his first moment of regret. But he took courage once more. "What place would you advise me to visit now?" he asked.

"The planet Earth," replied the geographer.

"It has a good reputation."

And the little prince went away, thinking of his flower.

## ☖ 16 ☖

So then the seventh planet was the Earth.

The Earth is not just an ordinary planet! One can count, there, 111 kings (not forgetting, to be sure, the Negro kings among them), 7,000 geographer, 900,000 businessmen, 7,500,000 tipplers, 311,000,000 conceited men — that is to say, about 2,000,000,000 grown-ups.

To give you an idea of the size of the Earth, I will tell you that before the invention of electricity it was necessary to maintain, over the whole of the six continents, a veritable army of 462,511 lamplighters for the street lamps.

Seen from a slight distance, that would make a splendid spectacle. The movements of this army would be regulated like those of the ballet in the opera.

First would come the turn of the lamplighters of New Zealand and Australia. Having set their lamps alight, these would go off to sleep. Next, the lamplighters of China and Siberia would enter for their steps in the dance, and then they too would be waved back into the wings. After that would come the turn of the lamplighters of Russia and the Indies; then those of Africa and Europe; then those of South America; then those of North America. And never would they make a mistake in the order of their entry upon the stage. It would be magnificent. Only the man who was in charge of the single lamp at the North Pole, and his colleague who was responsible for the single lamp at the South Pole — only these two would live free from toil and care: they would be busy twice a year.

When one wishes to play the wit, he sometimes wanders a little from the truth. I have not been altogether honest in what I have told you about the lamplighters.

And I realize that I run the risk of giving a false idea of our planet to those who do not know it. Men occupy a very small place upon the Earth. If the two billion inhabitants who people its surface were all to stand upright and somewhat crowded together, as they do for some big public assembly, they could easily be put into one public square twenty miles long and twenty miles wide. All humanity could be piled up on a small Pacific islet.

The grown-ups, to be sure, will not believe you when you tell them that. They imagine that they fill a great deal of space. They fancy themselves as important as the baobabs. You should advise them, then, to make their own calculations. They adore figures, and that will please them. But do not waste your time on this extra task. It is unnecessary. You have, I know, confidence in me.

When the little prince arrived on the Earth, he was very much surprised not to see any people. He was beginning to be afraid he had come to the wrong planet, when a coil of gold, the color of the moonlight, flashed across the sand.

"Good evening," said the little prince courteously.

"Good evening," said the snake.

"What planet is this on which I have come down?" asked the little prince.

"This is the Earth; this is Africa," the snake answered.

"Ah! Then there are no people on the Earth?"

"This is the desert. There are no people in the desert. The Earth is large," said the snake.

The little prince sat down on a stone, and raised his eyes toward the sky.

"I wonder," he said, "Whether the stars are set alright in heaven so that one day each one of us may find his own again... Look at my planet. It is right there above us. But how far away it is!"

"It is beautiful," the snake said.

"What has brought you here?"

"I have been having some trouble with a flower," said the little prince.

"Ah!" said the snake.

And they were both silent.

"Where are the men?" the little prince at last took up the conversation again.

"It is a little lonely in the desert..."

"It is also lonely among men," the snake said.

The little prince gazed at him for a long time.

"You are a funny animal," he said at last.

"You are no thicker than a finger..."

"But I am more powerful than the finger of a king," said the snake.

The little prince smiled.

"You are not very powerful. You haven't even any feet. You cannot even travel..."

"I can carry you farther than any ship could take you," said the snake. He twined himself around the little prince's ankle, like a golden bracelet.

"Whomever I touch, I send back to the earth from whence he came," the snake spoke again.

"But you are innocent and true, and you come from a star..."

The little prince made no reply.

"You move me to pity — you are so weak on this Earth made of granite," the snake said.

"I can help you, some day, if you grow too homesick for your own planet. I can — "

"Oh! I understand you very well," said the little prince.

"But why do you always speak in riddles?"

"I solve them all," said the snake.

And they were both silent.

## ♕ 18 ♕

The little prince crossed the desert and met with only one flower. It was a flower with three petals, a flower of no account at all.

"Good morning," said the little prince.

"Good morning," said the flower.

"Where are the men?" the little prince asked, politely.

The flower had once seen a caravan passing.

"Men?" she echoed.

"I think there are six or seven of them in existence. I saw them, several years ago. But one never knows where to find them. The wind blows them away. They have no roots, and that makes their life very difficult."

"Goodbye," said the little prince.

"Goodbye," said the flower.

## ♕ 19 ♕

After that, the little prince climbed a high mountain. The only mountains he had ever known were the three volcanoes, which came up to his knees. And he used the extinct volcano as a footstool.

"From a mountain as high as this one," he said to himself, "I shall be able to see the whole planet at one glance, and all the people…"

But he saw nothing, save peaks of rock that were sharpened like needles.

"Good morning," he said courteously.

"Good morning — Good morning — Good morning," answered the echo.

"Who are you?" said the little prince.

"Who are you — Who are you — Who are you?" answered the echo.

"Be my friends. I am all alone," he said.

"I am all alone — all alone — all alone," answered the echo.

"What a queer planet!" he thought.

"It is altogether dry, and altogether pointed, and altogether harsh and forbidding. And the people have no imagination. They repeat whatever one says to them… On my planet I had a flower; she always was the first to speak…"

## 20

But it happened that after walking for a long time through sand, and rocks, and snow, the little prince at last came upon a road. And all roads lead to the abodes of men.

"Good morning," he said.

He was standing before a garden, all a-bloom with roses.

"Good morning," said the roses.

The little prince gazed at them. They all looked like his flower.

"Who are you?" he demanded, thunderstruck.

"We are roses," the roses said.

And he was overcome with sadness. His flower had told him that she was the only one of her kind in all the universe. And here were five thousand of them, all alike, in one single garden!

"She would be very much annoyed," he said to himself, "if she should see that... She would cough most dreadfully, and she would pretend that she was dying, to avoid being laughed at. And I should be obliged to pretend that I was nursing her back to life — for if I did not do that, to humble myself also, she would really allow herself to die..."

Then he went on with his reflections: "I thought that I was rich, with a flower that was unique in all the world; and all I had was a common rose. A common rose, and three volcanoes that come up to my knees — and one of them perhaps extinct forever... That doesn't make me a very great prince..."

And he lay down in the grass and cried.

## ♛ 21 ♛

It was then that the fox appeared.

"Good morning," said the fox.

"Good morning," the little prince responded politely, although when he turned around he saw nothing.

"I am right here," the voice said, "under the apple tree."

"Who are you?" asked the little prince, and added, "You are very pretty to look at."

"I am a fox," the fox said.

"Come and play with me," proposed the little prince.

"I am so unhappy."

"I cannot play with you," the fox said.

"I am not tamed."

"Ah! Please excuse me," said the little prince.

But after some thought, he added:

"What does that mean — 'tame'?"

"You do not live here," said the fox.

"What is it that you are looking for?"

"I am looking for men," said the little prince. "What does that mean — 'tame'?"

"Men," said the fox.

"They have guns, and they hunt. It is very disturbing. They also raise chickens. These are their only interests. Are you looking for chickens?"

"No," said the little prince.

"I am looking for friends. What does that mean — 'tame'?"

"It is an act too often neglected," said the fox.

"It means to establish ties."

"'To establish ties'?"

"Just that," said the fox.

"To me, you are still nothing more than a little boy who is just like a hundred thousand other little boys. And I have no need of you. And you, on your part, have no need of me. To you, I am nothing more than a fox like a hundred thousand other foxes. But if you tame me, then we shall need each other. To me, you will be unique in all the world. To you, I shall be unique in all the world…"

"I am beginning to understand," said the little prince.

"There is a flower… I think that she has tamed me…"

"It is possible," said the fox.

"On the Earth one sees all sorts of things."

"Oh, but this is not on the Earth!", said the little prince.

The fox seemed perplexed, and very curious.

"On another planet?"

"Yes."

"Are there hunters on that planet?"

"No."

"Ah, that is interesting! Are there chickens?"

"No."

"Nothing is perfect," sighed the fox.

But he came back to his idea.

"My life is very monotonous," he said.

"I hunt chickens; men hunt me. All the chickens are just alike, and all the men are just alike. And, in consequence, I am a little bored. But if you tame me, it will be as if the sun came to shine on my life. I shall know the sound of a step that will be different from all the others. Other steps send me hurrying back underneath the ground. Yours will call me, like music, out of my burrow. And then look: you see the grain-fields down yonder? I do not eat bread. Wheat is of no use to me. The wheat fields have nothing to say to me. And that is sad. But you have hair that is the color of gold. Think how wonderful that will be when you have tamed me! The grain, which also golden, will bring me back the thought of you. And I shall love to listen to the wind in the wheat…"

The fox gazed at the little prince, for a long time.

"Please — tame me!" he said.

"I want to, very much," the little prince replied.

"But I have not much time. I have friends to discover, and a great many things to understand."

"One only understands the things that one tames," said the fox.

"Men have no more time to understand anything. They buy things ready all made at the shops. But there is no shop anywhere where one can buy friendship, and so men have no friends any more. If you want a friend, tame me…"

"What must I do, to tame you?" asked the little prince.

"You must be very patient," replied the fox.

"First you will sit down at a little distance from me — like that — in the grass. I shall look at you out of the corner of my eye, and you will say nothing. Words are the source of misunderstandings. But you will sit a little closer to me, every day…"

The next day the little prince came back.

"It would have been better to come back at the same hour," said the fox. "If, for example, you come at four o'clock in the afternoon, then at three o'clock I shall begin to be happy. I shall feel happier as the hour advances. At four o'clock, I shall already be worrying and jumping about. I shall show you how happy I am! But if you come at just any time, I shall never know at what hour my heart is to be ready to greet you... One must observe the proper rites..."

"What is a rite?" asked the little prince.

"Those also are actions too often neglected," said the fox.

"They are what make one day different from other days, one hour from other hours. There is a rite, for example, among my hunters. Every Thursday they dance with the village girls. So Thursday is a wonderful day for me! I can take a walk as far as the vineyards. But if the hunters danced at just any day would be like every other day, and I should never have any vacation at all."

So the little prince tamed the fox. And when the hour of his departure drew near —

"Ah," said the fox, "I shall cry."

"It is your own fault," said the little prince.

"I never wished you any sort of harm; but you wanted me to tame you..."

"Yes, that is so," said the fox.

"But now you are going to cry!" said the little prince.

"Yes, that is so," said the fox.

"Then it has done you no good at all!"

"It has done me good," said the fox, "because of the color of the wheat fields."

And then he added: "Go and look again at the roses. You will understand now that yours is unique in all the world. Then come back to say goodbye to me, and I will make you a present of a secret."

The little prince went away, to look again at the roses.

"You are not at all like my rose," he said.

"As yet you are nothing. No one has tamed you, and you have tamed no one. You are like my fox when I first knew him. He was only a fox like a hundred thousand other foxes. But I have made him my friend, and now he is unique in all the world."

And the roses were very much embarrassed.

"You are beautiful, but you are empty," he went on.

"One could not die for you. To be sure, an ordinary passerby would think that my rose looked just like you — the rose that belongs to me. But in herself alone she is more important than all the hundreds of you other roses: because it is she that I have watered; because it is she that I have sheltered behind the screen; because it is for her that I have killed the caterpillars (except the two or three that we saved to become butterflies); because it is she that I have listened to, when she grumbled, or boasted, or even sometimes when she said nothing. Because she is my rose."

And he went back to meet the fox.

"Goodbye," he said.

"Goodbye," said the fox.

"And now here is my secret, a very simple secret: It is only with the heart that one can see rightly; what is essential is invisible to the eye."

"What is essential is invisible to the eye," the little prince repeated, so that he would be sure to remember.

"It is the time you have wasted for your rose that makes your rose so important."

"It is the time I have wasted for my rose — " said the little prince, so that he would be sure to remember.

"Men have forgotten this truth," said the fox.

"But you must not forget it. You become responsible, forever, for what you have tamed. You are responsible for your rose…"

"I am responsible for my rose," the little prince repeated, so that he would be sure to remember.

## ♕ 22 ♕

"Good morning," said the little prince.

"Good morning," said the railway switchman.

"What do you do here?" the little prince asked.

"I sort out travelers, in bundles of a thousand," said the switchman.

"I send off the trains that carry them: now to the right, now to the left."

And a brilliantly lighted express train shook the switchman's cabin as it rushed by with a roar like thunder.

"They are in a great hurry," said the little prince. "What are they looking for?"

"Not even the locomotive engineer knows that," said the switchman.

And a second brilliantly lighted express thundered by, in the opposite direction.

"Are they coming back already?" demanded the little prince.

"These are not the same ones," said the switchman.

"It is an exchange."

"Were they not satisfied where they were?" asked the little prince.

"No one is ever satisfied where he is," said the switchman.

And they heard the roaring thunder of a third brilliantly lighted express.

"Are they pursuing the first travelers?" demanded the little prince.

They are pursuing nothing at all," said the switchman.

"They are asleep in there, or if they are not asleep they are yawning.

Only the children are flattening their noses against the windowpanes."

"Only the children know what they are looking for," said the little prince. "They waste their time over a rag doll and it becomes very important to them; and if anybody takes it away from them, they cry…"

"They are lucky," the switchman said.

## ♕ 23 ♕

"Good morning," said the little prince.

"Good morning," said the merchant.

This was the merchant who sold pills that had been invented to quench thirst. You need only swallow one pill a week, and you would feel no need of anything to drink.

"Why are you selling those?" asked the little prince.

"Because they save a tremendous amount of time," said the merchant. "Computations have been made by experts. With these pills, you save fifty-three minutes in every week."

"And what do I do with those fifty-three minutes?"

"Anything you like…"

"As for me," said the little prince to himself, "if I had fifty-three minutes to spend as I liked, I should walk at my leisure toward a spring of fresh water."

## ♕ 24 ♕

It was now the eighth day since I had had my accident in the desert, and I had listened to the story of the merchant as I was drinking the last drop of my water supply.

"Ah," I said to the little prince, "these memories of yours are very charming; but I have not yet succeeded in repairing my plane; I have nothing more to drink; and I, too, should be very happy if I could walk at my leisure toward a spring of fresh water!"

"My friend the fox — " the little prince said to me.

"My dear little man, this is no longer a matter that has anything to do with the fox!"

"Why not?"

"Because I am about to die of thirst…"

He did not follow my reasoning, and he answered me:

"It is a good thing to have had a friend, even if one is about to die. I, for instance, am very glad to have had a fox as a friend…"

"He has no way of guessing the danger," I said to myself. "He has never been either hungry or thirsty. A little sunshine is all that he needs…"

But he looked at me steadily, and replied to my thought:

"I am thirsty, too. Let us look for a well…"

I made a gesture of weariness. It is absurd to look for a well, at random, in the immensity of the desert. But nevertheless we started walking.

When we had trudged along for several hours, in silence, the darkness fell, and the stars began to come out. Thirst had made me a little feverish, and I looked at them as if I were in a dream. The little prince's last words came reeling back into my memory:

"Then you are thirsty, too?" I demanded. But he did not reply to my question.

He merely said to me: "Water may also be good for the heart…"

I did not understand this answer, but I said nothing. I knew very well that it was impossible to cross-examine him.

He was tired. He sat down. I sat down beside him. And, after a little silence, he spoke again:

"The stars are beautiful, because of a flower that cannot be seen."

I replied, "Yes, that is so."

And, without saying anything more, I looked across the ridges of sand that were stretched out before us in the moonlight.

"The desert is beautiful," the little prince added.

And that was true. I have always loved the desert. One sits down on a desert sand dune, sees nothing, hears nothing. Yet through the silence something throbs and gleams...

"What makes the desert beautiful," said the little prince, "is that somewhere it hides a well..."

I was astonished by a sudden understanding of that mysterious radiation of the sands. When I was a little boy I lived in an old house, and legend told us that a treasure was buried there. To be sure, no one had ever known how to find it; perhaps no one had ever even looked for it. But it cast an enchantment over that house. My home was hiding a secret in the depths of its heart...

"Yes," I said to the little prince.

"The house, the stars, the desert — what gives them their beauty is something that is invisible!"

"I am glad," he said, "that you agree with my fox."

As the little prince dropped off to sleep, I took him in my arms and set out walking once more. I felt deeply moved, and stirred. It seemed to me that I was carrying a very fragile treasure. It seemed to me, even, that there was nothing more fragile on all the Earth. In the moonlight I looked at his pale forehead, his closed eye, his locks of hair that trembled in the wind, and I said to myself:

"What I see here is nothing but a shell. What is most important is invisible..."

As his lips opened slightly with the suspicion of a half-smile, I said to myself, again:

"What moves me so deeply, about this little prince who is sleeping here, is his loyalty to a flower — the image of a rose that shines through this whole being like the flame of a lamp, even when he is asleep..."

And I felt him to be more fragile still. I felt the need of protecting him, as if he himself were a flame that might be extinguished by a little puff of wind...

And, as I walked on so, I found the well, at daybreak.

## 25

"Men," said the little prince, "set out on their way in express trains, but they do not know what they are looking for. Then they rush about, and get excited, and turn round and round..."

And he added:

"It is not worth the trouble..."

The well that we had come to was not like the wells of the Sahara. The wells of the Sahara are mere holes dug in the sand. This one was like a well in a village. But there was no village here, and I thought I must be dreaming...

"It is strange," I said to the little prince.

"Everything is ready for use: the pulley, the bucket, the rope..."

He laughed, touched the rope, and set the pulley to working. And the pulley moaned, like an old weathervane which the wind has long since forgotten.

"Do you hear?" said the little prince.

"We have wakened the well, and it is singing..."

I did not want him to tire himself with the rope.

"Leave it to me," I said.

"It is too heavy for you."

I hoisted the bucket slowly to the edge of the well and set it there — happy, tired as I was, over my achievement. The song of the pulley was still in my ears, and I could see the sunlight shimmer in the still trembling water.

"I am thirsty for this water," said the little prince. "Give me some of it to drink…"

And I understood what he had been looking for.

I raised the bucket to his lips. He drank, his eyes closed. It was as sweet as some special festival treat. This water was indeed a different thing from ordinary nourishment. Its sweetness was born of the walk under the stars, the song of the pulley, the effort of my arms. It was good for the heart, like a present.

When I was a little boy, the lights of the Christmas tree, the music of the Midnight Mass, the tenderness of smiling faces, used to make up, so, the radiance of the gifts I received.

"The men where you live," said the little prince, "raise five thousand roses in the same garden — and they do not find in it what they are looking for."

"They do not find it," I replied.

"And yet what they are looking for could be found in one single rose, or in a little water."

"Yes, that is true," I said.

And the little prince added:

"But the eyes are blind. One must look with the heart…"

I had drunk the water. I breathed easily. At sunrise the sand is the color of honey. And that honey color was making me happy, too.

What brought me, then, this sense of grief?

"You must keep your promise," said the little prince, softly, as he sat down beside me once more.

"What promise?"

"You know — a muzzle for my sheep... I am responsible for this flower..."

I took my rough drafts of drawings out of my pocket. The little prince looked them over, and laughed as he said:

"Your baobabs — they look a little like cabbages."

"Oh!"

I had been so proud of my baobabs!

"Your fox — his ears look a little like horns; and they are too long."

And he laughed again.

"You are not fair, little prince," I said.

"I don't know how to draw anything except boa constrictors from the outside and boa constrictors from the inside."

"Oh, that will be all right," he said, "children understand."

So then I made a pencil sketch of a muzzle. And as I gave it to him my heart was torn.

"You have plans that I do not know about," I said.

But he did not answer me. He said to me, instead:

"You know — my descent to the earth... Tomorrow will be its anniversary."

Then, after a silence, he went on:

"I came down very near here."

And he flushed.

And once again, without understanding why, I had a queer sense of sorrow. One question, however, occurred to me:

"Then it was not by chance that on the morning when I first met you — a week ago — you were strolling along like that, all alone, a thousand miles from any inhabited region? You were on your way back to the place where you landed?"

The little prince flushed again.

And I added, with some hesitancy:

"Perhaps it was because of the anniversary?"

The little prince flushed once more. He never answered questions — but when one flushed does that not mean "Yes"?

"Ah," I said to him, "I am a little frightened — "

But he interrupted me.

"Now you must work. You must return to your engine. I will be waiting for you here. Come back tomorrow evening…"

But I was not reassured. I remembered the fox. One runs the risk of weeping a little, if one lets himself be tamed…

## 26

Beside the well there was the ruin of an old stone wall.

When I came back from my work, the next evening, I saw from some distance away my little prince sitting on top of this wall, with his feet dangling.

And I heard him say:

"Then you don't remember. This is not the exact spot."

Another voice must have answered him, for he replied to it:

"Yes, yes! It is the right day, but this is not the place."

I continued my walk toward the wall. At no time did I see or hear anyone.

The little prince, however, replied once again:

" — Exactly. You will see where my track begins, in the sand. You have nothing to do but wait for me there. I shall be there tonight."

I was only twenty meters from the wall, and I still saw nothing.

After a silence the little prince spoke again:

"You have good poison? You are sure that it will not make me suffer too long?"

I stopped in my tracks, my heart torn asunder; but still I did not understand.

"Now go away," said the little prince.

"I want to get down from the wall."

I dropped my eyes, then, to the foot of the wall — and I leaped into the air. There before me, facing the little prince, was one of those yellow snakes that take thirty seconds to bring your life to an end. Even as I was digging into my pocket to get out my revolver I made a running step back. But, at the noise I made, the snake let himself flow easily across the sand like the dying spray of a fountain, and, in no apparent hurry, disappeared, with a light metallic sound, among the stones.

I reached the wall just in time to catch my little man in my arms; his face was white as snow.

"What does this mean?" I demanded.

"Why are you talking with snakes?"

I had loosened the golden muffler that he always wore. I had moistened his temples, and had given him some water to drink. And now I did not dare ask him any more questions. He looked at me very gravely, and put his arms around my neck. I felt his heart beating like the heart of a dying bird, shot with someone's rifle...

"I am glad that you have found what was the matter with your engine," he said.

"Now you can go back home — "

"How do you know about that?"

I was just coming to tell him that my work had been successful, beyond anything that I had dared to hope.

He made no answer to my question, but he added:

"I, too, am going back home today..."

Then, sadly —

"It is much farther... It is much more difficult..."

I realized clearly that something extraordinary was happening. I was holding him close in my arms as if he were a little child; and yet it seemed to me that he was rushing headlong toward an abyss from which I could do nothing to restrain him...

His look was very serious, like someone lost far away.

"I have your sheep. And I have the sheep's box. And I have the muzzle..."

And he gave me a sad smile.

I waited a long time. I could see that he was reviving little by little.

"Dear little man," I said to him, "you are afraid..."

He was afraid, there was no doubt about that. But he laughed lightly.

"I shall be much more afraid this evening..."

Once again I felt myself frozen by the sense of something irreparable. And I knew that I could not bear the thought of never hearing that laughter any more. For me, it was like a spring of fresh water in the desert.

"Little man," I said, "I want to hear you laugh again."

But he said to me:

"Tonight, it will be a year... My star, then, can be found right above the place where I came to the Earth, a year ago..."

"Little man," I said, "tell me that it is only a bad dream — this affair of the snake, and the meeting-place, and the star..."

But he did not answer my plea. He said to me, instead:

"The thing that is important is the thing that is not seen..."

"Yes, I know..."

"It is just as it is with the flower. If you love a flower that lives on a star, it is sweet to look at the sky at night. All the stars are a-bloom with flowers..."

"Yes, I know..."

"It is just as it is with the water. Because of the pulley, and the rope, what you gave me to drink was like music. You remember — how good it was."

"Yes, I know..."

"And at night you will look up at the stars. Where I live everything is so small that I cannot show you where my star is to be found. It is better, like that. My star will just be one of the stars, for you. And so you will love to watch all the stars in the heavens... They will all be your friends. And, besides, I am going to make you a present..."

He laughed again.

"Ah, little prince, dear little prince! I love to hear that laughter!"

"That is my present. Just that. It will be as it was when we drank the water..."

"What are you trying to say?"

"All men have stars," he answered, "but they are not the same things for different people. For some, who are travelers, the stars are guides. For others they are no more than little lights in the sky. For others, who are scholars, they are problems. For my businessman they are wealth. But all these stars as no one else has them — "

"What are you trying to say?"

"In one of the stars I shall be living. In one of them I shall be laughing. And so it will be as if all the stars were laughing, when you look at the sky at night... You — only you — will have stars that can laugh!"

And he laughed again.

"And when your sorrow is comforted (time soothes all sorrows) you will be content that you have known me. You will always be my friend. You will want to laugh with me. And you sometimes open your window, so, for that pleasure... And your friends will be properly astonished to see you laughing as you look up at the sky! Then you will say to them, 'Yes, the star always make me laugh!' And they will think you are crazy. It will be a very shabby trick that I shall have played on you..."

And he laughed again.

"It will be as if, in place of the stars, I had given you a great number of little bells that knew how to laugh..."

And he laughed again. Then he quickly became serious:

"Tonight — you know... Do not come."

"I shall not leave you," I said.

"I shall look as if I were suffering. I shall look a little as if I were dying. It is like that. Do not come to see that. It is not worth the trouble..."

"I shall not leave you."

But he was worried.

"I tell you — it is also because of the snake. He must not bite you. Snakes — they are malicious creatures. This one might bite you just for fun..."

"I shall not leave you."

But a thought came to reassure him:

"It is true that they have no more poison for a second bite."

That night I did not see him set out on his way. He got away from me without making a sound. When I succeeded in catching up with him he was walking along with a quick and resolute step. He said to me merely:

"Ah! You are there..."

And he took me by the hand. But he was still worrying.

"It was wrong of you to come. You will suffer. I shall look as if I were dead; and that will not be true..."

I said nothing.

"You understand... It is too far. I cannot carry this body with me. It is too heavy."

I said nothing.

"But it will be like an old abandoned shell. There is nothing sad about old shells…"

I said nothing.

He was a little discouraged. But he made one more effort:

"You know, it will be very nice. I, too, shall look at the stars. All the stars will be wells with a rusty pulley. All the stars will pour out fresh water for me to drink…"

I said nothing.

"That will be so amusing! You will have five hundred million little bells, and I shall have five hundred million springs of fresh water…"

And he too said nothing more, because he was crying…

"Here it is. Let me go on by myself."

And he sat down, because he was afraid. Then he said, again:

You know — my flower… I am responsible for her. And she is so weak! She is so naive! She has four thorns, of no use at all, to protect herself against all the world…"

I too sat down, because I was not able to stand up any longer.

"There now — that is all…"

He still hesitated a little; then he got up. He took one step. I could not move. There was nothing there but a flash of yellow close to his ankle. He remained motionless for an instant. He did not cry out. He fell as gently as a tree falls. There was not even any sound, because of the sand.

# ♔ 27 ♔

And now six years have already gone by… I have never yet told this story. The companions who met me on my return were well content to see me alive. I was sad, but I told them:

"I am tired."

Now my sorrow is comforted a little. That is to say — not entirely. But I know that he did go back to his planet, because I did not find his body at daybreak. It was not such a heavy body... And at night I love to listen to the stars. It is like five hundred million little bells...

But there is one extraordinary thing... When I drew the muzzle for the little prince, I forgot to add the leather strap to it. He will never have been able to fasten it on this sheep.

So now I keep wondering: what is happening on his planet? Perhaps the sheep has eaten the flower...

At one time I say to myself:

"Surely not! The little prince shuts his flower under her glass globe every night, and he watches over his sheep very carefully..."

Then I am happy. And there is sweetness in the laughter of all the stars. But at another time I say to myself:

"At some moment or other one is absent-minded, and that is enough! On some one evening he forgot the glass globe, or the sheep got out, without making any noise, in the night..."

And then the little bells are changed to tears...

Here, then, is a great mystery. For you who also love the little prince, and for me, nothing in the universe can be the same if somewhere, we do not know where, a sheep that we never saw has — yes or no? — eaten a rose...

Look up at the sky. Ask yourselves: Is it yes or no? Has the sheep eaten the flower? And you will see how everything changes...

And no grown-up will ever understand that this is a matter of so much importance!

This is, to me, the loveliest and saddest landscape in the world. It is the same as that on the preceding page, but I have drawn it again to impress it on your memory. It is here that the little prince appeared on

Earth, and disappeared.

Look at it carefully so that you will be sure to recognize it in case you travel some day to the African desert. And, if you should come upon this spot, please do not hurry on. Wait for a time, exactly under the star.

Then, if a little man appears who laughs, who has golden hair and who refuses to answer questions, you will know who he is.

If this should happen, please comfort me. Send me word that he has come back.

# 직독직해로 읽는 세계명작 시리즈

막힘 없이 읽다 보면, 어느 새 독해 실력이 쑥쑥!
막힘 없이 듣다 보면, 어느 새 듣기 실력이 쑥쑥!
막힘 없이 말하다 보면, 어느 새 동시통역 실력이 쑥쑥!

문법적으로 분석하다가, 모르는 단어 찾다가,
결국 문맥조차 제대로 파악하지 못하고 포기했던 영어 원작!
영어 원작에 대한 두려움이 자신감으로 바뀌게 됩니다.
이제 세계명작을 직독직해로 신나게 읽어 봐요!

수능 영어 준비도
문제없어요!